UP FRONT AND CENTER

New Orleans Music
at the End of the 20th Century

Jay Mazza

Foreword by Kermit Ruffins

THREADHEAD PRESS
New Orleans

To Adam –
Happy Graduation!

Jay

Library of Congress Cataloging-in-Publication data

Mazza, Jay.
  Up Front and Center: New Orleans Music at the End of the
  20th Century/Jay Mazza
  p. 299
Includes index.

Also by Jay Mazza

I Got the Fish in the Head: A Radiators Retrospective

Cover art by Isabelle Jacopin based on a photo by Nijme Rinaldi Nun of the crowd during a Rebirth Brass Band performance at the Maple Leaf Bar, 1991.

Author photo by Zach Smith

TABLE OF CONTENTS

For the Musicians of New Orleans
Past, Present and Future

Foreword

Looking back on my good old Rebirth Brass Band days, what stands out the most is traveling around the world, second lines, playing in the French Quarters for tips, and hard drugs. I left Lawless Junior High and went to Clark Senior High. Around about '81 or '82, I met Philip Frazier, and we started a band called The Group, which of course you know changed to the Rebirth.

We started playing in the French Quarters for tips every day after school and all day on weekends. We did well for teenagers—money wise. I used to walk or catch the bus to the lower 9th Ward where I would change clothes and then head back to the Tremé. Yeah, walking through the Tremé was like Mardi Gras. People everywhere—schoolteachers, lawyers, doctors, undertakers, pimps, whores, gangsters, prostitutes, drug dealers, dope fiends and musicians.

One night I was leaving Ruth's Cozy Corner walking down N. Robertson to the Lower 9th Ward with my bottle of Night Train wine and I remember a cold gun at my temple and this robber man saying, "Don't look at me nigga, empty yo fuckin' pockets." I did and I'm still here to talk about it. Where there is gold, there is trash.

The Rebirth saved my life. I was a rough neck in the lower 9th Ward. Making music and money humbled me, and I'm quite sure it does for many other kids playing music today. We started playing for social and pleasure club second line parades like the High Rollers, which was started by Trombone Shorty's mom and dad. We also played for the Money Wasters, the Tremé Sports and many other second line parades.

Before we knew it, we were off to Japan, Switzerland, Spain, France, Greece, Germany, Amsterdam, England and Canada. As for the USA, just name a place, we were there. Thanks to the great musicians before us, like the Dirty Dozen, the Olympia Brass Band etc., young kids were traveling the world making an honest living playing good old New Orleans music. 50 to 100 years from now, New Orleans jazz music will still be a lifeline for many, many young kids and families.

We were having the time of our lives. There is nothing like waking up in the morning to do these gigs. Learning a new song every day, having money all the time, and seeing things that your family and friends might never see. Being in the position to change and make history is an honor. For this little life we have, we are truly blessed.

Then there is that down time when the gig is over, you're hanging in the rough parts of town, you could easily get caught up in some drugs. I wasted five years on that shit. After five years, I hit bottom and you can't go no way but up after that. As I look back, I'm sorry for the bad influence I may have passed on during those times. But, I haven't done that shit in twenty-one years, thanks to God. Please stay away from drugs. I'll tell more in my book one day.

I'm still in New Orleans. It is the best place in the world to live. Where else can you go and listen to some of the best music in the world, come face to face with some of the best musicians, see second lines and other good shit. Not to mention, we have some of the best food, and the most loving, caring and beautiful people in the world. I don't have a doubt that we will look back and say ...What A Wonderful World!

Kermit Ruffins

Preface

This book is called "Up Front and Center" because that is where you will find me at musical performances. I have always preferred to be as close to the band as possible because that is where the magic of live music happens. I like to see the faces of the musicians as they interact with each other and create the sounds that move the bodies on the dance floor. I also favor that sweet spot because it puts me in the center of the crowd. Energy is concentrated. The musicians feed energy to the audience; the audience amplifies it and feeds it back. A feedback loop is created. The power of that interaction has never ceased to move me physically, emotionally and spiritually.

I first became aware of the power of live music while listening to rock bands play in concert halls or large arenas. When I moved to New Orleans in 1979, I had my first experiences in small clubs. I realized immediately that something had been missing. Since then, I have seen thousands of live music performances. Most of them have taken place in intimate venues.

While I have seen bands play in many other cities, it became clear when I was young that there is something profound and special about the music in New Orleans. It is why so many people gravitate to the city. It is why so many musicians move here. Music lives within the community unlike any other place in America. It is part of the cultural fabric. If you tune into it, you cannot help but feel it. It is rooted in the ancient communal traditions of humanity. The music creates unity; it bonds us together.

Over the twenty years covered in this book, I was out listening to music on an average of five nights a week. Factoring in multiple performances on a given night, festival days merging into festival nights, it is impossible to estimate how many shows I have seen. Luckily, I have kept a live music journal, also called "Up Front and Center," since April 4,1989. So I could count if I only had the time or inclination. But there is still so much more music to hear.

This book is written in a single voice. I have chosen to use the New Orleans Jazz and Heritage Festival as the central thread in the story since it weaves all of the music lovers and musicians together. The story of the Jazz Fest bookends this saga, which chronicles the many changes in the musical culture of New Orleans that occurred in the last twenty years of the 20th century. It covers numerous musicians and bands as well as the clubs and other settings in which they perform. But it is far from comprehensive or exhaustive since many of these artists are worthy of full-length treatments. If you are as passionate as I am about New Orleans music, you will undoubtedly be aware of some omissions because, while I have heard a lot of music, I have not heard it all. The story is told from the perspective of someone who was there—up front and center—grooving hard to the music.

Jay Mazza
January 5, 2012

Introduction

"The minute you land in New Orleans, something wet and dark leaps on you and starts humping you like a swamp beast."—Tom Robbins

When people talk about New Orleans, it has become commonplace for locals and visitors alike to bandy about the notion that the city is not really a part of America. To spin it towards the positive, people suggest it's the northernmost city in the Caribbean. The negative refer to it as a "third world country." All three of these ideas have become clichés—a smattering of inherent truth propping up a stereotype.

But when I first visited the city in the spring of 1979, all three characterizations were much closer to reality than they are today. There really was not much of a tourism infrastructure. There wasn't a music magazine. Neither the *Times-Picayune* nor the *States-Item*, the daily newspapers, had full time music writers though they did cover some of the bigger musical events. Neither had daily music listings though Vincent Fumar was well respected for his work covering popular music in the weekly "Lagniappe" section of the *Times-Picayune*.

The city was still flush with oil money, a boom that busted four years later, and there was not yet a need for efforts to develop the tourism economy. So there were few mechanisms designed to lure tourists to the city, and there were no means for them to find out what was happening culturally once they arrived.

The areas that are now considered "must-see stops" for the savvy tourist—the high end shopping along Magazine Street, the Faubourg Marigny, lower Decatur Street, the Arts District around Julia Street and the entirety of the Warehouse District—were yet to be developed. There were only two music clubs on Frenchmen Street, and one of them, the Faubourg (located where Snug Harbor is today), did more business as a restaurant.

The French Quarter was still a predominately residential neighborhood with a decaying infrastructure. The signature brick sidewalks and crosswalks in the Vieux Carre were installed as the city prepared for the 1984 World's Fair. Bourbon Street was already a long way from its heyday as the center of jazz in the earlier part of the 20th century. The T-shirt shops and tawdry strip clubs had already taken over. But their spread was being vigorously checked. Royal and Chartres Streets looked much as they do today, and the condo-fication of the surrounding streets had not yet begun.

Yet, the charms of the city were instantly evident as they are to visitors today and have been for nearly two centuries. The flowering gardens of the aptly named Garden District and the graceful architecture of the French Quarter still appear almost exactly the same over 30 years later. The same can be said of the stately majesty of St. Charles Avenue and the Uptown/University area.

As the city develops a master plan to turn the riverfront of the Mississippi into green space from Poland Avenue in the Bywater neighborhood to Napoleon Avenue uptown, it must be hard for today's visitor to imagine a New Orleans without the Aquarium of the Americas, Woldenberg Park, and its extension past the Moonwalk all the way down to Ursulines Street.

The only recreational access to the river was uptown behind the Audubon Zoo, an area still much beloved by students and nature lovers. "The Fly," as it was called, was a great spot to watch the ships go by and engage in games of love and sport, but it too lacked much infrastructure—it wasn't even locked at night and the batture was devoid of any river control mechanisms. The rest of the riverfront was still dedicated completely to industry where stevedores and river rats complemented the gray scenery of aging docks and creaky warehouses.

The Audubon Zoo, now the crown jewel of a local museum empire that features several other facilities including the Aquarium of the Americas, was a national disgrace. Its animal residents, whose descendents now enjoy one of the finest zoo settings worldwide, were trapped in confining cages with poor lighting amid squalid conditions that appalled the zoo's few visitors.

Tipitina's, which opened in 1977, and the Maple Leaf Bar, which opened in 1974, were the only pop music clubs of any renown outside of the French Quarter, and their fame barely spread across the city. Neither was air-conditioned, another fact of life in the 1970s and 1980s that is certain to baffle the modern day visitor.

The bands and musicians featured throughout this work have become standard bearers for the music of New Orleans across the country and the globe. But in 1979, they were all just beginning to become successful at plying their trade, or they were still in high school.

Modern jazz had a few more outlets including the famed Lu and Charlie's downtown, which closed in the late 1970s, and Prout's Club Alhambra. Uptown, Tyler's Beer Garden was on Magazine Street and Mason's Patio was on South Claiborne Avenue. But the local purveyors of modern jazz often couldn't make a living, and many had day jobs and/or played more popular R&B styles to make ends meet. During the late 1970s, Rosy's, located on Tchoupitoulas Street uptown, was one of the only places to regularly hear modern jazz performed by musicians from outside New Orleans. It was an upscale place with a top-notch sound system and less than 200 seats. Rosy brought in nationally known acts appealing to her diverse tastes. Legendary musicians such as Dizzy Gillespie, Ella Fitzgerald, Count Basie, Dave Brubeck, Ray Charles, Stan Getz and Rahsaan Roland Kirk played there amid occasional performances by local greats like James Booker, Professor Longhair and the Meters.

While still considered a city with great cuisine, the vanguard restaurants were of the decidedly white tablecloth, old school variety. The most popular restaurants were the grand dames of the French Quarter—Antoine's, Arnaud's and Louis XVI. For those on a limited budget, there existed a smattering of themed dining establishments like the Old Spaghetti Factory and Anything Goes, a crazy idea of a restaurant where all the waiters wore costumes and every booth had its own motif. Others favored the soul food offered by such dearly departed places as Chez Helene and Buster Holmes.

No one ate redfish; it was considered a trash fish only fit for bait or animal feed, because Paul Prudhomme had yet to blacken a filet. Lines between the Creole food of the city and its cosmopolitan inhabitants and the Cajun cooking of the country were firmly drawn. Try finding boudin in New Orleans in 1979.

Out in Acadiana, a limited effort to preserve Cajun culture began in 1968 with the formation of CODFIL—the Council for the Development of French in Louisiana. But the French patois, zydeco and Cajun music, and the indigenous cuisine of southwest Louisiana were not considered worth saving by the society at large. Speaking French, such a sign of sophistication in the city a mere hundred years earlier, was even made illegal in public schools in an effort to foster the Americanization of the Acadians. The council has since become a major force in the effort to encourage the retention of Cajun French and Cajun culture itself.

The same can be said in the city with respect to jazz. Preservation Hall was the one outlet for traditional jazz, and the city virtually disregarded the elders of the tradition even as those with direct links to the first days of jazz were dying off. It was not just the human links to the early days of jazz that were ignored; it was the buildings as well. In the early 1960s, the boyhood home of Louis Armstrong, now the namesake of the city's international airport, was razed to make way for government buildings. Dozens of other significant locales in the history of jazz were also demolished by design or neglect.

Around the same time, the gorgeous thoroughfare of North Claiborne Avenue was stripped of its ancient oak trees, said to have rivaled those along St. Charles Avenue, to build the I-10. Despite the loss of such natural beauty and the fracturing of the Tremé neighborhood, the artisans, craftsmen and musicians of the oldest black neighborhood in America still soldier on amid encroaching gentrification.

The culture of New Orleans, which Ellis Marsalis famously said "bubbles up from the street" and is now so revered by tourists and begrudgingly supported by city government, had been dying out for years. Jerry Brock, the highly respected music and cultural historian who started WWOZ with his brother because there was very little local music on the radio, remembers a mere seven or eight second line parades each season. Now there are over 40 social aid and pleasure clubs that march resplendent in feathered finery every Sunday from Labor Day until Father's Day.

Wavelength magazine, a precursor to *Offbeat* magazine, listed a grand total of sixteen Mardi Gras Indian tribes, seven uptown and eight downtown, and one tribe listed from the West Bank—the Mohawk Hunters who still exist today under the leadership of Big Chief Tyrone Casby. Currently, there are over 600 individual Indians in dozens of tribes. Clearly, the culture has rebounded.

Because of the success of the modern tourism industry, now most visitors to the city have at least some inkling about the indigenous black culture of jazz, Mardi Gras Indians and second lines. But back in 1979, even the New Orleans Jazz and Heritage Festival, which was celebrating its tenth anniversary with an unprecedented three weekends, was mostly populated by locals with a smattering of visiting musical cognoscenti. Many of the out of town aficionados were European.

New Orleans in the late 1970s was much more geographically isolated from the rest of the country. In the 21st century, it's a relatively easy trip getting to New Orleans. But during that period, Delta was the only airline that flew from the East Coast to New Orleans and there were no direct flights. The trip was considerably longer and much more expensive with a connection through Atlanta. Currently, it is routine to find a round trip flight for less than $250. It's hard to imagine that 30 years ago it cost closer to $400 to make the trip.

Now, savvy visitors can find out all about the culture from the local print media, and articles are just one click away in any search engine on the Internet. Mardi Gras Indian suits grace the collections of both the New Orleans Museum of Art and the Historic New Orleans Collection. The Backstreet Cultural Museum, which sends via e-mail the route sheets of most of the second line parades and information about events connected to the Mardi Gras Indian and jazz communities, is a resource for visitors and locals alike. Nationally and internationally published guide books take a cursory look at the culture and recommend key events, clubs and bands.

The significance of all these changes cuts both ways. On the one hand, the culture is much more viable today. Old timers say that the number of Indian tribes and social aid and pleasure clubs is as high as it has been since before World War II when the ranks of both sides of the culture were decimated by both wartime enlistment and the nascent Civil Rights movement.

World War II was one of the only times in the history of Carnival in New Orleans that the festivities were cancelled. It probably would not have mattered anyway since most of the able bodied men were in the military and many necessities were rationed. During the early days of the Civil Rights Movement, many blacks questioned the traditions including the wearing of blackface by the Zulu krewe, which was incorporated as a social aid and pleasure club in the first decade of the 20th century.

On the other hand, the culture has gradually been diluted. Among the Mardi Gras Indians, the fierce, often violent rivalries between downtown and uptown tribes are mostly a thing of the past. The violent confrontations that used to make outsiders wary of the Indians are also mostly dormant. It is easy to argue that the situation is much improved now that the fighting is mostly theatrical and Indians vie for who is the prettiest rather than who is the most feared.

But one can also argue that, as the culture changes, many of the revered traditions are being left by the wayside. Many an old time Indian has spoken out about young Indians disrespecting their elders, jumping positions in the tribe to become a chief before being properly inculcated into the traditions, and even failing to learn and understand the complicated system of signals that the tribes use to communicate.

The same arguments can be made about the second line culture. The legendary jazz musician and educator Danny Barker did not want a jazz funeral because the cultural antecedents had been diluted by modern day street culture. He wanted a dignified send off like his peers from the late 19th century, not a raucous street celebration. He wanted the musicians in uniform and the crowd to be respectful. It was only because some of his former students intervened that his widow reluctantly allowed a jazz funeral to occur. Barker died in 1994 illustrating that these concerns are not necessarily new.

I have identified five indicators of change that were in their nascent stages in the last years of the 1970s. Over the course of the next two decades, the city's arts economy and culture experienced profound growth that reverberates in numerous ways well into the 21st century.

1. The New Orleans music scene was in transition when this tale begins in the late 1970s. In pop music, the Meters, arguably the most important non-jazz act in the history of New Orleans music, had recently broken up amid years of friction between the members. The break up of the Meters fueled a second generation of funk bands that define a significant segment of the music of the last two decades of the 20th century in New Orleans.

2. The brass band tradition was beginning a long climb back into relevance after a decline that had threatened the very existence of the unique black culture of the city. Within twenty years, the brass band revival that produced the Dirty Dozen Brass Band extended to dozens of other bands and reenergized the social aid and pleasure clubs that are at the heart of the culture.

3. A new club, Tipitina's, had recently opened its doors with a mission to celebrate the greats of the R&B era. Tipitina's joined Preservation Hall, the bastion of traditional New Orleans jazz, as the second of two music institutions whose explicit purpose was to showcase the talent of an earlier era. Though its patron saint, the pianist and singer Henry Roeland Byrd, better known as Professor Longhair, passed away unexpectedly in January 1980 just as his career was being rejuvenated, Tipitina's became the standard for New Orleans nightclubs and exposed generations of concert goers, both local and visitor, to the wealth of musical talent in the city.

4. A music media infrastructure was emerging in the wake of the New Orleans Jazz and Heritage Festival's unprecedented success at showcasing the best music from New Orleans and Louisiana. Over the course of the next two decades, a new tourism-based

economy focusing on the music and culture of New Orleans, driven in part by this new media, replaced the collapsed oil-driven economy.

5. The development of jazz studies programs at the city's institutions of higher education, led by the University of New Orleans and Loyola University, created a new cohort of schooled jazz musicians that has increased the profile of modern jazz both locally and across the rest of the nation. Students who matriculated through the various programs over the last thirty years are among the leading jazz performers and educators across the country today.

Chapter 1

JAZZ FEST IN THE LATE 1970s AND THE EARLY 1980s

"I'm not sure, but I'm almost positive, that all music comes from New Orleans."—Ernie K-Doe

Looking back at the last decades of the 20th century and attempting to make sense of the period through a 21st century lens, it is clear the New Orleans Jazz and Heritage Festival, as entity, muse and inspiration, is the central thread running through this tale. From its humble beginnings in 1970 to its current status as the premier music festival in the world, the Jazz Fest, as it is known to all, is a river that flows through New Orleans carrying with it musicians who look to the music of New Orleans for inspiration. Music lovers and artists, businessmen and promoters have also ridden its stream and discovered the charms of New Orleans. They return each spring to bathe in its waters.

The Jazz Fest is also responsible for bringing musicians from outside its banks to the city. Thousands of musicians have taken residence in New Orleans over the decades and, in turn, influenced the direction of the flow of the music itself. Though purists would like to believe that real New Orleans music is created by native New Orleanians, many of the important players discussed in these pages were not born in their adopted hometown. As a port from its earliest beginnings, new blood has streamed into the city from every direction.

The history of the New Orleans Jazz and Heritage Festival actually begins a few years before the first festival took place. George Wein, the impresario behind the now world-famous event, was approached in the late 1960s about organizing a jazz fest in the city of the music's birth. He was already an old hand at outdoor music festivals having started the granddaddy of them all, the Newport Jazz Festival, in 1956. But circumstances conspired against the plan as it was conceived by the city—namely the fact that Wein, a gentile New Englander who loved traditional jazz, was a white man with a black wife. The city did attempt a modest jazz festival in 1968 and 1969.

The social milieu was shifting dramatically across the South, and within two years circumstances had changed enough for Wein to give New Orleans another chance. He hired two youngsters affiliated with Tulane University's jazz archive, Quint Davis and Allison Miner, to recruit talent. For the first two years, the festival's daytime Heritage Fair was held in Beauregard Square (now Congo Square) in the Tremé neighborhood on the edge of the French Quarter, and night concerts were held in the adjoining Municipal Auditorium. By 1972, though not actually turning a profit, the festival had outgrown the inner city location and moved to a horseracing venue, the New Orleans Fairgrounds, where it remains firmly lodged to this day.

Walking around the New Orleans Fairgrounds in the late 1970s was like being in another place and time. People brought their own food and drink, they flew canopies, and some hard-working souls actually pitched tents to shield their children from the blazing sun. The infield was set up in the same basic layout as it is today except that the blues, jazz and gospel tents had not been moved to the parking lot and the stages were more tightly bunched together inside both the dirt track and the inner grass track. The roster was considerably more local than it is today. A day at the Fairgrounds during this period was a far cry from today's Jazz Fest with each day meticulously planned and prepared in order to see every act on our wish lists. There were rarely any major crowd issues, and people generally planted themselves in one spot for the day or wandered around seeking out new sounds.

The line between performer and audience member was blurred since many of the most celebrated musicians also took part in the festivities. Keen-eyed festers could spot R&B musicians like Professor Longhair soaking up a gospel choir or brass band musicians rubbing shoulders with their country counterparts at a zydeco performance. One of the most famous photos in the early days of the festival features gospel icon Mahalia Jackson singing with the Eureka Brass Band as the group parades around the festival grounds.

By the early 1980s, the festival had added two gazebos where some of the most intimate performances took place. They were barely raised off the ground and fans could get up close to the musicians. On the first weekend of 1982, the list of gazebo performers reads like the headliners on the bigger stages today: Snooks Eaglin, Lucinda Williams, John Rankin, Spencer Bohren, David & Roselyn, Johnny Vidacovich and the Golden Eagles Mardi Gras Indian tribe all graced the stages of the two gazebos.

The early festivals also had the liberty to hire musicians who were out and out eccentrics. Foremost among them was Bongo Joe. He was a street performer from Texas whose given name was George Coleman. He built his own percussion set out of old 55-gallon drums along with various pipes that were filled with bird shot and sounded like maracas. He accompanied himself on the makeshift drum kit as he whistled, sang and told quirky little stories filled with social commentary. Bongo Joe played every festival back in that period, and his performances defined the inclusive nature of the event.

They also hired musicians who were legends in their specific genres. Many of the old time jazz masters like Willie and Percy Humphrey and Sweet Emma Barrett were still alive and they were treated like rock 'n' roll royalty. The early festivals also booked beloved bands from Cajun country that rarely performed in the big city. Cajun and Zydeco shows at clubs like Tipitina's and Mid City Lanes Rock 'N' Bowl did not become commonplace until years later.

Clifton Chenier, who billed himself as "The King of Zydeco," was the most celebrated of these performers. He was an incredibly charismatic performer who played the accordion like a banshee and sang his ass off in French. His brother, Cleveland, played the rubboard, or *frottoir*, like a man possessed. With a bottle opener in each hand, he coaxed intoxicating rhythms from the simple instrument.

Chenier always drew a huge crowd of people dancing in front of his stage as if their lives depended on this music and this man. Off to the side was an equally huge crowd just hanging out basking in the great man's glory. There were also a disproportionate number of men in cowboy hats and lots of people of both genders with boots on. Chenier, who died in 1987, was a real trooper and continued playing as his diabetes grew worse. His sheer tenacity was on display at his last performance at the Fairgrounds. One of his ailing feet was bandaged and blood could be seen seeping through, yet he kept on playing. Chenier helped define the inclusive nature of the New Orleans Jazz Fest in its early years.

Of course, the R&B legends of New Orleans also got their annual due at the Jazz Fest. At the top of the heap during this period was Earl King. King was a prolific songwriter, a brilliant guitarist and one of the most successful New Orleans artists from the 1950s rhythm and blues heyday. His song, "Come On, Part 1," was covered by many of the greats including Jimi Hendrix, and royalties from that song alone kept King in cash throughout the rest of his life.

King was an enigmatic performer who, in his later years, could put on an incendiary show, phone it in, or he could simply be a no-show. But going back closer to his heyday, the shows were nearly all over the top. King was a bear of a man given to wild suits and an even wilder stage persona. His eyes would bug out especially as he soloed. At the peak of any given solo he would clamp his eyes shut as if the intensity of the music would cause his eyes to eject from his head if he kept them open. He was sweating profusely even before he got warmed up, and the sweat seemed to pour from every pore often making his face look like a caricature.

His guitar playing was idiosyncratic, rooted in the blues, but with a swagger that transferred to his stage bearing. While he played, it often looked like the guitar was actually holding him up instead of vice versa. When he soloed, he had a tendency to play the same couple of notes over and over creating a hypnotic pattern that was bewitching in its complicated simplicity. No one else could solo like that even if they tried.

As a singer, King had the bluesman persona down pat even though his musical gifts transcended the genre. He projected a rough-around-the-edges stage presence, and his vocal phrasing could come across as that of a neophyte uncomfortable under the spotlight. But it was just an act, and King played it to the hilt. He threw himself into the performance and often seemed as if he were about to collapse as the set was ending.

King's idol was Guitar Slim, and each performance would inevitably include a few words of praise for his mentor followed by a scorching version of Slim's biggest hit, "The Things I Used to Do." King had a way of building a song from one crescendo to another. Each song, particularly the ballads, seemed like it was going to fall apart time and time again only to be pulled back together. Walter "Wolfman" Washington is one of the only other musicians with King's ability to deconstruct and refashion a song in the middle of playing it.

In a testament to the creative stage lineups that were the norm in the early years of the Jazz Fest and have remained hallmarks of the event's programming, Pete Fountain followed King, and then the Neville Brothers closed out Stage 1 in 1982.

Another feature of those early days was the inclusion of Mardi Gras Indian tribes on the roster. Big Chiefs Bo Dollis and Monk Boudreaux, of the Wild Magnolias and the Golden Eagles respectively, were hired to lure tourists to the first festival by parading from the French Quarter, and they have remained fixtures since the beginning.

However, the landscape of the Mardi Gras Indian community was considerably bleaker than it is today. Consider this—the first weekend of the 1982 Jazz Fest featured only four tribes over three days—the Wild Tchoupitoulas, the Black Eagles, the Golden Star Hunters and the Golden Eagles. The second weekend was not much better with just two tribes over the two days—the White Eagles and the Wild Magnolias. In the modern era, dozens of Indian tribes perform at the Jazz Fest with a number of tribes parading each day. However, there are still some tradition-minded tribes that choose not to participate in the annual event or are not on the radar of the festival's booking staff because they are newly formed.

Additionally, the tribes were not given choice stage times and none appeared on the big stages. This is not to suggest that the festival staff was discriminating against the Indians, for they had been a critical part of the festival experience since the first year when the

Indians trolled the French Quarter hoping to drag a few tourists back to the festival site in Congo Square. However, only a few tribes actually had a stage act. The others featured the hand percussion and call-and-response vocals that came undiluted straight out of their back-o-town practices. It was roots music that required no electricity for instruments or microphones.

Another aspect of the Jazz Fest that has gone by the wayside in later years was the official night shows sponsored by the festival. The booking agents were always very creative and booked like-minded acts in various genres. The best of the night concerts were held on the Riverboat President.

The Riverboat President experience during Jazz Fest is one of the most missed of all the attributes of those early festivals. While outside promoters still present shows on smaller boats, the experience is not the same as a couple of thousand fans sailing the Mississippi and dancing in unison until the wee-wee hours.

One particular evening from 1982 sums up the experience and warrants more detail. The "Caribbean Meets New Orleans" lineup on the Riverboat President starred Rita Marley with the Neville Brothers and Exuma providing support. While the Nevilles need no introduction, Exuma was an important player on the scene during this period because of his impact on the players in his band. He was a "junkanoo" musician who played acoustic guitar and sang songs from his home in the Bahamas. His style descended from slave traditions in the islands that included street parades with percussion instruments and vibrant costumes.

Exuma's drummer for a time was Ricky Sebastian who is now a well regarded drummer and music educator specializing in Afro-Caribbean rhythms both in New Orleans, where he has taught and played on and off for years, and in New York, where he is an in-demand session player and sideman. Ricky has a slippery sound on the drums and is able to move around the beat while keeping the tempo rock solid. He is a master on the ride cymbal and can play the clave beat like he was born in Cuba.

The guitar player with Exuma was Bruce "Weasel" McDonald. McDonald, who is mostly out of the music scene in New Orleans today, appears throughout this tale. He had a sterling sound on the Fender

Telecaster wringing crystal clear notes with a mixture of rock bombast and bluesy grit. He provided the perfect foil for Exuma's fairly simple acoustic guitar work.

Exuma's band also featured an incredible percussionist named Josiah Kinlock who played a vast array of instruments. He had chimes, ankle bells, wood blocks, junk bells (made out of found objects), clackers and gourds along with the requisite set of congas. He also played mouth harp and blew into whistles that he wore like a set of keys around his neck. Exuma wore small gourds tied around one ankle and was always stomping his feet while he played adding another layer to a sound that was already very percussive.

Surely one of the reasons why the "Caribbean Meets New Orleans" concert was such an amazing evening had to do with the hometown acts nearly upstaging Rita Marley. Exuma was a true professional who had performed all over the world before moving to New Orleans. He had already endeared himself to the community with his unique musical style and his effervescent personality. He was always able to turn it up a notch on stage, and his performance that night set the bar for the other two acts.

While the Nevilles were still in their infancy as a band, the group was also stocked with veteran performers, and they turned in an incredible hard-driving set that only featured two ballads—the requisite "Tell It Like It Is" from the golden voice of Aaron and a stellar version of the reggae classic, "Sitting Here in Limbo" sung with heartfelt emotion by Art Neville.

The crowd was very enthusiastic, cheering the bands with great enthusiasm and dancing with wild abandon. It was a Carnival crowd during Jazz Fest. An added advantage was the fact that there was no music on the Fairgrounds that day, so everyone was fresh rather than being sun-baked and a mite exhausted. Imagine Rita Marley sitting back stage smoking a spliff, and hearing the crowd going wild for the opening acts especially when Art Neville was singing a song so intimately connected to Jamaica and the reggae genre.

The reaction of the audience to the opening acts clearly energized her. When she hit the stage and the place went nuts, she knew she had to deliver. The energy was palpable and her performance, along with that of her great band, was ecstatic. The concert went quite late considering that she was scheduled to play the next day at the Fairgrounds. One of the highlights of the show was during the song, "One Love." Four of Rita and Bob Marley's children joined their mother on the chorus. If just for a moment, the bittersweet multi-generational performance transcended Bob's death of just over a year earlier.

During the summer of 1985 when Rockin' Sidney's "My Toot, Toot" was ubiquitous on the radio, the Riverboat President left town for renovations thereby insuring there would be no mid-sized shows until the boat returned.

By 1983, The New Orleans Jazz and Heritage Festival was growing considerably faster than anyone expected. That year, the organizers added the Economy Hall Tent that featured traditional jazz. They also began a long trend towards bringing international acts to the city. The Turtle Shell Band of Belize and the folkloric troupe from Haiti, Les Ballets Bacoulou D'Haiti, both performed on the Koindu stage (the precursor to the Congo Square stage) during the second weekend. But it was the appearances by Saxon Superstars of the Bahamas that had everyone talking the first weekend. The Saxon Superstars are a junkanoo group from Nassau. Their traditions dovetail perfectly with the Mardi Gras Indians of New Orleans, and it was the first time that many festers witnessed the deep connections between the various cultures of the African diaspora.

Junkanoo groups share many similarities with the Carnival cultures across the Caribbean including in New Orleans, Trinidad, Martinique and Brazil. They dress in handmade costumes and parade with various percussive instruments. Though there are plenty of similarities, there are also notable differences. The costumes of the Saxon Superstars are made of papier-mache and cardboard and are painted in bright colors. The group plays cowbells like the Mardi Gras Indians, but they shake them rather than playing them with a drumstick.

They didn't use drumsticks on any of their other instruments either. But they brought a wide range of percussive devices including goatskin drums, bicycle horns in various pitches as well as bugles and whistles. When they paraded around the infield of the New Orleans Fairgrounds, they created a spectacle that rivaled the biggest Mardi Gras Indian tribes. In another similarity to the Mardi Gras Indians, they brought up singers and electric instruments when they hit the Koindu stage. On stage, the music was more sophisticated than during the parade, which sounded to many like a cacophony of junkyard instruments. The Saxon Superstars left a lasting impression on everyone that year and helped usher in a new era of international performers at the Jazz Fest itself.

However, for many locals, 1983 was the beginning of the end of the Jazz Fest as they remembered it from its humble beginnings in Congo Square. Bringing your own food was still allowed although the ritual of bringing your own drinks had been banned the year before. The fest's organizers politely asked that everyone leave their little red wagons behind since the paved walkway was getting too crowded. They would eventually be officially banned putting a serious damper on the ability to bring in your own food. There was also griping in the media about the influx of well-heeled visitors from out of town. The argument was that the fest was too crowded and too expensive. These same arguments would surface again and again over the next few decades. Advance tickets were five dollars.

Chapter 2

NEW ORLEANS MUSIC VENUES IN THE 1980s

There are few who can visit her for the first time without delight; and few who can ever leave her without regret; and none who can forget her strange charm when they have once felt its influence."—Lafcadio Hearn

The opening of Tipitina's in 1977 was a landmark event in the history of New Orleans popular music. The establishment was named after a tune written by Henry Roeland Byrd, aka Professor Longhair, and the central concept of the club was to provide a venue for Longhair as well as his many peers from the heyday of the 50s R&B scene. It was started by a group of fourteen music freaks who formed a business akin to a co-op. The "fabulous fo'teen," as the ownership group came to be known, were slowly realizing that many of the musicians they usually only heard emanating from bar room juke-boxes around Mardi Gras and at the Jazz Fest every spring were still alive, and some were down on their luck and looking for work.

Professor Longhair was famously out of the music business and working as a janitor and occasional gambler when he was "re-discovered" by Quint Davis and Allison Miner. The group also embraced numerous other players from the 1950s such as Earl King, Snooks Eaglin and Jessie Hill.

The Tipitina's of today is a far cry from its humble beginnings. The original club, which was renovated before it re-opened in January of

1986 after an 18-month hiatus, was typical of many of the bars dotting the streets closest to the river. Prior to the lease being acquired by the ownership group, the location was a corner bar named the 501 Club after its address at 501 Napoleon Avenue. The 501 Club had occasional live music performances, but it was primarily a working class establishment catering to the dock workers whose place of employment was a mere quarter-mile away. There was also another separate establishment located next door to the 501 Club.

The new owners did away with the wall separating the two establishments and created a much larger space. The room was decorated in latter day hippie style with ratty, vinyl-covered couches along one wall. The bathrooms, which were both located along the General Pershing Street side of the building, were barely usable. They reeked of something old and decayed. A visit was always kept to the absolute minimum amount of time.

The two bar setup modern day customers are accustomed to was added during the 1986 renovation that also removed the drop ceiling, added the second floor balcony, back stage rooms, office space and, most importantly, air-conditioning. Before the renovation, the club had a single horseshoe-shaped bar extending from the Napoleon Avenue entrance to the bathrooms on the far side of the room. The renovation also put the front door on an angle—it was previously flush with Napoleon Avenue.

The surface of the bar was Plexiglas under which was displayed all manner of artwork, photographs, matchbook covers, newspaper clippings and other sundries. The bar's decoration clearly expressed the hippie ethic of the owners. Also part of that ethic was a service model based on as little effort as possible. But at least you always had something interesting to look at when the wait for a drink became interminable.

It was always a challenge to get through the narrow space on the Tchoupitoulas Street side of the bar, which was often crowded with regulars. But once you squeezed around the end, you were in a wide-open space that led up to the dance floor and the stage.

The Napoleon Avenue side of the building was the location of the juice bar (the original full name of the club was Tipitina's Piano and Juice Bar, but the juice bar barely lasted the first few years), the kitchen and a giant floor-to-ceiling fan that sucked air out of the club. The fan was critical in the warmer months because the original Tipitina's was not air-conditioned. The fan also provided an option for those music freaks short of cash on any given night. It was situated very close to the stage, and it was fairly easy to hear the music through the fan. Of course, they had to cope with the sound of the fan itself, but that was only a minor issue, and on a night featuring a big name act, it was common for a dozen or so folks to gather outside the fan. The other downside was the fact that the air blowing on them used to be inside the club and was of the superheated, sweat and smoke-charged variety.

For those who never experienced a crowded night in the heat of the summer, here is the best description I can muster because you really had to have been there to truly understand the level of discomfort. The walls literally sweated. Sometimes it was so humid in the place that the clouds of smoke seemed to be seeded with water. The smoke hung low in the room since there was not yet a second floor and balcony. Both bands and patrons alike were soaked to the bone within minutes. A trick learned early on was to bring extra shirts for changing between sets. The only respite was outside, where it was often noticeably cooler even in August, or underneath the meager ceiling fans that provided only a modicum of relief.

Still, everyone loved the place. The feelings that modern day visitors have for the club are rooted in its history, but there has always been an amazing vibe associated with Tipitina's. No one has ever been able to put a finger on exactly what created and sustains the magic, but no one has ever successfully denied its existence either. A college roommate of mine made this statement after a series of amazing nights where the music just kept getting better and better and the energy in the room made it feel as if the whole place was going to lift off and head into outer space—"Tipitina's is the greatest indoor spot on the planet." Few who spent any significant time during its 20th century heyday would argue.

The original Tipitina's had a kitchen that doled out hippie favorites and local cuisine to a mixture of neighborhood folks, students and music freaks who gravitated to the place at all hours. Monday's specials were vegetarian red beans and rice and veggie spaghetti. The spaghetti was one dollar a plate and the beans and rice was $1.50. Incidentally, in another nod to the "fabulous fo'teen's" hippie sensibilities, the kitchen served brown rice with the beans and meat eaters could get sausage on the side for an added price. It was one of the only places where you could get brown rice with your red beans in the entire city in the early 1980s, if not in the whole of the South.

Despite all of the attractions associated with the club, the "fabulous 'fo'teen" were constantly in dire financial straits connected to a plethora of problems. Some of the owners thought that if only the club were air-conditioned, the business would be able to survive the slowest and hottest months on the calendar. Numerous air-conditioning benefits were held at Tipitina's, but any monies collected went to service other outstanding bills. Nevertheless, the club remained without air-conditioning until it re-opened under new ownership in 1986.

Tipitina's eventually grew into the premier live music club we know today. It was the preferred venue for two generations of touring bands heading to New Orleans before the advent of the House of Blues. But in the early 1980s, it was not the only choice for live music uptown—three other clubs formed a holy trinity of music clubs in the Carrollton neighborhood and each had its own scene that differed slightly from each other and from the hippie aesthetic of Tips. Jed's was located catty corner from the Maple Leaf on the corner of Oak and Dante Streets, and Jimmy's was two blocks away on the corner of Willow and Dante Streets. The Maple Leaf is the only one of the three still presenting live music on a regular basis.

While Tipitina's underwent a major renovation before the grand reopening in 1986, the Maple Leaf has been a work in progress since it first opened in 1974 as an uptown jazz and chess place that was supposed to cater to a more sophisticated, literate crowd. It was also without air-conditioning and the ambiance in the hotter months was similar to that of Tipitina's with the exception of the grand patio that is still one of the main draws to the Oak Street establishment. Over the years, the space where the ladies restroom is now located has served many functions. It was once a laundromat and also a delicatessen called Fat Boy's.

The upgrades at the Maple Leaf, including the central air-conditioning, have been so gradual that only a longtime regular might notice the differences. Some of these enhancements also include the wood dance floor, a wide range of draft beer selections, larger restrooms, and as of the spring of 2007, a state-of-the-art sound system.

Without a doubt, Jimmy's was the rock club during this period. Its larger size allowed it to draw more touring bands amid the local multi-band bills that drew lots of students. Numerous bands broke into the city's collective consciousness after a successful night at Jimmy's including local and touring new wave acts. Jimmy's was a bare bones place that could have been described as a dump, although that term could be used to describe most of the music clubs in the city at that time. The non-descript brick building featured a raised area by the bar in the back of the club that offered great sightlines to the stage. But the room itself lacked significant air-conditioning, which was a big problem when it was crowded, and the acoustics left something to be desired.

Jed's, on the other hand, attempted to develop in amenities what it lacked in ambiance. It was not located in an historic building like the Maple Leaf or Jimmy's, but was on a corner lot with a split-level design that allowed for multiple sightlines. Plus, the place was air-conditioned! By the time it became Tupelo's Tavern in 1981, they had tables accessorized with umbrellas inside—very upscale indeed.

In the late 70s and early 80s, Jed's booking policy walked the musical line between the Maple Leaf and Jimmy's while skewing towards local new wave bands that couldn't get booked elsewhere. There was a lot of overlap since many of the more popular bands played all over town. Jed's hosted the occasional touring rock act. Elvis Costello, the Psychedelic Furs and the Jam played there early in their careers. But their bread-and-butter was local rock and new wave acts along with occasional appearances by musicians from the R&B scene.

Jed Palmer, the namesake of the club, closed the bar in October of 1981 telling the media he was retiring. He surfaced soon enough as the owner of F&M's, a late night college hangout on Tchoupitoulas Street that did not present live music. During the 1984 World's Fair in New Orleans, Palmer got back into the live music business with Jed's Lookout—one of several live music venues at the fair.

Jed's re-opened Thanksgiving weekend in 1981 as Tupelo's Tavern under new ownership and a no punk music policy. The hardcore aspect of the style was fading in popularity, though Tupelo's continued booking national and international acts that were part of the punk-new wave continuum such as Oingo Boingo and Billy Idol. By 1983, Tupelo's Tavern was on its last legs and closed within the year.

What made these three clubs so special had a lot to do with their proximity to each other and their hours. The music at Jimmy's usually ended earlier. The Maple Leaf and Jed's (and later Tupelo's) often vied for who stayed open the latest. Either way, on a good night it was easy to walk between the three clubs and see three completely different bands with three completely different crowds. The scene was similar to what has evolved on Frenchmen Street since those days.

Another option emerged when the Willow Inn, a neighborhood bar located across Dublin Street from Jimmy's, changed hands and was renamed Carrollton Station. By the summer of 1983, they began presenting live music adding a fourth club to the walkable neighborhood.

At the other end of the spectrum uptown was Tyler's Beer Garden, which was located on Magazine Street just downtown of Jefferson Avenue. Though still basically a dump, it was a jazz club that fostered an air of sophistication, which had a powerful effect on the college crowd. It was where students took their visiting parents after they grew tired of Bourbon Street. It was the hot spot for that hot date. Tyler's had an oyster bar and table service with a crew of waitresses drawn from the uptown colleges.

The big draw during this period at Tyler's was the James Rivers Movement on weekend nights. Rivers, who is still active on the scene today, is an urbane multi-instrumentalist who always carries himself with an air of dignity. He plays all manner of woodwinds from the saxophone family as well as flute and bagpipes. Though he played the part of the quintessential modern jazz player, he wasn't averse to adding some showmanship to his act. He had one particular flute with a harmonica strapped to it. He would play a lick on the flute and then quickly switch to the harmonica. He was very adept at going back and forth between the two instruments and always found a way to tastefully end the musical phrase.

Rivers' show at Tyler's was a sophisticated act that drew touring jazz players, celebrities and even rock 'n' rollers. The legendary swing musician Woody Herman, who was getting up in years at the time, was a special guest in the fall of 1979. All I remember is how old he seemed and the blues song he sang in a croaky voice. The tune had the hilarious refrain, "Your sister smoked in bed, now she's dead." A year or so later, Herman, tired of the incessant touring that is a jazz-man's life, opened his own club in the Hyatt Regency downtown and played every weekend with his band, the Thundering Herd.

Besides Rivers on the weekends, Tyler's also had a stunning weeknight schedule. You could expect to see the Taste of New Orleans, which featured George Porter, Jr. on bass, David Lastie on saxophone, David Torkanowsky on piano and Herlin Riley on drums. Torkanowsky, Riley and the bassist James Singleton played in various combinations in those years with the saxophonist Fred Kemp and the trumpeter Clyde Kerr, Jr. Willie Tee, the prolific composer and keyboardist behind the Wild Magnolias Mardi Gras Indian funk project, held down Wednesdays for a period, and a very young and precocious Leslie Smith sang on Tuesdays. The drummer Johnny Vidacovich was a regular as well. He formed Astral Project, the longest-running modern jazz band in New Orleans and an institution in its own right along with Singleton, the pianist Mike Pellera and the guitarist Lon Price. The saxophonist Tony Dagradi and the guitarist Steve Masakowski replaced Pellera and Price to form the group we know today.

Business at Tyler's Beer Garden also was suffering along with the local economy, and in 1985 they had to cut back their schedule to four nights a week. They also started veering away from the straight ahead modern jazz formula that had sustained them for years. The club closed for about six months in 1987, and Tyler's II opened briefly in the space on the corner of Oak and Dante Streets in the building formerly occupied by Jed's and Tupelo's Tavern. Tyler's finally closed for good and ended an era of live jazz uptown.

By May of 1987, the club that housed Jed's and Tupelo's Tavern had changed hands again and was re-named Muddy Waters. The booking policy at Muddy Waters in their first couple of years mirrored that of its predecessors and skewed towards local rock and hardcore bands. But the club eventually began focusing more on New Orleans funk.

There were a few clubs that presented live music downtown. Modern jazz had Lu and Charlie's, which closed in the late 1970s, and Prout's Club Alhambra, which hosted Jazz Fest night shows in this period. Preservation Hall didn't have the cachet it has today, but it was a critical cog in traditional jazz presenting the standard bearers of the genre in the same barebones setting that is visited by tourists today.

The opening of Preservation Hall in 1961 reflected the opening of Tipitina's nearly two decades later. As the public's fancies changed, swing and then modern jazz replaced the traditional jazz of New Orleans in the public's imagination creating a need for a place like Preservation Hall, just as rock 'n' roll, replacing R&B, created a need for a place like Tipitina's.

The Old Absinthe Bar on Bourbon Street was a blues joint that attracted touring musicians particularly from the world of rock 'n' roll. In the early 1980s, Mason Ruffner, an incredibly talented blues guitarist out of Fort Worth, Texas began playing at the club before being embraced by blues cognoscenti all over town. He was a regular at the club until 1985 when he was signed to CBS Records and left town shortly after. But for a while he was New Orleans' own blues guitar hero.

A black blind drummer named Willie Cole powered Ruffner's band during his stretch playing on Bourbon Street. A number of international stars including Jimmy Page of Led Zeppelin and Bruce Springsteen watched in awe as he attacked the guitar while Cole pounded the skins. Some of the stars, including local heroes like Earl King, even chose to sit in creating a feeling among the musical cognoscenti that the Old Absinthe Bar was much more than just a tiny club on Bourbon Street. The sit-ins by major stars allowed the club to develop an aura that grew until it was eventually turned into a daiquiri shop much to the dismay of preservationists in New Orleans and music lovers across the globe.

While Frenchmen Street is regarded today as a "musical arts district," it was still largely a commercial district for much of the early 1980s. There were two clubs, the Dream Palace, located where the Blue Nile is today, and the Faubourg, located where Snug Harbor is today. All of the buildings housing clubs today were businesses that kept daytime hours or were vacant storefronts. At night, it was a downright desolate neighborhood.

The Dream Palace was a favorite of the gangs of hippies that descended on the club from neighborhoods all over New Orleans. The club had a mural of the cosmos on the ceiling, faux brick arches and hosted mostly rock bands. Another book could be written about the various changes in ownership and décor at the Dream Palace. The schedule was haphazard and the stage was moved more than once from the front of the building to the rear and back again. For a period, there was no roof at all over the back part of the club. The Dream Palace closed for good in 1983 and reopened a few months later as Club Marigny just in time for Carnival.

Two blocks down the street was the Faubourg where jazz was the music of choice. It changed hands in 1983 and George Brumat, who had recently sold his interest in the Port of Call restaurant, took over laying the groundwork for what became a New Orleans institution. The club was christened Snug Harbor, and though their booking policy remained mostly the same as when it was called the Faubourg, the leadership of Brumat eventually raised the profile of the club to international renown.

Across the Mississippi River, Sherman Bernard, who currently owns one of the larger production companies in the city, held court at his club, Ole Man River's. It was a sit down venue that contrasted nicely with the free-for-all vibe at Tipitina's and the other rock clubs in town. Ole Man River's catered to touring rock and blues acts such as George Thorogood and the Destroyers and Johnny Winter. During its heyday in the early 1980s, the club also featured punk acts such as the Ramones, Talking Heads and Siouxsie and the Banshees. The Police played there on their first U.S. tour, as did U2. But Ole Man River's was an event destination due to its distance from the city and the lack of suitable public transportation for fans from the east bank.

While the racism of the segregated South was definitely not a prominent feature of living in cosmopolitan New Orleans during the 1980s, there were still plenty of vestiges of the segregation era that had ended a mere fifteen years before I arrived in the Crescent City. Certain bars and restaurants still had a separate service window that opened onto the street outside to serve blacks, and plenty of establishments still had buzzers on their doors to control admission. There were also innumerable black clubs dotting the city. They were mostly in back-of-town neighborhoods, and some featured live music. But none ever advertised. Looking back, it's important to note that shows went a lot later in those days. Now it's rare for a club show in New Orleans to last past 3 AM except around Carnival or during the Jazz Fest. The black clubs went even later.

The Rose Tattoo was one of the few black clubs that was not located on an out of the way street or in a rough neighborhood. It was directly across Napoleon Avenue from Tipitina's, and the room resembled the layout of the original Tipitina's. It was a long, narrow building with the main entrance on Napoleon Avenue, half a block off the corner of Tchoupitoulas Street. The bar ran parallel to Napoleon and extended from the corner about two-thirds of the length of the building. At the far end of the bar was a small dance floor surrounded by a few tables and a makeshift stage.

If the original Tipitina's had the well-worn feel of an old riverfront bar, the Rose Tattoo looked and felt exactly like the bar in the movie "Animal House" where the frat brothers go to see Otis Day and the Nights. It was dark, really dark. The only significant illumination came from the genuine disco ball rotating on the ceiling. The ball threw white refracted light throughout the entire bar creating a vaguely psychedelic haze when combined with the cigarette smoke.

Walter "Wolfman" Washington was one of the regulars at the Rose Tattoo during this period. He was regarded mostly as the bandleader for the great R&B vocalist Johnny "The Tan Canary" Adams, but he also performed with his band Solar System. The group featured two musicians who played with Washington throughout his career—the bassist Jack Cruz and the drummer Wilbert "Junkyard Dog" Arnold. Cruz is still ably handling the bass duties for Washington's current outfit, the Roadmasters. Arnold passed away late in 2008.

"Wolfman" was playing mostly blues at that time with a bit of R&B and soul mixed in, but the band just oozed that elusive New Orleans vibe that made his style so different from Chicago or Mississippi delta style blues. Washington's singing back then was rather rudimentary, but his guitar playing was intense. He used techniques gleaned from a variety of styles and influences, and it sounded like he was literally wringing the notes out of the guitar. His rhythm playing was sublime.

The two other musicians also carried themselves with authority. Arnold had chains around his drum set. Some claimed it was to remind him of the days of slavery, but he often played so hard that the drums would gradually migrate away from him. The chains kept them in place. Cruz, though just a youngster transplanted to New Orleans from the East Coast, was a monster. He laid down the most serious groove this side of George Porter, Jr., and the three of them made a hell of a racket that sounded like heaven to many ears.

Towards the end of its existence, the Rose Tattoo began branching out to feature young white bands playing punk rock. But for years, it was a black club that catered to the working class men who toiled on the nearby Mississippi River.

Dorothy's Medallion, another black club, was located on Orleans Avenue just off of Bayou St. John in the Mid City neighborhood. It attracted a more moneyed crowd and was the king (or queen) of the super-late night crowd. Dorothy's, as everyone called it, was a real late night joint in a town filled with late night joints. When the music at the other clubs ended around 3:30 or 4 AM, Dorothy's was just getting started. The band on weekend nights, with Walter "Wolfman" Washington as the leader, didn't even start until after 2 AM. Weekend performances at Dorothy's Medallion routinely ended long after the sun had come up.

Mostly everyone sat at tables with a lively scene at the bar. The drink menu featured "set ups," and Dorothy, the owner, would often be behind the bar with her huge blond wig and oversized eyeglasses. They sold half pints of liquor and small bottles of various mixers. The "set up" came with a couple of glasses and a small bowl of ice cubes, and patrons made their own drinks.

The star of the show was the vocalist Johnny Adams. The band usually played a long opening set of instrumentals before Adams would stroll in, impeccably resplendent in a brightly colored suit. Wolfman usually had horn players on this gig, and the band gradually worked the crowd into a frenzy in anticipation of the arrival of Adams. The music was more R&B than the straight up blues of the Rose Tattoo. All of the musicians stretched out, taking long languorous solos, and a tune could go on for an indeterminate amount of time. But it wasn't jamming per se—the sound didn't fit into any set category. It was bluesy jazz or jazzy blues. When Adams started his long string of records for Rounder Records in 1984, he used jazz musicians on all of them except for his debut, *From the Heart*, which featured Washington's band.

Adams is generally regarded as an R&B vocalist, but he had a jazz singer's phrasing and his sets usually included a jazz standard or two. He was a vocalist who was respected by the band as a musician. He could scat along with the band or trade phrases with the lead instruments. He also was a gifted mimic who could play a wicked mouth trombone that sounded right at home among the other instrumentalists. His singing voice could go from a whisper to a wail depending on whether he was singing a ballad or a roadhouse stomper. He was great at getting up into the higher registers, and he could sing falsetto like his namesake bird. He was one of Aaron Neville's musical heroes.

Adams paid close attention to his posture, and though he didn't move much on stage, his presence and intensity were riveting. Sometimes it looked like he was gripping the microphone with all of his strength, and the tiniest little gesture—a clenched fist, a raised hand or an outstretched arm—communicated volumes. He was a consummate gentleman both on and off the stage. He always made it appear as if you were doing him a favor by listening to his music. When his scintillating set ended, Adams would immediately walk off the bandstand right into the crowd. He would extend his hand to anyone and everyone and effusively thank the audience for coming. Regardless of whether he was playing in a tiny back-o' town club or on the big stage at Jazz Fest, Adams had the ability to make you feel like he was entertaining you in your own living room.

During this period, Dorothy's was *his* living room, and the place was always packed. They also had cage dancers—hugely over-weight black women dressed in minute outfits who would gyrate to the music in a makeshift cage by the side of the stage. After seven years in business, it was disheartening to learn that the venerable Dorothy's Medallion, where so many had witnessed many a dawn, was closing. There has never been another club like it.

Johnny Adams and Walter "Wolfman" Washington moved on as well. Adams continued to perform around town and Washington debuted his long-running band, the Roadmasters. Out of Adams' shadow, he began to develop his own singing voice, and the new band's sound starting veering into funky territory.

* * *

Of course, there were larger venues presenting live music in New Orleans. A Warehouse, as it was formally known, was a legendary concert venue that hosted all of the greats from the sixties includ-ing the Doors and Pink Floyd amid southern rock bands such as the Allman Brothers. It opened in January of 1970 with a double bill of original bluesy Fleetwood Mac and the Grateful Dead. The place was a bare bones facility that was literally a riverfront warehouse before it was converted into a concert hall. It lacked air-conditioning and had holes in the walls. The floor was covered with huge carpets that reeked from all manner of liquids and substances spilled by wob-bly-legged hippies. It looked like the ceiling might cave in at any moment, and the horrible condition of the bathrooms rivaled those at Tipitina's and CBGB's in New York. It was located in a rough neigh-borhood on Tchoupitoulas Street on the way downtown. Kids from the nearby St. Thomas housing project would ask you for a dollar to "watch" your car. But despite the various inconveniences, it was a great place to see a show.

By the late 1970s, the sixties acts that were the mainstay of A Warehouse during its heyday were no longer drawing crowds as a new style, new wave/punk, rose up in response to the crass mate-rialism that was infecting popular music. Newer bands like Elvis Costello and the Attractions, Squeeze and the Clash had graduated from the small clubs and earned gigs at A Warehouse. The promoters booked local acts to open for the headliners. The Cold, a new wave band fronted by the vivacious singer Barbara Menendez with Vance Degeneres (brother of Ellen) on bass, opened for Costello and the great New Orleans vocalist Lee Dorsey, known for such classics as, "Working in a Coalmine" and "Ride Your Pony," opened for the Clash in 1981.

The Saenger Theater on Canal Street was also a venue for touring acts. In early August of 1981, Peter Tosh, one of the greatest singers and songwriters from reggae's golden age, made an appearance at the downtown theater. The great contemporary bluesman Taj Mahal opened the show, and he gave the audience a generous helping of his good-natured personality and a pleasant lesson in the blues. But everyone was waiting for Tosh who appeared late amid a cloud of smoke. The music itself was smoking from the first notes. During the song, "African," which was a staple of Tosh's live set, he name-checked a list of locales in an effort to spread the theme of African unity that was part of the songwriter's oeuvre throughout his career. After singing, "If you're from Jamaica, you are an African; if you are from Canada, you are an African; if you are from America, you are an African," he got really local with the audience and earned huge cheers. He sang, "If you are from New Orleans, you are an African; if you are from Gretna, you are an African; if you are from the West Bank, you are an African." On and on he went, name-checking other local spots as the crowd went wild.

There were also some clubs during that period that could be called dance clubs or discos. But they were concentrated on Bourbon Street and in an area of Metairie called Fat City. The city itself was isolated from mainstream American culture in such a way that even disco, which took the country by storm in the late 70s and early 80s, barely made any inroads. Sure, the Meters recorded a song called "Disco is the Thing Today" on their last album, *New Directions*, but that record was arguably a last hurrah rather than an actual statement of musical intentions.

Chocolate Milk, a local rival of the Meters, recorded some music that could be called disco. They were signed to RCA Records from1975 to 1983 and had a series of Top 20 R&B hits.

As far as I know, New Orleans never had a movement against disco, like the episode that resulted in a massive destruction of dance records at Comiskey Park in Chicago, because New Orleans has always had its own distinctive musical style. However, the fact that disco never really gained a foothold in New Orleans doesn't mean that people didn't dance. On the contrary, dancing was omnipresent in the clubs of New Orleans in the 1970s.

Dancing to live music was a way to commune with other music freaks and to connect with the band. It was a requisite of life in the city. You rarely saw couples locked into a specific style—they generally just hit the floor and moved to the music however they felt it. There was no learning curve for newcomers, and there was no difference between the dance floor and the rest of the club. It just seemed like everyone was dancing to the music in his or her own way, and the bands always seemed to play better with a crowd of music lovers pushed up front on the dance floor.

New Orleanians developed their own style of dancing by mixing various elements mirroring the mélange of cultures that came together to create the vibrant pastiche of the city's ethnic makeup. While jazz became sit-down music as it migrated north, acquiring an air of sophistication and moving out of bar rooms and into concert halls, it remained dance music in New Orleans. So there is also a genteel aspect to dance here.

Chris Kenner, a 1950s era songwriter who achieved considerable fame among the cognoscenti for his great tunes, wrote a song, "The Land of 1000 Dances," that reflects this aesthetic. The song names dozens of dance steps from "the pony" to "the mashed potato" and "the alligator." It musically sums up the connection between the city, clearly "the land" in the title, and dancing.

The concept of the second line has also strongly influenced the role of dancing in New Orleans culture. In the early days of jazz, strong ties still existed connecting the slaves to their various African cultures. Those ties have lessened over the ensuing centuries, but the ritual role of dance in the cultures of Africa was transferred, along with the musical rhythms, to the citizens in New Orleans. Over time, the influence of those connections came to spread through the various ethnicities in the city. Now everyone, from uptown bluebloods to working class African-Americans, understands what you do when the band is playing and you have an umbrella in your hand.

Another element that factors into this equation is the influence of the counterculture of the 1960s. Since New Orleans was so far removed from mainstream America, it took a little longer for the counterculture ethic to take hold, just as punk did not emerge in New Orleans until several years after it became the rage in London and New York. Social commentators have argued that the lag time between New Orleans and the capitals of culture in fashion, music and other elements of popular culture is five years.

But once the counterculture movement reached the city, it quickly merged with her many other bohemian attributes and developed a staying power that rivaled much bigger cities. When I arrived in 1979, it felt like the sixties were still going on though many of the quaint vestiges of that era, like psychedelic light shows and food co-ops, had fallen out of fashion elsewhere.

There is a shared energy between the audience and the band when everyone is dancing. It is earthy and primal, and it connects the audience and the band like an umbilical cord. It is like being tied into another frequency that encourages some form of unspoken communication. Besides being palpable, it is powerful—there is no resisting this level of intensity; everyone simply has to join in. One of the reasons that this form of communication between a band and an audience occurs has to do with the dancing. That is also why the feeling is so hard to find elsewhere in today's society. Because elsewhere, out in the great beyond that is mainstream America, people generally don't dance to live music.

I have seen many of the same bands that play regularly in New Orleans in other cities, including music meccas like New York and San Francisco, and though the bands usually play their hearts out, inevitably the feeling is not the same. The missing factor is dancing for the pure joy of movement; dancing that empties the mind and creates spiritual unity in the audience while providing a connection to the musicians.

This dancing ethic is one of the things that has changed in New Orleans over the past thirty years. As the country has become more homogenous with the consolidation of regional radio, interstate highway systems and cookie cutter fast food restaurants among hundreds of other factors, some of the cultural mores that have always separated New Orleans from the rest of the United States have gradually seeped in.

Among the most sinister of these new values is the suppression of dancing. It used to be a rarity; now it is commonplace. People sit on the dance floor; people ask dancers to sit down. People put chairs on the dance floor. While I have no problem with sitting per se, although I think it interferes with the spirit of the music, I do object to what I have termed the imposition of external values. Just because that's the way you do it at home, does not mean that is the way we do it here.

Chapter 3

THE MUSICIANS AND BANDS OF THE LATE 1970s AND THE EARLY 1980s

"Funny thing is, people in New Orleans expect music, not just at parties, but all the time"—Record Ron

While I have already touched upon a number of the important players from the last 25 years of the 20th century in New Orleans, the city had an amazing abundance of incredible musicians in nearly every genre. Many of them, particularly the modern jazz players, crossed genres to play R&B, funk, or the blues on a regular basis. Their ability to move easily between genres is based on an inherent tension that blooms because they have mastered a rare dichotomy—the music can be loose and tight at the same time. This tension is very compelling to the ears. It provides a push-pull effect that attracts listeners because a lack of balance can occasionally be sensed, as if the song could fall apart at any moment. But it rarely ever does.

The basis of the tension is connected to the role of the rhythm section. New Orleans has always produced great drummers going back to the earliest days of jazz in the city. Their ability to syncopate the beat provides openings for the other musicians to explore the spaces between the actual notes of a given song.

Primary among these musicians were the saxophone players Alvin "Red" Tyler, Fred Kemp and Earl Turbinton. Earl Turbinton was by far the most eccentric of the many great saxophonists who dotted the musical landscape of New Orleans. He was a disciple of John Coltrane and actually spent time with the innovator when he was in New Orleans in the 1950s. During the 1960s and early 1970s, he recorded with B.B. King, Allen Toussaint and the great jazz-fusion player, Joe Zawinul. He was reportedly invited to join the seminal fusion band, Weather Report. In the 1960s, he often performed with his brother, Willie Tee (Wilson Turbinton), in both jazz and pop bands. He was a member of the Gaturs—a seminal New Orleans funk band, and he played on the Wild Magnolias' groundbreaking synthesis of funk and Mardi Gras Indian music that Willie Tee produced.

Turbinton nicknamed himself "the African Cowboy" after a conversation about Ronald Reagan's presidency, which was wrecking havoc on the arts and arts education. Turbinton disparagingly called the president "a cowboy" and then stated that what America needs is an African cowboy. After the saxophonist made a sojourn to Africa, the nickname stuck. He played regularly at Snug Harbor and other venues, and his act and appearance gradually became decidedly more African-inspired. His set at the Jazz Fest in 1986 was billed as the "African Cowboy Anthology" and featured African percussionists. Turbinton presided over the affair like a chieftain, blowing long lines in the manner of Coltrane, his idol.

Despite his brilliance, Earl Turbinton suffered through a range of personal and medical problems that came to a head in the early 1990s. Arriving home at three in the morning with a friend in late 1994, we heard Turbinton on the radio station WWOZ. He was on the air for over an hour alternating between playing solo saxophone and ranting and raving about Jesus and his love for prostitutes and other marginalized characters. It was completely over the top, and the deejay, an inexperienced substitute, was overwhelmed and unable to control the "interview."

On another occasion, Turbinton strolled into Kermit Ruffins' regular gig at Donna's Bar and Grill on N. Rampart Street with a snifter of brandy in one hand and his saxophone in the other. Seemingly high on himself and/or cocaine and/or alcohol, he approached the bandstand with nary a word to Ruffins. He just assumed sitting in was his god-given right. When the time came for his solo, he was unable to generate enough saliva to wet the reed of his horn—a necessary step before playing the instrument. Without hesitating, he dipped the reed into the brandy glass, inserted it into the horn and proceeded to deliver one of the most incredible solos of his distinguished career. He then picked up the glass and walked straight out the front door without exchanging words with anyone in the bar.

Earl Turbinton didn't record much of his own music, but a striking example of his talents on the alto and soprano saxophone can be heard on his album, *Brother For Life*, which he recorded with Willie Tee. Towards the end of his life, he also recorded with Johnny Vidacovich, Labelle, Champion Jack Dupree and others. Turbinton died in August 2007 after a stroke silenced his horn.

Alvin "Red" Tyler, whose love of modern jazz was stifled by the shifting whims of the marketplace, was a legendary saxophonist in R&B circles. He performed as a rhythm and blues sideman on hundreds of singles during the 1950s R&B heyday by the likes of Fats Domino, Little Richard, Aaron Neville and Lee Dorsey. He released two jazz records on Rounder Records in the 1980s. Like many of the bebop stylists of the Crescent City during the 1950s, Tyler often worked pop gigs to keep his hand in the game as well as to earn some extra bucks. Incidentally, Tyler also worked a day job as a route salesman for a liquor company for most of his adult life.

He backed the great New Orleans vocalist Germaine Bazzle on countless gigs. Bill Huntington, a veteran bassist with a sumptuous tone who is still active on the scene, was also a regular sideman for gigs with Bazzle and dozens of other leaders. Alvin "Red" Tyler was a longtime member of Dr. John's band. He also gigged regularly with Professor Longhair and the eccentric keyboard genius James Booker. Towards the end of Booker's life, Tyler backed the pianist at the Maple Leaf in a group called "The Heavenly Angels" that included Johnny Vidacovich and James Singleton.

Tyler wasn't a player given to showing off. His demeanor on stage was playful, and he had a great ear. He was always listening to the other musicians, and his solos reflected a deep understanding of the history of the music. His tone was buttery, and he could play a ballad with deep conviction communicating the essence of a song as if he were a singer. His idols were the bebop greats Charlie Parker and Dizzy Gillespie, but when he led his own group at the Jazz Fest, which he did nearly every year, he knew intuitively that the crowd was out to have a good time. So, his song selections reflected good time jazz rather than complicated tunes demonstrating his musical prowess. Alvin "Red" Tyler died on April 3, 1998 leaving a void that has yet to be filled.

Fred Kemp was another saxophonist with a pedigree similar to Tyler's although his playing could not have been more different. If Tyler's tone was like a cool breeze, Kemp could bluster like a growing storm. His long tenure playing with Fats Domino sometimes showed with his brawny approach to soloing and ensemble work. He played in the Tremé Brass Band and also worked with Bo Dollis and George Porter, Jr. among many others. He was a member of Wardell Quezergue's big band and recorded with the Neville Brothers, the Dirty Dozen Brass Band, Champion Jack Dupree, Robbie Robertson (on the album *Storyville*), Snooks Eaglin, Dave Bartholomew, Aaron Neville and Allen Toussaint.

Kemp's jazz playing can be heard on two Rounder recordings: the New Orleans Saxophone Ensemble effort from 1992, which features five of the greatest New Orleans saxophonists in modern jazz—Earl Turbinton, Edward "Kidd" Jordan, Roger Lewis (of the Dirty Dozen on baritone) and Tony Dagradi along with Kemp, and a recording of the Ed Frank Quintet that also appeared on Rounder in 1992.

Kemp was an adventurous musician who never hesitated to take a chance. In 1983, he played in a short-lived but significant band called the Metrics. A performance in April was scheduled at Tipitina's, and the show was broadcast on WWOZ using an effective but primitive technique. A microphone connected to the studio's console on the second floor was dropped through a hole in the ceiling of the uptown club.

The Metrics featured Zigaboo Modeliste and George Porter, Jr., founding members of the Meters, the keyboardist David Torkanowsky and the guitarist Scott Goudeau. Goudeau played in early versions of the guitar supergroup, Twangorama, but during this period his tasty guitar licks and sterling tone could mostly be heard in the jazz setting. He brought a jazz sensibility to the set that was seriously augmented by the presence of Kemp.

The Metrics' show featured a mixed bag of song selections including several from the Meters' catalog. The band stretched out letting Goudeau and Kemp take the lion's share of the solos. They also played some funky jazz reflecting Kemp's predilection for groove-based jazz. The Metrics performed at the Jazz Fest that year, reprised the show at Tipitina's with another performance in late May, and then promptly disappeared.

Fred Kemp passed away in June 1997. His funeral could not have been more dignified. The trumpeter Milton Batiste of the Olympia Brass Band played taps after his body was laid to rest. Later, a large group of musicians and friends gathered at Joe's Cozy Corner in the Tremé neighborhood to play and reminisce about the horn man's life.

Another player from this period who was a significant contributor to the music of New Orleans was the pianist Ed Frank. He was an arranger and a wonderful accompanist even after a stroke essentially turned him into a one-handed musician. He is not well known among the general public, but every musician knew him while he was alive. He played with everyone in town, and his legacy lives on in one song, "Fruit Punch," which he co-wrote with Fred Kemp. The song is fast becoming a *new* New Orleans standard widely performed by musicians who are generations younger.

One of the greatest testaments to the stature of a New Orleans musician is the size of the turnout and the location of the musician's funeral. Ed Frank passed away in February of 1997. His jazz funeral was massive with over 50 musicians parading through the French Quarter. The number of musicians is noteworthy but not as significant as the fact that it swept through the French Quarter and stopped in front of Preservation Hall for a dirge. As I stood on the side listening to this massive band play the most beautiful, saddest song, I saw a young woman softly sobbing through the entire dirge. After the music stopped, I was compelled to speak to her about the gentle musician's impact on her life. She said she didn't even know him and had just stumbled upon the jazz funeral—it was the music that had moved her to tears.

It was not just jazz greats who were still on the scene in the late 1970s and early 1980s. The aforementioned James Booker played an enigmatic solo gig every Tuesday night at the Maple Leaf Bar and other assorted gigs around town including at the Toulouse Theater (now the home of One-Eyed Jack's) where he played before and between theatrical shows. Booker is now regarded as the Piano Prince of New Orleans—he was actually billed that way on the Maple Leaf's schedule. He has been deified as one of the greats, second only to Professor Longhair. He was a wiry guy given to rather flamboyant attire with wild, unkempt hair. He wore an eye patch with a star embroidered on it. Towards the end of his life, Booker had descended into alcohol and drug related despair. Although he could still occasionally impress listeners with his incredible talent, he was personally and professionally far removed from the recordings that defined his genius. In the late 1970s and early 1980s, he was mostly cantankerous and loud with a speaking voice that was as shrill as his singing voice. His music was random and his playing haphazard.

The stories from this period tend to revolve around his extravagant behavior including urinating on stage, falling out of taxicabs, and carrying a starter pistol he used to threaten a crowd whose behavior he didn't like by putting the gun to his head. But Booker was truly a musical genius—that much has never been in doubt. His studio recordings and the memories of those who heard him as a younger man, though he was only 48 when he died, clearly demonstrate his genius.

On November 8, 1983, James Carroll Booker III, the piano prince of New Orleans, died in a wheelchair waiting to be admitted to Charity Hospital in downtown New Orleans. His death, coupled with that of Henry Roeland Byrd, aka Professor Longhair in early 1980, Roosevelt Sykes in July 1983, and Isidore "Tuts" Washington in August 1984, represented the end of an era in New Orleans. Though Sykes and Washington were considerably older than Booker and "Fess", the four, along with the expatriate pianist "Champion" Jack Dupree and funk pioneers Willie Tee and Eddie Bo, were part of a continuum of piano-playing bluesmen in the city. Curiously, during this period when Dupree was living and playing in Europe, Willie Tee was playing mostly jazz gigs and Bo was not playing at all. Willie Tee died in 2007 after a brief illness and the loss of his brother, Earl Turbinton. Longhair and Booker became icons whose lives are regularly celebrated while the memories of Sykes, Washington and Dupree, who died in 1992, remain only in the minds of their small group of dedicated fans and the dwindling numbers of people who actually knew them.

Another player from this era, whose death in 2009 shook a large section of the musical community of New Orleans, was the great guitarist Snooks Eaglin. Beginning in the early 1980s, Eaglin began appearing around town with a combo featuring George Porter, Jr. and Zigaboo Modeliste from the Meters. Every single musically inclined individual, whether a player or simply a music lover, described their first experience hearing Snooks as "mind-blowing." His guitar technique has variously been described as stupendous, amazing, brilliant, idiosyncratic, confounding, dazzling, infectious, mesmerizing, inspired, gifted, exceptional, unusual, bewildering, mystifying and astonishing. It was all of the above and more. He didn't use a pick, opting instead to use his fingers in a variety of ways to coax an incredibly wide range of sounds out of the guitar.

Porter and Modeliste were the perfect backing band for Eaglin because they were completely locked together in rhythm from their years of playing together. Though Eaglin's playing could be explosive, his style was very laid back and off-the-cuff, and he was liable to switch directions musically at any moment including right in the middle of a tune. Both Porter and Modeliste were able to follow his every move and turn on a dime.

Eaglin had such an encyclopedic knowledge of songs in nearly every genre that he has been called "the human jukebox." A blind musician, he loved to interact with the crowd and often took requests. His playing suffered to a small degree as he aged, but in his prime he was a musician's musician. You could always tell the guitar players in the audience at an Eaglin show. They all had their eyes glued to his hands trying to figure out exactly how he was ringing so much music from his instrument.

* * *

There are dozens, perhaps hundreds, of other veteran players who were in their prime during this period. Rather than attempt to discuss them all, I've limited my discussion to musicians who flew under the radar or have not been covered ad nauseum. Now the subject turns to once young musicians who are veteran players today. Of course, as with the veterans who are still living as this tale begins, it would be impossible to cover them all. So the list is restricted to those players who grew up to leave a mark on the musical culture of the city.

The five members of the Radiators came together in January 1978 in the garage of Ed Volker, the keyboardist and principal songwriter. Each of the musicians, the guitar player and vocalist Dave Malone, the lead guitarist Camile Baudoin, the drummer Frank Bua and the bassist Reggie Scanlan had already made an impression as young musicians. Scanlan's resume was by far the most advanced of the five players because of stints performing in the bands of Professor Longhair and James Booker. Malone and Scanlan were members of another band, Road Apple, at the time of that fateful first jam session that led to the formation of the Radiators. Bua, the oldest of the quintet, had played in some of the first 1960s style psychedelic rock bands to emerge in New Orleans including the Palace Guards. He was also a member, along with Baudoin and Volker, of the Rhapsodizers—a well-regarded ensemble that was an occasional backing band for Earl King and eventually morphed into the Radiators.

After the five played together that first time, the musicians immediately disbanded their other bands and made plans to form a new band. Clearly, the rapport between the five musicians was significant. The band immediately took over the Rhapsodizers' weekly gig at Luigi's, a pizza place in Gentilly, as their base of operations and played there for free every Wednesday in their early years.

The Radiators had a part time percussionist and vocalist, Glen "Kul" Sears, who was heavily into the Grateful Dead and brought some of that influence to the band. Additionally, their loose style of playing had a lot in common with the Grateful Dead's opened-ended approach to live music. Both bands shared the same sentiment about instrumental solos, and they loved to jam. But during this period, before the advent of "jam bands," this loose-limbed, fly-by-the-seat-of-your-pants style of playing was uncommon in popular music, and many Deadheads in New Orleans gravitated to the Radiators because of the similarities in their approach to the music. The Radiators and the Grateful Dead also shared the same attitude about taping their shows. Both bands encouraged taping, and tapers at Radiators shows were common by the early 1980s. The spread of the tapes among like-minded music lovers helped each band develop its fan base. Volker dubbed their sound "fishhead music" when asked to pigeonhole their style by a local writer. The fans became "fishheads," which reflected the nickname of the aficionados of the Grateful Dead.

The Grateful Dead and the Radiators also shared several other musical characteristics that separated them from other popular bands at the time. They didn't usually play with set lists, letting the crowd and the vibe determine the next song. They also liked to segue from one song into another creating an unbroken chain of music. With both bands, this could go on for the length of a set. But more significant was the fact that both bands shared a similar affection for what is now called "Americana" music. Both groups were fascinated by the role of country music and the blues in the developing style of rock 'n' roll. They both played cover songs exploring connections between the various styles. While Sears was known to sing the occasional Dead song (he also fronted a Grateful Dead cover band called Remedy at the time), he was more likely to be called up during a Radiators show for a cover tune like "Turn On Your Lovelight" that was in both bands' repertoire.

However, there were differences as well. While the Grateful Dead played a few small rooms very early in their career, the Radiators were a bar band throughout their existence. The members of the group relished the "up front and center" connection with their fans, and they were rarely forced to confront the realities associated with playing to crowds so large that they couldn't see the audience members in the front row. They also rarely played to sit-down audiences and never lost the invigorating effect of seeing a large crowd dancing ecstatically to their music.

Another important part of the appeal of the Radiators that disappeared for the Grateful Dead when they graduated to larger stages was the personal connection to their fans. Throughout their 33+ years of existence the members of the Radiators retained strong connections with individual fans thus fostering a sense of community. That community had a sustaining effect for both the musicians and the fans. It never devolved when the group became more popular as some longtime fans of the Grateful Dead community alleged.

In the summer of 1981, Ed Volker began playing a series of solo gigs listed as his alter ego, Zeke Fishhead. The June issue of *Wavelength* magazine—the monthly source for musical information at the time and the precursor to *Offbeat* magazine—highlighted his gig at Tipitina's with these words, "rarely does Zeke play solo." Despite that pronouncement, Volker played solo at least once a month over the course of the summer and into the fall. In *Wavelength*'s 1983 band guide, the repertoire of his solo act was described as, "From ancient songs to the stuff I wrote this afternoon."

Volker also configured bands featuring some of the members of the Radiators with other like-minded players. These groups were musical free-for-alls and were given whimsical monikers like Bwana Dik and the Headhunters or Waldo and the Peppers (clearly named for the Robert Redford aviator film, "The Great Waldo Pepper"). Another group featured the Radiators' guitarist and singer, Dave Malone, with his younger brother, Tommy, on guitar and his wife, Suzie, on vocals backed by the Radiators' rhythm section. Fittingly, this band was called the Malones.

In 1981, two members of the Radiators, the bassist Reggie Scanlan and the keyboardist/vocalist Ed Volker, formed a trio with the band's erstwhile percussionist and guest vocalist, Glen "Kul" Sears (Sears would become an official member of the Radiators later in 1982). The group was called Blind, Crippled and Crazy after the O.V. Wright gutbucket classic. That summer, they started a twice-monthly Monday residency at the Maple Leaf alternating with the duo act of John Magnie (later of the subdudes) and Leigh Harris (Little Queenie).

Blind, Crippled and Crazy stripped the Radiators' sound down to its core—Scanlan played an upright acoustic bass, Volker had a basic keyboard set up, and Sears arrived with a set of congas. The songs they played mined the same roots as the tunes in the Radiators' repertoire, but the band delved deeper into the blues. Sears sang a few songs each set, but Volker dominated the shows. Their music was described in the 1983 *Wavelength* magazine band guide as, "raggy, acoustic music about prison, wimmen, drink, railroads." That about sums it up.

It should be noted that the Radiators were the first rock band in New Orleans to start their own record label. Beginning in 1978, Croaker Records released two singles and two albums by the Radiators until they won a best of the unsigned bands contest and were signed to Epic Records, a major label, in 1986. It was the third such signing in New Orleans since the Meters were signed a decade earlier. Zebra, a heavy metal band popular in Metairie but never gaining much traction in the city, released three albums on Atlantic Records in the early 1980s. The Red Rockers, a power pop band featuring John Thomas Griffith, a future member of longstanding rock band Cowboy Mouth, were very successful locally before moving to the Northeast. Their song "China" was one of the first videos to appear on MTV. On the strength of that song, they were signed by Columbia Records and released one album before disbanding.

The Radiators and their rabid fishhead fan base were poised to spread fishhead music over the FM airwaves of America, but after three albums and two incredibly cheesy videos the relationship ended. The Radiators never signed with a major label again, but they endured for over three decades with their original lineup intact, based on the strength of their live performances and the deep and abiding dedication of their fan base. Their label lived on as well and released two more albums in the early 1990s. The five original Radiators finally broke up in 2011 after over 33 years playing together.

While the Radiators are arguably the most successful rock band to emerge from this era, Little Queenie and the Percolators were the more popular act at the time. The Radiators were still developing the "fishhead music" sound that came to define them, but the Percolators were a fully formed band. Little Queenie, nee Leigh Harris, was a sprite with formidable vocal talents still on display all these years later, but she is no longer based in New Orleans. Though still quite young, she was a front woman who could roar and purr while keeping all eyes on her small frame.

Tommy Malone, then barely in his twenties, was the guitarist for the Percolators, and he also sang. He is now a member of the subdudes and a well-respected musician nationally. Even at such a young age, Malone was already showing the prodigious technique that has served him well throughout his long career. His playing had hints of the blues but with a clear, precise tone that was jazzier than that of most of his peers.

Kenny Blevins was a time-keeping monster of a drummer. His cymbal accents were impeccable, and his playing was firmly rooted in the drum tradition of New Orleans. In his career, Blevins played and recorded with many important Louisiana acts such as Sonny Landreth, John Mooney, George Porter, Jr., Earl King, Zachary Richard and Michael Doucet of Beausoleil as well as roots rock star John Hiatt. He eventually relocated to Nashville and spent years as a highly regarded studio musician.

Little Queenie and the Percolators, which also included future sub-dude John Magnie on keyboards and accordion, were one of the hottest bands on the scene and managed to garner some national attention before breaking up at the height of their success though the various members have continued to collaborate over the ensuing years. The band was uncanny with respect to their ability to communicate with each other. The Percolators had some great songs including the only one they ever released during their heyday, the iconic "My Darling New Orleans." The song, which name checks so much of what New Orleans is all about in a style presaging rapping, was written by the local poet Ron Cuccia and was released as a 45 rpm single. By late in 1982, Little Queenie and the Percolators were just a fond memory. Leigh Harris debuted her new band, Backtalk, at the Maple Leaf after working all summer in the duo setting with John Magnie. The band featured her new husband, Bruce McDonald of Exuma's band, on guitar.

As it is in New Orleans today, musicians rarely played with just one group. Tommy Malone hooked up with the bassist and singer Becky Kury to form the Cartoons after her main band, the Rhapso-dizers, broke up. Johnny Ray Allen and Steve Amadee, who would go on to form the subdudes with Malone, were also in the band.

Kury was essentially the front woman of the Cartoons and her vocals were soulful and warm. She could wail like the proverbial banshee, but she also projected a vulnerability that endeared her to other musicians and to the male members of the audience. After the demise of the Cartoons, Becky Kury ended up playing bass in an unusual band called RZA, which was fronted by a woman who dressed and acted like a man. Lenny Zenith was her stage name, and she was part of a sizable group of young people who were mining the punk-pop-new wave continuum fashionable around the world in the late 1970s. Kury died prematurely and is remembered as a seminal figure on the scene. For many years following her death, the wall on the Broadway side of the K&B drug store (now a Rite Aid) at the corner of St. Charles Avenue sported the semi-cryptic message, "Becky Kury Lives." Every time it was painted over, which was often, the phrase reappeared overnight clearly vexing the building's owners.

Among the punk/new wave bands, the Cold was the most successful on the local scene. They did a cool, albeit greatly altered, version of the Rolling Stones' "Paint It Black." The Normals were also fairly popular, but their sound was raw and considerably more edgy than the Cold's pop-punk confections. There were also a number of other new wave-style bands playing around town including the Uptights, the Models, the Sheiks and the Look. Paul Sanchez and Fred LeBlanc, two of the other principals in Cowboy Mouth, were in a band called Godot.

For a brief period, a band called the Wyldabeats existed though they mostly played the Tulane and Loyola fraternity circuit. Their tenure was unremarkable but for the fact that their lead singer, a vivacious Newcomb co-ed from Tennessee named Holden Miller, captured the imagination of the post-new wave rock scene in New Orleans with her next band, Tribe Nunzio.

Another band that was fairly successful during this period was the whimsically named Waka Waka (after the sound of the Pac-man video game character). They played a punky version of ska, the high energy Jamaican precursor of reggae, and they were popular enough to get several gigs at Tipitina's. Waka Waka's rhythm section, the bassist Vernon Rome and the drummer Damon Shea, eventually joined forces with the guitarist Jeff Treffinger, along with Miller on lead vocals, to form Tribe Nunzio. Treffinger went on to become one of the founders of the Mermaid Lounge, the 1990s music hot spot in the Warehouse District.

A lot more could be written about the punk/new wave scene in New Orleans during the late 1970s and early 1980s including discussion of a short-lived Faubourg Marigny club called the Beat Exchange that catered to the new wave crowd. But with the exception of the musicians named above, the scene had little impact on the overall development of music in New Orleans.

The popular music of the day wasn't the only music being presented in local clubs—many other genres were represented as well. The Maple Leaf had zydeco and Cajun bands regularly. A popular rockabilly band called the Rockabyes featured two stalwarts of the local scene, the guitarist Cranston Clements and his bassist brother, David. Another well-liked band, also led by a pair of brothers, Buddy and Bruce Flett, was A-Train. They were from north Louisiana, and played scorching, soulful blues.

There was also another female singer, Allison Young, who was popular during this period. She played in the late 1970s rootsy combo, the Nightriders, but by 1983 she had put together what was perhaps her best band. Allison and the Distractions featured the songwriter and bassist John Meunier from Little Queenie and the Percolators along with the guitarists Charlie Reagin and Jimmy Gennaro, the synthesizer guru Dave Goodman and the future Walter "Wolfman" Washington and Roadmasters' saxophonist Tom Fitzpatrick. They rehearsed for months before hitting the scene with a great batch of original songs and solid covers. Young had matured considerably since her early years playing with Nightriders, and the band was as tight as anyone playing at that time. Their blend of danceable pop and hard-hitting R&B was perfectly suited to the music freaks constantly looking for the newest thing. Allison and the Distractions quickly began playing regularly at the bigger rooms in town—Tipitina's, Jimmy's and the Dream Palace.

Since the band featured a vivacious lead singer and a key member of Little Queenie's band, comparisons were inevitable. Certainly there was some indebtedness to the groundwork laid out by the Percolators, but Young was her own woman who found a niche. However, it is arguable that Allison and the Distractions may not have had as much success if Little Queenie had been able to keep her full band together.

What is interesting to note is that Barbara Menendez, Becky Kury, Allison Young and Leigh Harris were women fronting their own bands in an era when to do so was fairly uncommon in popular music. These four local gals were alone amongst the boys and held their own convincingly.

The late 1970s and early 1980s was an incredibly fertile period for New Orleans rock. Though the Radiators stand alone as the only band to make it out of the 20th century with their lineup still intact, the period was a proving ground for many of the players who ultimately made music their life's work. Many of the musicians who were youngsters then are now the veterans of today's scene.

Chapter 4

THE BEGINNINGS OF A MUSIC MEDIA INFRASTRUCTURE

"Where words fail, music speaks."—Hans Christian Andersen

There were two daily newspapers in New Orleans in the late 1970s, the *Times-Picayune* and the *States-Item*. The two papers merged in 1980, and both were notorious for rarely including coverage of events pertaining to the musical culture of New Orleans or the black community from which much of the culture originated. In fairness, they were not exactly running out to cover the changes occurring in pop music either. There were occasional features about pop styles, but the regular music coverage was limited to classical music. Two publications with limited circulation—the *Louisiana Weekly* and the *Vieux Carre Courier*—were the only publications regularly covering jazz, soul and R&B. Only the *Louisiana Weekly* still exists today.

There were also other niche publications, such as the New Orleans Jazz Club's, *Second Line*, but they weren't aimed at the general reading public. There were also a few tourist publications, but they didn't come close to covering what was really happening on the music scene.

Figaro, a for-purchase (50 cents) alternative weekly, was published from 1972 until 1981 with music listings and ads for music clubs along with musical picks in the "Eight Days a Week" section. However, this section of the weekly concentrated mostly on the new rock scene, and it was not an easy section for readers to navigate because of vague headings, poor layout, overly long articles and very small print. There was also a problem with tone that often led to condescending copy.

In a telling and ironically still relevant article titled "The Media's Music Void," which appeared in *Figaro* in October 1979, the now highly esteemed New Orleans writer, Jason Berry, opined about media coverage in the local press. He wrote, "There's a large hole in the workings of the local news media and it is the coverage of music—the musicians themselves and what they are playing, club life, the changing tides of musical styles, records and business deals." Berry singled out the weak coverage of the two daily papers by observing that the only musicians receiving press were the "winners" such as Fats Domino, Allen Toussaint, Dave Bartholomew and Professor Longhair. He wrote that coverage was limited to, "periodic profilers and then of course the adoring pieces that inevitably begin to appear in the spring before fest." In a somewhat scathing tone, Berry didn't even spare the publication in which the piece appeared, "Bunny (Matthews—the music writer for *Figaro*) covers rock music, some Rhythm and Blues and very little jazz." The article concluded with Berry's assertion that the major reason the press ignores music is because television does the same. Citing *Austin City Limits*, he noted there was no regular television show about music in New Orleans at the time.

Interestingly, a couple of weeks before *Figaro* passed into media history, the magazine published "the Definitive Music Guide" by Almost Slim, aka Jeff Hannusch, a well-respected writer who still works in the music media today. It was far from definitive and was actually a last gasp at relevance for the publication.

A local photographer and music aficionado, Pat Jolly, published a pamphlet-sized calendar of listings, the now legendary "Jolly Jazz Calendar." But the catch-22 about the calendar was that the only way for a tourist to get one was to pick it up in one of the clubs whose listings graced its narrow pages.

The atmosphere began to change in November of 1980 when *Wavelength*, a monthly music magazine, and *Gambit Weekly* fired up their presses for the first time. *Wavelength* was published by Patrick Berry and edited by Connie Atkinson. Atkinson is currently a well-regarded academic working out of the University of New Orleans.

Wavelength, while occasionally lapsing into gossip and petty disputes between various competing interests, changed the outlook of the business community and opened numerous doors for other publications and writers. It can be argued the magazine taught the rest of the media that money actually can be made from the music itself. Yet even as late as 1983, the publisher and editors at *Wavelength* were very aware of the void in local music coverage. Their advertising slogan for selling subscriptions read, "New Orleans music—we'll help you find it."

By 1988, just short of celebrating ten years of fabulous coverage of the music scene, *Wavelength* magazine was experiencing problems. The publisher, Pat Berry, left town to pursue a career with Windham Hill Records leaving the editor, Connie Atkinson, to run the publication. She published the magazine herself for nearly two years before Jim Green, a Texan who purchased Tipitina's and orchestrated its grand reopening in January of 1986, and his wife became involved. The arrangement with Green as publisher and Mientje Green as marketing director lasted all of three months. The demise of the first significant publication devoted to New Orleans music was approaching, and they finally closed their doors in 1989.

While *Wavelength* only lasted a decade or so, it was the precursor to *Offbeat* magazine, which began as a tourist rag focusing on what its publisher, Jan Ramsey, believed was a missing market segment. *Offbeat* is now the grandmother of all local music publications and serves a major part of the music community.

Gambit Weekly remains in business. From its beginnings, it was dedicated to serious coverage of the music community, but unlike *Wavelength*, it also features politics, community news and extensive coverage of the other arts. *Gambit* eventually promoted a typesetter named Geraldine Wyckoff into a music columnist in 1986. Over the ensuing years, Wyckoff, a dedicated modern jazz fan and aficionado of the traditional jazz community, set a standard for local music writing and introduced countless numbers of mostly white, middle class readers to the nuances of the music community, particularly its African-American cultural components. *Gambit Weekly* let Wyckoff go amid downsizing in the early years of this century, but it has remained a source of information about the music scene. However, the paper has never managed to attract another writer with Wyckoff's deep knowledge and sense of the jazz community.

While the print media was gaining steam with respect to music coverage, the radio dial was still grossly underrepresenting New Orleans music. This is ironic considering the role radio played in the 1950s when deejays were the ultimate tastemakers with the ability to make or break every new release. Simply put, from the advent of the British Invasion in the early sixties until WWOZ 90.7 FM first went on the air in 1980, there was essentially no New Orleans music on the radio.

Of course, WWOZ changed all that. The station's first studio was on the second floor of the building that housed the music club, Tipitina's. Before they actually had a physical space from which to broadcast, the station presented pre-recorded programs. In the early days, their broadcast hours were limited from between 9 AM and 10 PM. The decidedly homegrown operation gradually developed into a key component of the music community. While initially dedicated to the great music of New Orleans and the surrounding areas of Acadiana, it eventually began covering all kinds of roots music including African and Caribbean genres. After the Brock brothers moved on to other endeavors, WWOZ struggled through numerous personnel and ownership changes until its license was acquired by the New Orleans Jazz and Heritage Foundation, the non-profit organization that owns the New Orleans Jazz and Heritage Festival. The station is now on solid financial footing and continues to be a major player in the local music community.

Smatterings of local music could be heard on WWNO, the community radio station associated with the University of New Orleans. In late 1980, WWNO presented a series of live shows sponsored by the Contemporary Arts Center and a group called "Musicians for Music." The series featured musicians who are still stalwarts of the local scene—the guitarist Jimmy Robinson and his band, Woodenhead; the drummer Johnny Vidacovich and his trio; the pianist Ellis Marsalis; and the singer Leigh Harris and her accompanist, the pianist Larry Sieberth.

In October 1981, WWNO inaugurated a new program called "Jazz Tonight." The show didn't focus exclusively on New Orleans music but featured "American improvisational music." By the end of 1981, WWNO was broadcasting jazz in the evenings from Wednesday through Saturday, and they also presented a show called "Blues in the Night." By early 1982, WYLD, a commercial radio station targeting the black community, got into the game. They presented a show called "Extensions from Congo Square" on Sunday afternoons.

WTUL, the station owned by Tulane University, was one of the first college radio stations in the country. However, the student deejays didn't play much New Orleans music in the late 1970s and early 1980s although they did feature local acts on the short-lived "New Wave Hour" and some of the programmers occasionally injected local R&B songs into the mix. In the decades since, it has become a typical college radio station playing indie rock and other styles not heard on commercial radio. But in the latter part of the 20th century, it was very different from anything else on the extremely limited dial in New Orleans. Since the classic rock format had not yet been invented, the student programmers on WTUL were almost exclusively into the music of the 1960s and early 1970s. Considering what a wasteland rock radio had become amid the excesses and grandiosity of the big hair bands against which punk rock revolted, 91.5 FM was a very friendly place on the dial.

Every spring the station hosted the WTUL Rock On Survival Marathon, an annual fundraiser. Three disc jockeys would take requests for 24 hours each, and the main quad on campus hosted live performances. The marathons were an opportunity for students and a great many local music lovers to hear up-and-coming acts as well as more established bands. The marathon was a highlight of the spring festival season from the late 1960s until 1992. Pressure from the neighborhood about noise and crowds, coupled with Tulane's new restrictive alcohol policy, forced the station to alter its longstanding policy of being free and open to the public.

By 1979, around the time Berry's scathing indictment of the local media appeared in *Figaro*, there were rumblings of a new focus on New Orleans music on local television. WYES, a public station, hired Peggy Scott Laborde, a producer who has since produced hundreds of programs featuring New Orleans music. In 1981, the station aired a series called "Jazz Now" with programs featuring Astral Project, Ramsey McLean and the Lifers with Ron Cuccia and the Alvin Batiste and Kidd Jordan Ensemble. *Wavelength* magazine opined that the new series, "looks like a real step forward for music programming on local television." Also in April 1981, the producer John Boyer started an ambitious series of musical performances called "Jazz Excursions." In January 1982, the show featured modern jazz from Ellis Marsalis and his sons as well as traditional jazz from Al Belletto and Pete Fountain. WYES also provided a venue and production facilities for outside producers. The station made a major commitment to New Orleans music and arts when the "Steppin' Out" program, which had appeared on WLAE beginning in 1986, moved to WYES in 1988.

In the early 1980s, Channel 26, a commercial station, began its "Homegrown Series." The first season featured the Radiators and the New Jazz Quintet. Both bands were recorded playing in the station's studio. For the second season they recorded the pop/new wave band, the Cold, live at Jimmy's Music Club. The Neville Brothers appeared in November 1981, and Little Queenie and the Percolators appeared in February 1982. The long-lived rock band Dash Rip Rock, fronted by the guitarist and singer Bill Davis, and the bluesman John Mooney were among other acts featured on Channel 26.

From 1983-1986, the acclaimed filmmaker Jim Gabour was the producer, director, writer and host of a successful series called "Music City." The program won the ACE award for best local cable music program in the United States from the National Academy of Cable Programming/National Cable Television Association three years in a row. It was also picked up by A&E and by ITV in the United Kingdom.

In hindsight, this coverage of local music was a great development in a city that has consistently undervalued its cultural capital, and it certainly helped the careers of many of the musicians involved. Most of the featured acts are still active in the music scene today. But the notion of getting New Orleans music on television never translated into anything permanent such as "Austin City Limits." Arguably, there is currently less local music on television in New Orleans than there was 30 years ago.

I would be remiss in this section not to mention the wonderful feature film, "Piano Players Rarely Play Together." Stevenson Palfi directed this fascinating study of three generations of piano players from New Orleans. It features Isidore "Tuts" Washington, Henry Roeland Byrd, aka Professor Longhair, and Allen Toussaint. The film was recorded in the period leading up to the unexpected death of Byrd and includes priceless footage of his funeral in 1980.

Other factors contributing to the development of a music media infrastructure in New Orleans were the formation of Blacktop Records and the increasing presence of Rounder Records, a roots music label out of Massachusetts. Rounder Records was started in the late 1960s to showcase the bluegrass and other string music traditions of the United States. Their first release was a 1969 recording by the Nevada-based singer-songwriter Utah Phillips. By 1975, their catalog branched out and began including Irish and African styles.

In 1976, Rounder released *Louisiana Cajun French Music from the Southwest Prairie, Volumes 1 and 2* and an album by the Balfa Brothers. The two volumes were the first major compilation recordings of rural Louisiana music to hit the American record stacks, but they were certainly not the last. Since those three albums, Rounder has been a key player releasing a large number of Zydeco and Cajun music albums.

In January 1979, Rounder's *10th Anniversary of the New Orleans Jazz and Heritage Festival* compilation hit the streets nationwide. The recording featured live performances from a mixed bag of artists including self-proclaimed "Zydeco King" Clifton Chenier & his Red Hot Louisiana Band doing the jump blues classic, "Caledonia;" the Onward Brass Band with Louis Cottrell performing the brass band standard, "Paul Barbarin's Second Line;" Eubie Blake doing "Charleston Rag;" and in what must have been a major coup for the producers, jazz legend Charles Mingus presenting "Theme from a Movie." The record also features stalwarts of the New Orleans music scene as well as more sounds from Cajun country. This landmark recording proceeded to affect major changes in New Orleans music that still reverberate today. Following the success of the live record, the profile of the Jazz Fest began growing leading to the event becoming the cultural behemoth it is today. For the next thirty years, Rounder Records focused heavily on New Orleans music helping to create a lasting representation of the musical climate of the city in the last decades of the 20th century.

By 1983, while continuing to mine the fertile territory of Southwest Louisiana for Cajun and Zydeco acts, Rounder began to branch out into the uncharted territories of New Orleans music, which had been grossly underrepresented nationally since the heyday of the 50s R&B scene. That year, Rounder released James Booker's most important studio album, *Classified*, as well as a live recording of *New Orleans Piano Wizard* in addition to Tuts Washington's *New Orleans Piano Professor* and two albums by Clarence "Gatemouth" Brown.

In 1984, the label did the whole world a gigantic favor when they started a series of releases by Johnny Adams, also known as the Tan Canary, which continued until the great vocalist's death in 1998. Rounder eventually released thirteen recordings of new material by Adams. In 1986, Rounder again turned the world's ears onto some groundbreaking music coming out of New Orleans when they released the Dirty Dozen Brass Band's *Live: Mardi Gras in Montreaux*. While the Dozen left the label for greener pastures after that one release, *Live: Mardi Gras in Montreaux* set the stage for other brass band recordings including four original releases by the Rebirth Brass Band that informed the world of the great changes occurring in the brass band tradition.

From the beginning of this prolific run until the volume of releases started to subside in the late 1990s, Rounder has released nearly a hundred albums of New Orleans music (counting numerous compilations). The label resurrected the careers of the vocalist Irma Thomas, the blues pianist "Champion" Jack Dupree, and the guitar slinger and longtime Adams sideman, Walter "Wolfman" Washington. They released the first albums by the R&B vocalist Chuck Carbo, the Meters' bassist George Porter, Jr. and the Mardi Gras Indian Big Chief Monk Boudreaux. They also recorded jazz players like Alvin "Red" Tyler, Tony Dagradi, Earl Turbinton with his brother Willie Tee and David Torkanowsky. By the late 1990s, Rounder started recording a new generation of New Orleans musicians before they eventually reduced their New Orleans-related output at the turn of the new century.

Rounder Records played an extremely important role in increasing the worldwide profile of New Orleans music. With a wide distribution system, especially as the label grew, they were able to introduce large numbers of listeners to the wealth and breadth of music coming out of New Orleans. Numerous artists, both veterans like Washington and Thomas and relative newcomers like the Rebirth Brass Band, benefited from this high profile especially when it came to touring the world. Having an album out on Rounder allowed New Orleans musicians entré into markets that clearly would have been inaccessible without international distribution.

Back in New Orleans, in 1981 Blacktop Records began a nearly twenty-year run of fine New Orleans releases. Founded by the brothers Nauman S. Scott, III and Hammond Scott, Blacktop specialized in blues and R&B, but they also released a number of significant recordings in other genres. Rounder initially distributed these recordings allowing Blacktop's artists access to the same markets.

R&B legends Earl King and Snooks Eaglin called Blacktop home for most of the label's existence. Eaglin recorded four studio records for the label and also a live release. The label paired King, one of the most prolific songwriters from the heyday of the 1950s R&B scene, with the great Rhode Island band, Roomful of Blues, resulting in his comeback album, *Glazed*. They also released two highly regarded studio albums by King, 1990's *Sexual Telepathy* and 1993's *Hard River to Cross*. Blacktop released two live albums recorded at Tipitina's by the Neville Brothers, *Neville-ization, Volumes 1 and 2*. At the end of the label's run, they also recorded an album each by the second-generation bluesman Chris Thomas King and the pianist Henry Butler.

Part of the label's mission was to highlight the less commercially successful acts from earlier times that were still alive and well. Their Blacktop Blues-A-Rama series, recorded live during a yearly showcase of unsung blues and R&B acts in the midst of the New Orleans Jazz and Heritage Festival, was a precursor to the now popular Ponderosa Stomp. While the recordings are important, particularly the releases by Snooks Eaglin and Earl King, Blacktop also provided a significant amount of studio work for New Orleans musicians during the label's existence. Though the bulk of their releases were not New Orleans artists per se, they often recorded in the city and booked studio time with numerous local players including David Torkanowsky, George Porter, Jr. and the drummer Herman Ernest.

The same can be said for Rounder Records—they usually recorded in the city and used local musicians as backing players.

The bulk of these recordings on Rounder and Blacktop records were recorded at Ultrasonic Studios on Washington Avenue. Two other prominent studios were active at the time—Allen Toussaint and Marshall Sehorn's Sea-Saint Studios in Gentilly and the Studio in the Country on the Northshore of Lake Pontchartrain. However, both Sea-Saint and Studio in the Country focused on mostly national acts.

Three records stores uptown catered to fans of independent, local and non-mainstream musical groups: the Metronome, located on Pleasant Street just off Magazine Street near the corner of Louisiana Avenue; Leisure Landing, located on Magazine between Nashville and Jefferson Avenues; and the Mushroom, which is still in business on Broadway just off the Tulane University campus. The Metronome was the upstart challenger, but they did not last through the 1980s, moving to Atlanta in May 1987. Leisure Landing became part of the national Sound Warehouse chain. Less than six months after the Metronome left the city, Tower Records opened its doors on Decatur Street in the French Quarter to compete directly with Sound Warehouse. Of the two national chains, Tower stocked the widest and deepest catalog of New Orleans and Louisiana music and helped fuel the growth of the two labels and their artists.

Each of the four parts of the music media infrastructure in New Orleans—print, radio, television and the recording business—grew considerably over the last twenty years of the 20th century. But unlike the hotel and restaurant businesses, which have very effective lobbying organizations, there has never been a concerted effort among the various entities to create an all-encompassing music "business." So, while New Orleans is known worldwide for its restaurants, fine hotels and other elements of the tourism economy, other cities, especially Nashville, Tennessee and Austin, Texas, which branded itself "the live music capital of the world," have claimed the music mantel. Even with the rise of the Internet and the decentralization of the music business across the globe, New Orleans, arguably one of the birthplaces of American music, still lags behind in the business of music.

Ironically, the federal flood, which destroyed New Orleans and threatened the very existence of the music community following Hurricane Katrina in 2005, left new mechanisms in its massive wake to support the musical arts in the city. National funding organizations such as the Threadhead Foundation (which supports this book), the Backbeat Foundation, Music Rising and grassroots efforts like the Roots of Music educational program have filled a void left by local and national budget cuts and the lack of a centralized music business infrastructure.

Chapter 5

THE METERS AND THE SECOND WAVE OF FUNK

"Life is a one way ticket, there ain't no second time around. You better get your kicks before you're six feet in the ground."—Dr. John

Of all the bands and musicians dotting the musical landscape of New Orleans as the R&B generation of the 1950s gave way to the soul and rock 'n' roll of the 1960s, none captured the imagination quite like the Meters. The keyboardist Art Neville, a veteran of the 1950s scene (he recorded the now classic version of "Mardi Gras Mambo" with his band, the Hawkettes, in 1954), led the band. His band mates, George Porter, Jr. on bass, Leo Nocentelli on guitar and Joseph "Zigaboo" Modeliste on drums, were on average 10 years younger than the already established leader.

The quartet's instrumental sides from the late1960s showcased the unique drumming skills of Modeliste, and one of those songs, "Cissy Strut," became a sensation reaching #23 on the national charts.

Art Neville had a steady relationship with the producer, songwriter and pianist Allen Toussaint dating back to when the eldest Neville was a solo artist known for regional hits such as "Cha Dooky Do" and "All These Things" in the late 1950s and early 1960s. So when Toussaint and his business partner, Marshall Sehorn, opened Sea-Saint Studio in the Gentilly section of New Orleans in 1973, Neville was a natural to lead the house band, which included the other three members of the Meters. With the impeccable production skills of Toussaint they backed up a slew of local and regional acts. As the fame of the house band and Toussaint grew, numerous internationally known artists including Paul McCartney, Patti Labelle, Lowell George, and Robert Palmer were recruited by Sehorn to record at the studio.

The music of the Meters changed as the 1960s gave way to the 1970s—they added vocal parts contributed by all the members, and eventually they created some of the most lasting music to come out of the Crescent City since the heyday of the R&B scene in the 1950s. Their classics, "Cissy Strut," "Hey Pocky Way," "They All Axed For You" and "Fire on the Bayou," are now funk standards, and many of the riffs and beats laid down by the band have found new life as hip-hop samples. The Meters are among the most sampled bands in the history of rap music.

The Meters were the seminal funk band from New Orleans, and with the exception of James Brown and George Clinton's various bands, they became one of the most important funk bands in the country. Though they had a local rival in the form of Chocolate Milk, that band lacked the staying power to weather the juggernaut of disco in the late 1970s. Significantly, the Meters were highly respected by many of the bands of the British Invasion including the Rolling Stones and the Beatles. Ironically, this respect ran counter to the fact that the British Invasion was blamed for the demise of the R&B period that led to the formation of the Meters in the first place.

Despite achieving great success in the studio, performing as the opening act for the Rolling Stones on their 1975 tour and playing private parties for stars such as Paul McCartney, the band never had much monetary success while the original quartet was still intact. With its members in all sorts of emotional, financial, personal and drug-related turmoil, the Meters broke up. While the breakup was traumatic for fans of the band, it also had an upside that reverberates to this day. The dissolution of the Meters paved the way for a second generation of funk bands.

The first band to form in the wake of the Meters' demise was the Neville Brothers. Art Neville and Aaron Neville had considerable success in the R&B world of the 1950s, and Charles was a well-respected jazz musician, so the brothers considered forming a band together. Youngest brother Cyril, who performed with the Meters in their latter years, became a catalyst towards forming the family band.

While the Meters were critical darlings and loved by musicians, they never achieved worldwide acclaim or significant album sales while they were still active. The Meters' fame has been retroactive, and their first reunion concerts in the mid-2000s attracted much more attention than any of their shows during their initial heyday when they played local hot spots like the Nitecap on Louisiana Avenue and the Ivanhoe in the French Quarter. But with the success of the Nevilles, New Orleans music was again in the international spotlight. Another style of New Orleans music had captured the attention of the world mirroring the trajectory of jazz in the early part of the 20th century and during the 1950s peak of R&B. The Nevilles earned an endearing sobriquet that is as accurate today as when they first achieved international fame—they are the heartbeat of New Orleans.

The Nevilles first began appearing on the stage at Tipitina's, which became the band's de facto home even as the members became stars around the world. In another example of the uncanny synergy surrounding the music scene in New Orleans—the brothers formed the family band around the same time that Tipitina's opened its doors for the first time. In the early days of the group, the supporting players in the band switched around a lot. Ivan Neville, Aaron's son, played some keyboards as did Gerald Tillman, a temperamental prodigy who died young. In June 1982, *Wavelength* magazine's gossipy "Last Page" said with characteristically thinly veiled derision, "Gerald Tillman had left the Neville Brothers Band for the third time, breaking the record previously held by Reynard (sic) Poché."

Ivan Neville, Gerald Tillman and the guitarist Renard Poché represented another generation of musicians inside the Neville orbit. Though still very young at the time, they were all capable musicians who also performed together in other Meters-inspired bands such as Black Male.

A perusal of the first two Neville Brothers records, 1978's eponymous debut and 1981's *Fiyo on the Bayou*, gives little insight into who was on the gig on any given night. *The Neville Brothers* lists Eugene Synegal on bass and Newton Mossop, Jr. on drums. The bassist and the drummer listed on *Fiyo on the Bayou* are David Barard and Herman Ernest, both of whom played with Dr. John for years. There were also fluctuations in the membership of the rhythm section, which finally coalesced with Daryl Johnson on bass, "Mean" Willie Green on drums and Brian Stoltz on guitar in 1983. Johnson and Stoltz were with the group for most of 1980s. Green has been the drummer since he first joined the band.

Whenever Ivan Neville would join the band, the four younger musicians would open the show in a configuration dubbed the "Special Forces Band." They would play an instrumental song called "The Switch." Only Green played his primary instrument. Neville played the bass, Johnson played guitar and Stoltz played keyboards.

For modern day fans of the Neville Brothers, it's important to note that during this period Art Neville was clearly the star of the show. While Aaron is obviously the most recognized by mainstream America today, his early solo success in the 1950s was mostly reflected through one song, "Tell It Like It Is." He performed it at virtually every show along with another ballad, "Arianne." Years later, after his success with Linda Ronstadt, Aaron's presence began to dominate the band.

The origin of Aaron's relationship with Ronstadt deserves some explication. During the economic recession of the early 1980s, an organization called New Orleans Artists Against Hunger and Homelessness presented their first benefit concert in October 1986. The group's mission reflected a harsh reality across the city and the nation. Linda Ronstadt was the headliner for the first relatively low-key show that also featured Branford Marsalis, Rita Coolidge and the Radiators. Aaron Neville was one of the organizers of the event, along with Allen Toussaint, and when he met and performed with Ronstadt, the door opened for him to become a major pop star in his own right. His solo career took off after his first collaboration with Ronstadt.

Art Neville, on the other hand, was coming off considerable success with the Meters. His huge hit, "Mardi Gras Mambo," which he recorded as a teenager with the Hawkettes, was a local standard that was on every jukebox and was ubiquitous during Carnival season. A

Neville Brothers show circa 1980 was almost always a tour-de-force as the band pulled together all of their various influences including the 1950s R&B that put Art and Aaron on the charts for the first time, Jamaican reggae, American jazz and a healthy dose of the funk that the Meters made famous. The shows were always well paced since all of the musicians were veteran performers.

Each member got his moment in the spotlight. Cyril, the youngest by ten years and the most politically focused of the four brothers, was a minor player in the early days mostly singing backing vocals and playing congas. Within a few years, Cyril's culture-based consciousness began emerging on stage and affected the songwriting of the group. Aaron, bulging muscles and facial tattoos belying that angelic voice, was at center stage providing vocal harmonies and playing his cowbell when he wasn't singing like the leader of the heavenly choir. Charles set up to one side with his studied hep cat coolness and saxophones on display. Art unmistakably directed the show from behind his bank of keyboards.

A central part of the Neville Brothers collective persona was in the personage and omniscient presence of their legendary maternal uncle, George Landry, also known as Big Chief Jolly of the Wild Tchoupitoulas Mardi Gras Indians. Landry was an amateur pianist, and his style on the keyboard influenced his nephew Art. While Landry directly influenced Art's work as a pianist, the music of the Mardi Gras Indians influenced all four of the brothers. The Indian chant, "Brother John," was almost always a part of the set along with its musical sibling, "Iko, Iko." The two songs were usually segued together. "Meet Da Boys On the Battlefront," an Indian song credited to Landry, also made regular appearances on set lists in the 1980s.

In the early days of the band, the Nevilles would occasionally appear on stage with members of the Wild Tchoupitoulas. In the fall 1981, the group was an opening act, along with George Thorogood and the Destroyers, for the Rolling Stones in the Louisiana Superdome. The boisterous crowd was in no mood for the costumed performers and, seemingly unaware of the brothers' connection with the headliners, actually booed the band.

The first time all four brothers appeared together on a recording was the self-titled album, *The Wild Tchoupitoulas*, which appeared in 1976 on Mango Records, a subsidy of Island Records. It is one of the most important records of New Orleans music to ever have been released. The gorgeous vocal harmonies set the stage for the family band's sound. The Meters provided the instrumental backing for the Wild Tchoupitoulas recording, and the sparse yet incredibly funky sound that was their trademark has always been present in the music of the Neville Brothers. The classic instrumental tunes that defined the Meters' early years were represented by a single song, the often-covered "Cissy Strut."

It was the Meters' songs with vocals, such as "Fire on the Bayou," "People Say," "Africa," and "Hey Pocky Way" from the latter part of their career, that were sustained by the Nevilles. Those songs also remained the core selections for the bands featuring various other members of the Meters that popped up after the dissolution of the original outfit.

The music of the Neville Brothers was fresh and novel to many of their listeners. Though they were clearly not the Meters—the vocal harmonies were far beyond what that band was capable of—and despite the presence of Charles Neville and his saxophone, they were not a jazz band either. They played funk derived from the seminal sounds of the Meters, but they also rocked. Screaming electric guitar, not the syncopated rhythm work of Leo Nocentelli in the early Meters, has been part of their instrumentation since day one. Their music has a flow, a natural rhythm that winds its way almost insidiously through the body. It is visceral but not in the rock 'n' roll sense. Quality rock n' roll tends to throw body punches at the listener, and pummels the crowd into submission and/or ecstasy. But funk acts like your friend, even as it hits you over the head with rhythm and groove and knocks you around with the beat.

Up front and center at a Neville Brothers' performance, particularly at Tipitina's during Jazz Fest or Mardi Gras, was like having an out-of-body experience. Your senses were pulled in so many directions that the easiest solution to this stimuli conundrum was to simply close your eyes and listen to these masters play. Your hips moved to those funky bass lines like your brain had abandoned your cranium for points south. Art's percolating organ and Charles' sax gently massaged "Mean" Willie Green's staccato beat. A crisp, piercing guitar solo rang out. Then those magnificent voices, intimately connected by blood, overwhelmed you with astonishing vocal harmonies. The pacing of the shows was masterful. Just when you thought you couldn't take any more of the relentless funk, the band brought down the sound to a feathery whisper. Aaron's ethereal voice filled the room, and you literally heard women swoon and gasp. Then the funk hit you again until Art set up a reggae groove and sang "Sittin' Here in Limbo" as a colorblind love vibe permeated the smoky confines of the club. Though I don't ever recall the whole crowd holding hands and swaying together with peace signs in cartoon balloons over our heads, it sure felt that way.

While the Nevilles were arguably the first significant funk band from New Orleans to emerge after the breakup of the Meters, the end of that seminal band led to a full-fledged funk movement that continues to this day. Each of the other members of the Meters became bandleaders in their own right. Almost immediately after the Meters called it quits, the four members moved on to other musical pursuits. Art Neville, as discussed above, formed his iconic family band with his three brothers.

During the late 1960s and early 1970s, Aaron, Art and Cyril Neville had developed considerable experience performing together in Art Neville and the Neville Sounds—a group that played regularly around town. As Art began focusing more on the Meters, Aaron and Cyril began playing with the keyboardist Sam Henry's group, the Soul Machine. Cyril also performed with big brother Art in the Meters at the end of their storied run, and he appeared as a percussionist on all but one of their studio albums.

Charles Neville's career was a peripatetic one before he returned to New Orleans in 1977 to join the family band. He spent time in the Navy, at Angola Penitentiary, and touring with blues acts Bobby "Blue" Bland and B.B. King. He also found inspiration for his modern jazz sound in New York City where he lived as an on-again-off-again heroin addict and played with Billy Higgins and George Coleman. The Nevilles' autobiography, *The Brothers Neville*, written with David Ritz and published in 2000 provides scintillating and occasionally salacious details.

Leo Nocentelli and Zigaboo Modeliste formed a new version of the Meters, billed as the New Meters, and recruited the bassist Tony Hall and the keyboardist David Torkanowsky to fill the big shoes of George Porter, Jr. and Art Neville. With Neville out of the picture, Modeliste was the leader of the band on stage and Torkanowsky ably played Art Neville's parts on the keys, but they suffered a bit musically because no one could replace the great keyboardist's vocals. This version of the group was capable of bringing first-rate funk and a singular groove anchored by the rat-a-tat-tat of Modeliste's trademark drum style. Hall's playing was sterling—an in-the-pocket style that allowed plenty of room for the other musicians to solo.

Nocentelli, on the other hand, had begun a radical style shift. Long time fans of the guitarist argue that his style morphed from a groove-based rhythm player to a shredding lead guitarist complete with over-the-top pyrotechnic runs and insanely fast single note solos after he left New Orleans and moved to Los Angeles. But the evolution was beginning prior to the dissolution of the original band. Those early shows with the New Meters suggest that his transition to a guitar god was cemented when he was unburdened by playing with his peers and further distanced from the sparse instrumental sound of the group in their early days.

While Modeliste had to handle the lion's share of the vocal duties, since Neville and Porter were out of the picture and Torkanowsky and Hall were busy filling those gigantic shoes, Nocentelli was freed up to roam the edge of the stage and tear off one wild solo after another. The fact that the crowds ate up his guitar hero antics only seemed to encourage his new style.

Joyride was George Porter, Jr.'s first musical vehicle following the breakup of the Meters. The band featured Bruce McDonald and Ricky Sebastian on guitar and drums respectively, and Gerald Tillman and Sam Henry on keyboards. Sam Henry is a veteran journeyman player who has recorded and performed with most of the key players from the era including Allen Toussaint, Deacon John, James Rivers, Johnny Adams, Walter "Wolfman" Washington and Earl King.

Joyride represented a new direction for the bassist. They were raw, and they were edgy. It felt as if the band could fall apart at any time, thus creating that familiar rock 'n' roll tension. The music wasn't beautiful like an Aaron Neville ballad—it was greasy and overwhelmingly powerful like the spicy version of Popeye's Fried Chicken. Additionally, the songs were unfamiliar. Joyride's material was fresh, and the lyrical sentiments from the classic chorus, "I get high every time I think about you," to the simple, yet profound message of "Happy Song"—"don't let the madness get you, don't let the sadness get you—" resonated deeply.

The Meters and the Neville Brothers essentially operated out of the same songbook in the late 1970s and early 1980s. They just played different versions of the same songs. The Meters featured sparse instrumentation while the Nevilles added harmony vocals and jazzy sax work. But Joyride was a new band, essentially cut from the same cloth, but wearing a new style of clothes. It wasn't so much an update as it was a new direction in funk; a new school with as much rock 'n' roll edge as a full-fledged rock band.

There were two reasons for the edgy new style. One was the guitarist Bruce McDonald. He hails from Cajun Country and was a founding member of Coteau, a band out of the bayou that is considered significant because they were one of the first bands to add a rock edge to traditional Cajun music. McDonald's biggest claim to fame on the New Orleans music scene is that he composed "Happy Song," the set closer or encore for George Porter, Jr. for the better part of twenty-five years. McDonald was active on the scene through the early 1990s, and he will pop up several more times in this tale.

The other factor contributing to Joyride's edgy style was the presence of Gerald Tillman in the band. Tillman is one of the unsung geniuses of the New Orleans funk tradition. He died in 1986 at the age of 31, but before he passed away he earned the moniker "Professor Shorthair" because of his skill on the piano, and his ability to create something new from the old tried and true material. The nickname was also an homage to the great Professor Longhair.

In his early twenties, he played organ on the first Neville Brothers album and was the second (or third if Ivan Neville was with the band) keyboardist in some of the earliest incarnations of the band. He performed with most of the second wave of Meters-inspired funk musicians including the multi-instrumentalist Renard Poché in the seminal group Black Male (which also supplied the first Neville

Brothers rhythm section). He also led his own band, G.T. and the Trustees, and he co-founded the Uptown Allstars with Ivan Neville.

Tillman was the architect of what became known as the uptown sound. He re-arranged a number of the classic tunes from the Meters' catalog by changing the tempo or the syncopation. Cyril Neville, who eventually took over the Uptown Allstars, has long championed Tillman's rearrangements of the classic Meters tunes and he makes sure no one ever forgets the enigmatic composer and performer. His versions of the tunes live on when performed by Cyril Neville and Ivan Neville.

In March 1981, George Porter, Jr.'s Joyride played on Tulane University's main quad amid the glorious meteorological ambiance of an early spring day in New Orleans. The occasion was the WTUL Rock On Survival Marathon. The band played new tunes written by Porter and McDonald. Only one Meters standard graced the set list that day, but the new version of "Africa" was completely re-worked and rearranged with Tillman's deft touch. Slowed down and with a Caribbean-style lilt that Sebastian swung on the drums as if he were in the islands, it exploded into a powerful jam at the end.

George Porter, Jr. had recently cut off his long hair, and the remnants of his braids were hanging down like a talisman from the headstock of his bass. He owned that stage—for the first time in his career he was the one true leader of the band. His now-trademark uvula-shaking shriek was in fine form, and the crowd responded to his exhortations like he was a shaman. He stalked the stage like a man possessed while encouraging the other musicians on every solo.

George Porter, Jr.'s Joyride only existed for a short time; the few recordings of the group include a studio album that was not released until well into the 21st century. But during the band's brief tenure they set the tone for Porter, Jr's long term project, the Runnin' Pardners, and for the future of New Orleans funk itself.

At this point in the tale, it's important to shed a little more light on the personage of Gerald "Professor Shorthair" Tillman considering his legendary status and the legacy of his accomplishments. That he was a virtuoso player and an amazing arranger was never in doubt, but his troubles were mostly of his own making. Despite his propensity for problematic behavior, Tillman was extremely well respected among the musicians, and he was usually able to recruit the best players for his own band, alternatively listed as the Gerald Tillman Band or G.T. and the Trustees. That group played a couple of times on Tulane's quad during the 1983 fall semester. There was nearly as much confusion surrounding the personnel in Tillman's various ensembles as with the bands that emerged in the wake of the break up of the Meters. Tillman played with a drummer, Gerald Trinity, who also played in early versions of the Neville Brothers and with the bassist Roger Poché whose brother, Renard, a crucial member of the extended Neville family, was Dr. John's guitarist during 1981-82.

Two other drummers, James Ledet and Reggie Cummings, were childhood friends of Ivan Neville and were regulars on the scene filling in where necessary. Ledet was actually the very first Neville Brothers drummer, and Cummings earned a co-writer credit on "Dance Your Blues Away," a favorite song in the 1980s Neville Brothers' repertoire. G.T. and the Trustees also occasionally (depending on scheduling and remuneration) included bigger name players such as Willie Green and Daryl Johnson, the Nevilles' rhythm section, and often featured Cyril Neville himself on congas and vocals. The saxophonist Alonzo Bowens was usually part of the band as was the guitarist Bruce Blaylock.

In the summer of 1982, with students gone and the tourism economy barely alive, gigs were hard to come by. In order to get paid, George Porter, Jr. and Zigaboo Modeliste put aside whatever differences may have still been lingering over the breakup of the Meters. They played a gig at Jimmy's billed as Jimmy Ballero and the Renegades. The group was a trio ostensibly led by Ballero, a journeyman guitarist and singer. Due to the sparse crowds that were out and about on a weeknight in the middle of the summer, they set up their stripped down band on the raised area right next to the bar rather than using the main stage. Porter sat on a barstool. The drums were set up on the floor, and a small section of tables and chairs was arranged creating an intimate arrangement that had the audience practically on top of the band. It allowed for superior viewing, but there was no dance floor at all.

The stage set up was a precursor to Porter's trio gig with Johnny Vidacovich, and the band pursued a jazzy approach to funk. Ballero is an underrated guitarist capable of hanging with the two legends of the Meters. The show provided a chance to really appreciate the chops of both Porter and Modeliste in a sit down setting. It is the contention of serious students of the Meters, as well as other musicologists, that Modeliste's drumming style was the critical factor that set the Meters apart and helped them earn a place in music history.

Modeliste's playing was incredibly supple because he was always messing around with the rhythm with what musicians call the "one," playing accents on his ride cymbal or snare drum that made the beat feel as slippery as wet mud. This is the central appeal of his playing, especially to other drummers, and it works because he has an uncanny ability to play all around the central beat without ever losing it. It can be a jarring experience at first because the slippery nature of the beat can deceive the ears.

Porter, Jr.'s playing was usually over the top with the wicked bass gymnastics that cause mouths to hang open in awe of the sheer funkiness of the music. He played guitar early in his career, and he took elements from a guitarist's style and mirrored them on the bass. But with this trio, he stripped down his playing to the raw essentials and unmasked his inner jazzman.

Despite the opportunity to hear these legendary players up close and personal, a strange energy permeated this gig. Some of the problems that caused friction within the Meters were still visible because Porter was clearly rankled by Modeliste's propensity for talking too much between songs and occasionally in the middle of a tune. Yet, the show was proceeding nicely. It was low key, with each player taking turns leading the band when Gerald Tillman walked in and it quickly became obvious that he wanted to sit in with the band.

There was no keyboard, Tillman's instrument of choice, on stage. Tillman could play anything, but the three players were very reluctant to give up their instruments. This state of affairs was a given considering the volatile nature of Porter and Modeliste's relationship and the collective insecurity within any new group. Tillman was an unpredictable personality. Within a short amount of time, he created quite a ruckus and the sparse audience was overtaken with a bit of group anxiety since he appeared to be confronting the musicians while they were playing.

After realizing his situation was untenable, Tillman got his hands on the microphone and proceeded to attempt to sing. It went off poorly and the evening went from downright bizarre to truly weird. Tillman took the microphone and went out into the audience trying to get members of the crowd to participate. I remember fear—is he going to approach me with that crazed look in his eyes?

Tillman continued to perform sporadically over much of the early 1980s. He continued his work rearranging the classic songs from the Meters' catalog, and Cyril Neville regularly included the new versions in his live shows. Sadly, Professor Shorthair died in September of 1986 before seeing the full effects of his work or becoming aware of his legacy.

The four original members of the Meters spent much of the early part of the 1980s trying to reinvent themselves and crawl out of the giant shadow cast by the legendary group. There were numerous hints in the media of a full on reunion including a show the week before Mardi Gras in 1981 at the Saenger Theater. The headliner was Dr. John, and the ticket listed the original Meters as being part of the show along with Joyride and the Radiators. But given the well-documented conflicts between the members of the Meters and the timeline, it is highly unlikely that the band that night featured all four original members even though the word "original" appeared on the ticket.

Modeliste worked on his jazz chops with a new group called the Survivors led by bassist Ramsey McLean. That group featured Charles Neville and Reggie Huston on saxophones, Charmaine Neville (Charles' daughter) on vocals and John Magnie on keys. Huston went on to be a long time member of Charmaine Neville's band.

In May 1983, fans of the Meters were excited to see the names Nocentelli and Modeliste scheduled to appear with Jimmy Ballero and the Renegades at Jimmy's. Nocentelli had already relocated to Los Angeles and was preparing for a tour with the blues shouter, Etta James. He was given a featured billing for James' show at Tipitina's on September 17, 1983.

Nocentelli's return to New Orleans set the stage for an attempt at a full-fledged reunion. The band was scheduled to perform at Tipitina's, and I was in attendance that night. There were some serious highlights including a great instrumental opener and a long medley that centered on the classic tune, "Hey Pocky Way." The four musicians seemed able, at least for one night, to put their differences aside in front on an ecstatic crowd. Tellingly, they also performed their latter day song, "My Name Up in Lights," from the *New Directions* album. That tune, with the pleading chorus, "I've got to… get my name up in lights," defined the ego problems plaguing the group since the early 1970s.

The four members of the Meters played together one more time at Tipitina's on December 28, 1983, Modeliste's birthday. They played a couple more shows during Jazz Fest week in 1984; their last full performances together until the celebrated reunion of 2000.

At the end of 1985, Joseph "Zigaboo" Modeliste filed a $20 million lawsuit against Allen Toussaint and Marshall Sehorn (the owners of Sea-Saint studios where the Meters recorded their magic), Jerry Wilson and Cosimo Matassa, the legendary producer from the 1950s. Modeliste alleged the defendants were responsible for a widely circulated bootleg recording of the Meters' performance at Rosy's, the fabled club on Tchoupitoulas Street, in the mid-1970s.

The charge was copyright infringement. The other members of the Meters eventually settled the suit deepening the rift between them and virtually insuring no more reunions would take place. Over the course of the ensuing sixteen years, there would be other near-reunions, with three of the four original members playing a gig or with all four on stage for a song or two, but the financial issues, lawsuits and ego problems always manage to derail any other attempts at reuniting the band for a full performance.

Still, the music of the Meters defines 20th century funk. The role each of the four musicians played in altering the direction of New Orleans music cannot be overestimated, and the influence of Art Neville, George Porter, Jr., Leo Nocentelli and Joseph "Zigaboo" Modeliste extends far beyond the boundaries of the Crescent City. Nocentelli and Modeliste decamped permanently to the West Coast and influenced a whole new generation of musicians in Los

Angeles and San Francisco respectively. When the jam band movement coalesced in the 1990s, New Orleans-style funk became a national obsession and spawned dozens of groups in America and overseas. Tellingly, rappers and hip-hop artists have made the music of the Meters among the most sampled grooves of the last century proving the foursome created powerful art that defies genre, time and place.

Chapter 6

THE BRASS BAND REVIVAL

"Down in New Orleans where the jazz is hot, the Tremé area is right on top"—Kermit Ruffins

Danny Barker's return to New Orleans in 1965 from a successful career as a jazzman in New York instigated a renewal of the brass band tradition and its cultural components, especially the social aid and pleasure clubs' tradition of the Sunday second line parade. Barker, who played guitar and banjo, sang and wrote numerous classic tunes including "Don't You Feel My Leg," sung by his wife, "Blue" Lu, and "Save the Bones for Henry Jones" which was a huge hit for Nat King Cole. His career in the Big Apple was punctuated by stints as a sideman for a veritable who's who of jazz stars from members of the original generation such as Bunk Johnson and Sidney Bechet to swing legend Cab Calloway. Barker was also a writer, historian and raconteur, and his arrival back in New Orleans heralded a sea change in the way New Orleanians regarded the earliest generations of jazz musicians.

Some of Barker's first work back in the city was as an assistant curator at the New Orleans Jazz Museum where he worked from 1965 to 1975. He also began a light performance schedule generally hiring younger musicians as his mentoring was both on and off the bandstand. By the mid-1980s, Barker's notoriety in New Orleans had spread outside of the Tremé neighborhood, and his contributions to the musical community were being more widely recognized. In 1983, he performed at Tulane University's Dixon Auditorium. The event was billed as "Save the Bones—An Evening of Reminiscence, Anecdote and Song."

His act had a bit of kitsch. Since he was an accomplished story-teller, each song was preceded by a story or lengthy lesson in the history of the music. His performance was so polished as he sang his whimsical songs while playing banjo or guitar that it hardly seemed to be an act at all.

Barker returned home only to discover that the traditional jazz community in New Orleans, which was thriving when he left some thirty-five years earlier, was stagnated by an aging musician popula-tion. Many of the musicians from the earliest years of jazz were still living but had few opportunities to perform.

Preservation Hall, which transitioned from an art gallery to a performance space under the guidance of Larry Borentstein in 1961, became a venue to "preserve" the old styles under the lead-ership of Allan Jaffe. But despite the new venue, societal pressures were beginning to affect the larger, segregated city and region. The changing culture, driven by the incipient black empowerment movement, was on the verge of rejecting all of the old traditions partially because of the impact of integration.

For generations, the social aid and pleasure clubs provided a safety net for black New Orleanians. They served as an informal social network and provided various forms of insurance including burial coverage, which often included a jazz funeral, to dues-paying members. With the advent of societal change, the old mechanisms were seen in some quarters as vestiges of a bygone era.

Even before the landmark Brown v. Board of Education Supreme Court decision in 1954, doors were opening for black citizens. Con-ventional insurance was becoming more available to black custom-ers. Increasing educational opportunities for blacks eventually led to the development of a viable black middle class as well as a politi-cal base. However, the downside was the devastation of the black commercial districts along Dryades Street in the Central City neighborhood and along N. Claiborne Avenue in the downtown area. A long decline, still evident in those neighborhoods today, began when the previously whites-only stores along Canal Street began begrudgingly opening their doors to black citizens.

Since the beginnings of the jazz age, the 6th Ward and the Tremé neighborhood comprised the center of the town musical scene. "The Tremé," as it is popularly known, is the oldest black neighborhood in the country and is also the home of St. Augustine Catholic Church, one of the oldest integrated parishes in the United States. The area has percolated with music and musicians since the 1700s. It is where Congo Square is located and is a mere short walk from the French Quarter and the center of commerce in the city.

Congo Square is significant because it was the place where slaves and free people of color gathered on Sundays throughout the years leading up to the Civil War. The city of New Orleans was the only municipality in the slave-owning states allowing such gatherings. Historians believe that the retention of old-world rhythms, dances and instruments by the slaves and former slaves played an important role in the creation of jazz. Those special Sundays were replicated in later generations by the annual second line parades sponsored by the social aid and pleasure clubs.

Amid these societal changes, Barker noticed that a few notable brass bands such as Dejan's Olympia, the Onward and the Pinstripe, mainly featuring older musicians, were still working in New Orleans. There were no young bands, and no one was leading an effort to get young musicians involved in learning the traditions of New Orleans jazz. So Barker approached the pastor of the Fairview Baptist Church, and with the blessing of the church he started a band of youngsters in 1971. He began teaching them the traditions and songs associated with jazz and the culture of social aid and pleasure clubs, second lines and jazz funerals. He also instilled in his charges the importance of promptness, proper attire and the role of the musician in a society that still marginalized African-Americans.

It is fair to say that each member of the Fairview Baptist Church band went on to become an important musician, and each has contributed in numerous ways to the current revival of the brass band tradition. Some of the musicians who matriculated through the band include the clarinetist Dr. Michael White, a music historian and founder of the Original Liberty Brass Band; the trombonist Lucien Barbarin (a snare drummer at the time); the tubist Anthony "Tuba Fats" Lacen, a mainstay of the traditional jazz scene before his passing in 2004; the trumpeter Leroy Jones, a veteran of Harry Connick, Jr.'s big band who founded the Hurricane Brass Band in 1974 around the core of the Fairview band; and the trumpeter Gregory Stafford, the leader of the Young Tuxedo Brass Band, a member of the Original Liberty and Hurricane Brass Bands, and a traditional jazz stalwart. A young Wynton Marsalis also performed with the Fairview Baptist Church Band.

Not all of the alumni of the Fairview Baptist Church Band stayed focused on traditional jazz. Gregory Davis, currently in charge of bookings for the jazz tent at the New Orleans Jazz and Heritage Festival, co-founded the Dirty Dozen Brass Band in 1977. The Dirty Dozen became famous for updating the tradition. They took the sounds they learned under the tutelage of Barker and added elements of newer music popular at that time including modern jazz from the likes of Duke Ellington, Dizzy Gillespie and Charlie Parker as well as jump blues, and soul music. At first, this updating of the tradition was not popular, and the more tradition-minded members of the music community rejected the modern sounds although the younger generation of dancers and parade followers quickly embraced the new music.

The transition between styles was not absolute since they continued to play in the traditional style depending on the gig. And it was gradual. As late as January 1982, the Dirty Dozen was being billed at Tipitina's as, "a fine 8-piece traditional marching jazz band," though the same issue of *Wavelength* magazine later suggests, "the Dirty Dozen began with what we consider traditional jazz, but fused it with modern elements and Caribbean influence." By 1983, the band guide in *Wavelength* described them as, "new New Orleans traditional jazz." Regardless, the band persevered and led the way for other contemporary brass bands including the Rebirth Brass Band.

There have been some personnel changes over the 33+ years of the band's existence, but the core of the Dirty Dozen Brass Band at the beginning of their career included the aforementioned Gregory

Davis on trumpet and the saxophonist Roger Lewis. The first version of the band also included two musicians more closely associated with the traditional side of the genre—the bass drummer Benny Jones and the tuba player Anthony "Tuba Fats" Lacen. However, Lacen was an innovator in his youth, and his new approach to the bass parts of brass band music had a major influence on the next generation of tuba players. Jones is still active on the scene with the Tremé Brass Band.

It was the addition of the sousaphonist Kirk Joseph, along with the modern jazz sensibilities of Lewis and Davis, that led to the ground-breaking style of the band, particularly Joseph's radical new stylistic approach and the effervescent gurgling of his iconic instrument. The first Dirty Dozen album, *My Feet Can't Fail Me Now*, was released in 1984, and the song selections demonstrated early on that this was a band to be reckoned with. They included New Orleans standards such as "Li'l Liza Jane" and "St. James Infirmary" alongside Charlie Parker's bebop cut, "Bongo Beep," and Duke Ellington's classic, "Caravan."

Though it took five years before the band cut their first album, success came quickly following the release in 1985 of their now legendary recording from the Montreaux Jazz Festival, *Live: Mardi Gras at Montreaux*. That album was released on Rounder Records. Their next, *Voodoo*, featuring Dizzy Gillespie, Branford Marsalis and Dr. John, appeared on a major label. Columbia Records was their home through 1992.

During this period, the band was on the road nearly all year round, and performances in New Orleans were rare, celebrated occurrences. In some quarters, the Dirty Dozen was accused of neglecting their community obligations with respect to performing at second line parades, jazz funerals and other traditional functions. But, the group was becoming an international sensation. They appeared on the recordings of other musical celebrities including Elvis Costello and the Neville Brothers.

The National Geographic Society was so impressed with the changes in the traditional musical culture of New Orleans that they came to the city in 1989 to film a program for their *Explorer* television series. They staged a meeting of two generations of brass bands in the city deep in the Tremé neighborhood. The set up was contrived to create a "the Dirty Dozen Brass Band meets the Olympia Brass Band" vibe. They filmed each band marching through the streets separately and then staged the meeting with the two bands approaching each other on an otherwise empty block in the Tremé. Of course, this would never happen in real life. Yet, it was a wild afternoon that ended with the musicians and a smattering of fans chatting in front of the Candlelight Lounge on N. Robertson Street. The footage was edited into a program called "New Orleans Brass: Young Musicians Join Their Elders in Reviving the Vibrant, Vivacious Tradition of New Orleans Brass Marching Bands." It aired regularly for years.

The brass band tradition has always been a dynamic one, but most of the changes in repertoire and style were gradual throughout the 20th century. This new avant-garde approach to the traditional brass band music of New Orleans was a more radical shift that did not endear them to the older generation. But younger folks were deeply impressed by this new hybrid sound. Though no one knew it at the time, a musical revolution was beginning.

In 1983, a group of high school students from Joseph S. Clark High School in the Tremé neighborhood of New Orleans formed a band that, over the ensuing decades, has become a New Orleans institution and has spawned dozens of other bands. The Rebirth Brass Band followed in the footsteps of the Dirty Dozen Brass Band and became the second brass band to impact the traditions in the genre's nascent revival.

The group originally called itself the ReBirth *Jazz* Band, and that name and spelling was used throughout the band's early years. The sousaphonist Philip Frazier and the trumpeter Kermit Ruffins were the leaders, and their first gigs were working for tips on the streets of the French Quarter. After school they would walk the few short blocks from the Tremé to the tourist district, and they quickly became enamored of the easy bucks to be earned with the trumpet case open.

The Rebirth has had considerable personnel turnover since their beginnings. The early version of the band also included Frazier's younger brother, Keith, on bass drum, Keith "Wolf" Anderson on trombone, Kenneth "Eyes" Austin on snare drum, Reginald Steward on trombone and Gardner Ray Green on trumpet. Anderson was the only member of the band who was not born in New Orleans, though he moved to the city at a young age. He was the most musically sophisticated of the young musicians, and he took on a leadership role as well. The Frazier brothers are the only original members still in the band.

They played their first professional gig on May 4th for a convention at the Sheraton Hotel on Canal Street. Exactly one year later, they made their first recording for the Arhoolie record label during the 1984 Jazz Fest. It was a live album recorded on the fly in the Grease Lounge—a tiny hole-in-the-wall in the Tremé just off N. Claiborne Avenue.

Though both their musical skills and the production values on the record are extremely raw, Rebirth was clearly "here to stay." They chose that phrase as the title of their first album. The record featured originals, a few classics from the New Orleans R&B canon and two modern jazz standards—Herbie Hancock's "Chameleon" and Thelonious Monk's "Blue Monk."

Early on, the Rebirth Brass Band didn't have many gigs outside the Tremé neighborhood, their home turf, but by 1987 the band was starting to come into its own. They opened a series of shows for the Neville Brothers at Tipitina's, and Cyril Neville became a champion for the group as he would also be for the next new brass band to emerge on the scene, the Soul Rebels.

By the mid-1990s, a group of young musicians who had been mentored by Milton Batiste of the Olympia Brass Band began shaking things up by adding hip-hop to the brass band mix. Cyril Neville heard them performing their own music and dubbed them "the Soul Rebels". Like the Dirty Dozen and the Rebirth before them, the Soul Rebels were simply updating the tradition with the music of their contemporaries. A DJ on WWOZ, Davis Rogan, who was broadcasting "The Brass Band Jam" on WWOZ at the time, championed them and the new direction in a letter to the editor after the 1960s legend, John Sinclair, panned their record in *Offbeat* magazine. Sinclair's curt reply in an editor's note to the young man—"Get a life."

Despite the protestations of the older generation, the Soul Rebels and other brass bands that followed them continued injecting rap into the brass band sounds. Observers detected a sense of déjà vu harkening back to the "moldy figs," a group of jazz purists who rejected the earliest changes in jazz in the 1920s and similar minded folks who were against the innovations of the Dirty Dozen. But if there were naysayers among the younger generations, they were immediately silenced when the Soul Rebels released their debut recording in the middle of August 1994. The record included one of the most definitive songs to ever emerge from the brass band genre—"Let Your Mind Be Free." It was a song designed to raise consciousness in the inner city and began with the prophetic lines, "Walking 'round in the Sixth Ward, everybody's asking who we are." It wasn't long before the Soul Rebels were challenging Rebirth for the top spot in the local brass band hierarchy.

In January 1987, the Rebirth Brass Band played a rare club date at Snug Harbor. But more importantly, they inherited the Glass House, a tiny ramshackle bar in the Central City neighborhood, from the Dirty Dozen Brass Band in late March. The Dozen had been playing Mondays for a few years, but their success on the national and international stage precluded any more intimate shows in the ghetto. The Rebirth began playing on Thursday nights.

The Glass House was located on S. Saratoga Street between Second and Third streets; a mere two blocks from the corner of Lasalle and Washington and A.L. Davis Park, important meeting spots for the uptown Mardi Gras Indian tribes and the second line community. Prior to the wholesale name changing that occurred across the city, A.L. Davis Park was known as Shakespeare Park—a name that reoccurs regularly in song lyrics and in historic accounts of the fabled 1950s-era nightclub, the Dew Drop Inn, which was also located in the immediate area. Needless to say, no one writes songs about A.L. Davis Park.

The Glass House shared none of the characteristics of the Rose Tattoo and Dorothy's Medallion—except having a predominately black clientele. It was not an inviting place like Dorothy's, and the neighborhood was considerably more intimidating than the familiar corner of Tchoupitoulas and Napoleon. Simply put, the Glass House was a ghetto bar with extremely raucous regulars. When the Rebirth played, it was always packed to the point of overflowing. Like most of these neighborhood joints, many of the patrons came from the surrounding blocks and they were some of the roughest blocks in one of the most dangerous sections of the city.

The crack cocaine epidemic that was destroying inner city neighborhoods across the country was in full swing in Central City. There was no police presence whatsoever, though crime in the area was out of control. The New Orleans Police Department was wracked by corruption, and several officers were eventually arrested for aiding and abetting criminal drug gangs. So there was clearly an element of danger associated with going to the Glass House. The shows didn't start until well after 11 PM and lasted until after 3 AM.

Stepping into the Glass House completely overwhelmed the senses. It was hot, it was loud, and it stunk. While the Dirty Dozen had updated the hundred-year-old tradition with modern jazz and old school R&B and soul, Rebirth's new take on the brass band traditions was all about the funk. It's important to note that most of the inner city black bands had two different approaches to playing music depending on who was in the audience. When they played to a predominantly white crowd, the music was a little more controlled, the show was more regimented, and the set list was more defined.

In the 'hood, all bets were off. At the Glass House there was rarely a break between songs, and most nights they wouldn't stop playing for the duration of the 45-minute set. Sometimes it seemed like they only stopped twice over three sets. There were no microphones, so there was very little singing, and if there was any singing at all, it was exclusively of the call-and-response nature. There were no stage lights, and what little illumination there was in the bar came from the Christmas lights strung as permanent fixtures along the walls and over the bar. There was no stage. The tables were pushed to one side and the band would set up behind a row of chairs at the far end of the rectangular building. There was a rickety old window unit that didn't provide much in the way of air-conditioning. The row of chairs was a meager barricade, and to this day I wonder how they were even able to play amid the mayhem that occurred a few feet away.

But play they did. Describing the music at the Glass House is difficult even to someone fully aware of the potency of the band in the current era. They were still young, very green in the larger sense of the music business, but the band was tight. The rhythm section was what hit you first because of the sheer volume at which they played. I saw Kenneth "Eyes" Austin play snare drum with the band a few times before Ajay Mallory replaced him. Mallory was a former drum major with St. Augustine High School and led the city's premier high school marching band as a teenager. His power on the snare was undeniable. In those days, he could hit with such a force that the reverberation carried across the room. But he wielded the power with accountability, and he often held back so that the meaning of each power shot increased exponentially. He was also a finesse player with an innate sense of syncopation that developed profoundly under the tutelage of his teachers. Mallory has been in and out of the Rebirth and other brass bands since then, vacillating back and forth between a career in music and other more stable occupations. He has a very able replacement in Derrick Tabb, the current snare drummer for the Rebirth.

Mallory's rhythm section partner in the Glass House period was the longstanding bass drummer and original member, Keith Frazier. Because of his short stature, "Bass Drum Shorty" has been called the secret weapon in the band since he can barely be seen over his instrument. Keith Frazier's rock solid rhythm playing sets the tone for the band. In the New Orleans brass band, the bass drum has a cymbal attached to it allowing the musician additional opportunities to accent the basic rhythm and create a polyrhythmic sound. Frazier uses a screwdriver in his cymbal hand. The metal-on-metal contact allows the sound to travel further; certainly something that is important when playing without microphones. But it also creates a trebly wash of sound that meshes perfectly with the higher register of the trumpets.

While some would call Keith Frazier the secret weapon, it is my contention that Philip Frazier's groundbreaking work on the sousaphone is what set Rebirth apart. Though he was clearly influenced by Kirk Joseph of the Dirty Dozen, Frazier's use of the "elephant call," a higher pitched honking blast in the middle of a bass line, has defined Rebirth since the early days. The elephant call directly impacts the dancers because it creates a crescendo effect that raises the intensity level up to the next notch. Philip Frazier has the ability to directly control a crowd using this technique. I have seen him do it in clubs, at big concerts and at second line parades in the street especially under bridges like the interstate overpass along N. Claiborne Avenue. The effect is invariably the same. With each repeated blast, the crowd's energy surges to the point where everyone who is able is jumping up and down. Meanwhile, the band is blowing away like mad. Imagine what would happen if he kept it up indefinitely.

Reginald Steward and Keith "Wolf" Anderson were the trombone players during the Glass House period. Though Anderson was musically the most advanced in the band, Steward was no slouch as a young man. The two were both adept at "tailgating," a technique that creates tension as the musicians play bleating lines slightly behind the beat. Anderson, in particular, was the showman in the early group, eagerly getting down with the crowd and exhorting them to go crazy.

The front line included the saxophonist John "Prince" Gilbert and the trumpeters Kermit Ruffins and Derek "Dirt" Wiley. Wiley was a quiet, unassuming player who left music to become a preacher. He was replaced in the band by a child prodigy, Derrick Shezbie, who joined the band at the age of 10 and never looked back.

Ruffins is one of the best-known New Orleans musicians who has forged a successful solo career since leaving the Rebirth in the 1990s where he was just beginning to develop his fun-loving persona. Now he is known more as a vocalist, and though he sang a bit with Rebirth in the early days when they played at Tips and other more established clubs, it was his hot trumpet playing that set the tone for the band. Philip Frazier and Ruffins were often referred to as co-leaders. Frazier handled the business of the group, but Ruffins was the on-stage leader. However, he would often defer to Frazier with each new song selection calling out, "whatcha got Phil?," before the beginning of the next tune.

Gilbert was older than the other members and was a rollicking free spirit on the bandstand. Since the saxophone is the hardest instrument to hear in a setting without microphone, he had a penchant for leaving the tiny stage area especially when the place was filled with out of control dancers.

Picture the scene—all the bar stools are occupied. The dancers, led by a frenetic fellow with the whimsical nickname, "Ice Cream," are going full tilt spinning and whirling like so many manic tops. The band is playing something exceedingly funky at top volume. It's dark, there are sweaty bodies all around, and everyone in the place is feeling the music utterly and completely. The energy swells with every "elephant call," and suddenly it seems as if the music is every-where. No longer coming from just the stage—it's surround sound live and direct. John "Prince" Gilbert has commandeered a bar stool and is bent over his horn blowing like crazy behind the dancers with a sly look in his eyes.

When the Rebirth played at the Glass House it was the wildest scene imaginable. There are enough stories about the Glass House to fill another book—here are a few more.

There is a long-standing tradition among trumpet players of a certain disposition, Kermit Ruffins among them, to play up against a willing woman's private parts. They say that the sensation of com-pressed air coming through the bell of the trumpet can be very stim-ulating (check out the cover of Rounder Records' *New Orleans Brass Bands—Down Yonder* for a photographic depiction of the practice that was shot at the Glass House).

One night in the Central City club, a particularly willing woman sat down on the one of the chairs at the front of the dance floor and Ruffins went to work on her. After a few minutes of spirited blowing (pun intended), the crowd mostly stopped dancing and gathered in a circle. The woman had her eyes clenched tightly shut and Ruf-fins continued to blast a long winding solo. She was not just play-ing along; basking in the attention. She was feeling it deeply, and everyone in the place would have agreed that something more sig-nificant was going on than a fan simply enjoying a trumpet solo up close and personal. When the solo ended, the woman appeared visi-bly embarrassed when she realized most of the room had witnessed such an intimate moment.

On another night, the power went out and the whole neighbor-hood was plunged into darkness. Since the band didn't require any electricity, they just kept playing. There were no windows in the Glass House and it was pitch black inside. They only had one flash-light behind the bar, so it was virtually impossible to sell liquor, thus defeating the whole purpose of owning a bar. After a few minutes, it was clear the power wasn't coming on any time soon, but the band had no intention of taking an early break.

In those days, Rebirth played with a fury that welled up from their collective creative energy and individual frustrations. The money they made from the meager two-dollar cover collected in a cigar box by the Frazier brothers' sisters at the door was not their sole motivation. They were as consumed playing the music as the crowd was listening and dancing to it. It was a symbiotic relation-ship—the band needed the crowd as much as the crowd needed the band.

So, the night the lights went out, they kept on playing. The snare drummer, Ajay Mallory, went outside and moved his car, a giant Cutlass, so he could aim the headlights right into the front door. Though it was completely blocking S. Saratoga Street, the car provided enough light for the bar to continue doing business. The rest of the set was illuminated, and the dancers created oddly over-sized shadows that raced around the room in time to the relentless Rebirth beat.

Summers in New Orleans are impossibly hot, and spending time in a club with inadequate air conditioning (or none at all) requires suspension of the normal rules of interpersonal interaction. Since there were a number of patrons of the Glass House who chose not to use antiperspirant or deodorant, they began to stink, badly, over-whelmingly, by half way through the first set.

On another night during the depths of summer when the air-conditioner couldn't have cooled a small, empty room never mind a crowded bar filled with frenetic dancers, I had a very strange bod-ily reaction. When the first set ended I was drenched in sweat, and raced outside as quickly as possible to escape the suffocating condi-tions. As soon as I got out the door, an instant chill came over me, and goose bumps formed on my arms despite the fact that it had to be over eighty degrees outside. I felt like I had walked into a refrig-erator. After a second or two, my body recovered, but it had been briefly fooled. It must have been over 115 degrees inside for me to have such a physical reaction.

Besides beginning a regular gig on Thursday nights at the Glass House, the group also made their first appearance at the New Orleans Jazz and Heritage Festival in 1987. Inexplicably, the hot group of young men from the Tremé was booked into the relatively staid Economy Hall Tent. They tore the roof off the place and many of the traditional jazz fans just sat there with their mouths hanging open.

Their appearance at the prestigious local festival coupled with the hiring of Allison Miner, one of the founders of the Jazz Fest, as their first manager allowed the Rebirth to move up to the next level since the Jazz Fest was now attracting larger numbers of booking agents for other festivals. Rebirth spent the month of June playing major festival dates in Europe including the Montreaux Jazz Festival and the North Sea Jazz Festival. The group never looked back and summers on the road became the norm.

By 1991, the Rebirth Brass Band was beginning to resemble the Dirty Dozen with respect to the impact of their innovative approach and their growing international reputation. New brass bands began popping up in the brass band community including the Soul Rebels, who have since grown into one of the most respected units in the tight-knit community despite having a lot of personnel changes, the Little Rascals and the New Birth Brass Bands. By the end of the 1990s, the city was literally crawling with young musicians seeking to emulate the Rebirth. Bands with arcane or whimsical names such as the Highsteppers and the Looney Tunes came and went as members moved from one ensemble to the next. The style even infected musicians in other locales. The Black Bottom Brass Band formed in Japan and Mama Dig Down's Brass Band formed in Wisconsin among other examples.

Due to the profound impact of the Dirty Dozen and Rebirth Brass Band, what was at first considered sacrilege among the traditional standard bearers has now morphed into the tradition itself. Young bands are expected to learn the traditions, but they are also free to add elements of popular music to the sound. Now it is common for brass bands to feature bits and pieces of hip-hop, reggae and other genres, as the music has become hybridized. Additionally the number of musicians performing in brass bands has exploded exponentially since the 1960s. Danny Barker's goal to revitalize the brass band tradition has literally come true. Even the devastation following Hurricane Katrina could not dampen the impact. Currently, there are more young people learning the brass band traditions and repertoire than ever before in the modern history of New Orleans music.

Chapter 7

THE WORLD'S FAIR AND THE SAGA OF TIPITINA'S

"Calling out around the world, are you ready for a brand new beat, summer's here and the time is right for dancin' in the streets"—Marvin Gaye/Ivy Hunter/William "Mickey" Stevenson

Tipitina's financing was already on shaky ground by the summer of 1983. One local report suggested that the loosely organized consortium of owners (the fabulous "fo'teen" founders and a shadowy group of shareholders that reportedly included members of the Neville family and Professor Longhair's widow) was $47,000 in debt.

But the rest of the city was in a veritable tizzy about the arrival the following June of the World's Fair, officially known as the Louisiana World's Exposition, scheduled to run from May 12-November 11, 1984 on reclaimed riverfront space in downtown New Orleans. Reaching a feverish pitch six months before the gates were set to open, anticipation in the local press and among culture lovers across the city was running high from the moment New Orleans was selected as the American site. Determined to use the World's Fair as a giant tourist magnet, promoters hoped to pull first time visitors to the city from across the globe and entice them to return again and again to revisit the magic. The goal was nothing short of creating a sensational event rivaling anything the nation had ever seen. The power brokers in the city made decisions as if they were unaware of the deep recession gripping the country.

The economy had been in a bust phase since the late 1970s, and South Louisiana was greatly affected since the oil boom, which left much of the Gulf Coast flush with cash, had also ended. Inflation was causing economic hardships across the land. Clubs in New Orleans actually had discounted "recession nights" to try to lure locals to part with their hard earned dollars. The French Quarter, then mostly a dying residential neighborhood, was spruced up with new sidewalks complete with brick crosswalks, and the public was primed for this important six-month long celebration. A new festival, located in and named after the historic neighborhood, was conceived as part of a strategy to get locals to visit the district and spend money in the restaurants, bars and shops. However, very few locals actually went to the French Quarter Festival that first year.

Amid all the anticipation and media hype over the fair, rumbles of discontent among both the citizenry and the many planners and organizers began growing in volume during the early planning stages. The single day admission price, fifteen dollars, was deemed excessive. Cries of racism emitted from members of the black community who feared being left out of both the dollars to be earned from lucrative contracts and access to the event itself. A gondola over the Mississippi River to ferry visitors from the West Bank and a monorail around the giant site became symbols of the optimistic grandiosity of the plans. The idea of a giant open-air amphitheater to be built on the banks of the mighty Mississippi for big time touring bands and torn down at the end of the fair's run struck the music community in particular as completely ill-advised and poorly thought out.

Other civic leaders suggested that the estimates for the number of out of town visitors were grossly exaggerated considering the state of the national economy and the unbearable summer weather in New Orleans. These dire predictions proved prophetic at the end of the six-month run when organizers revealed that the only day the fair hit its expected daily average attendance was the much-hyped opening day.

Despite negative talk from some quarters, expectations were very high for music fans and local musicians. The fair took a page from the New Orleans Jazz and Heritage Festival and was designed to showcase the talents of Louisiana artists as well as national and international stars. The organizers suggested there would be "at least fifteen stages" in addition to the amphitheater. The event promised to be world class in every way.

The music press began soliciting for performers for the World's Fair in late 1983. Jed Palmer, late of Jed's University Inn on Oak Street, decided to get back into the promotions game and started a new business, Jed's Lookout, on the top floor of the Federal Fiber Mills building. He was aggressive with his advertising taking out full-page ads hyping the new venue months before opening.

While the promised fifteen stages never materialized, there were still considerable options for hearing live music at the fair on a regular basis. Located on the downriver end of the fair site and affording great views of Algiers Point and the ill-advised gondola system built to fly the non-existent droves of visitors over the Mississippi, the temporary Louisiana World Exposition's Quality Seal Amphitheater (its full corporate-sponsored name) actually had a well-thought out design complete with bleacher seats that dried quickly after an intermittent summer rain and a curtained proscenium that could be left open allowing a clear view of river traffic behind the performers. Admission required a separate fee, and the booking policy was skewed towards run-of-the-mill mainstream acts. Among my peer group, we shook our heads at the logic behind booking Air Supply, Neil Sedaka, Andy Gibb, and Sheena Easton.

Yet there were a few standout shows. Neil Young played a blistering version of "Down By the River" as riverboats, tugs and assorted work vessels could be seen plying the muddy waters just over his shoulders. The Temptations and the Four Tops appeared on a double bill. Their exquisite vocals wafted over the entire fair site and their choreographed dance moves impressed even the most jaded hipsters in attendance. Ray Charles, Gladys Knight, Charlie Pride, James Taylor and Randy Newman, Jessie Colter and Waylon Jennings, George Jones and Willie Nelson also played over the fair's six month run. Elvis Costello took the opportunity of an early fall show to wax philosophically about the state of American politics. During one song he ad-libbed lyrics addressing the upcoming presidential elections. He wondered why Americans would want to elect George

H.W. Bush, Ronald Reagan's two-term vice president, to succeed him in the highest position in the land.

The amphitheater didn't feature too many local bands except as opening acts, but they did put on one notable show at the end of that long hot summer. Dubbed "Rockin' on the River," the lineup included the Radiators, the instrumental rock band Woodenhead, Deacon John and Pop Combo among others. At 1 AM the show was still going on in front of a scattering of exhausted, overheated fans who were waiting on the headliners—a reunited version of the Cold.

My favorite venue presented non-stop music courtesy of a Lazy Susan-style stage configured to allow two bands to be set up at the same time. When the first band finished their set, the stage simply rotated 180 degrees and the next band, which had been setting up behind the curtain, cranked up. When the band before the Radiators failed to finish "Mustang Sally" in the allotted time, the stage began turning while they were still playing. The Radiators emerged in front of an enthusiastic audience playing their version of the R&B classic without missing a lick.

Elsewhere on the sprawling fair's grounds, an Italian Village was built. Just past the village, an Australian-themed club, Sheila's, opened on Fulton Street and presented live music for free (with fair admission) every night of the week. There was a long stretch toward the end of the fair's six-month run when the Neville Brothers played every Wednesday night. But the presence of these new venues and an unrelenting push towards keeping the tourist dollars on the fair site didn't bode well for other local businesses.

Locals who purchased the season passport, which allowed unlimited admission, generally had good things to say about their experiences at the fair. But nearly every other entity associated with the fair lost money in droves. The World's Fair itself was a giant financial bust—bankrupt with executives leaving town in disgrace, and hundreds of contractors left holding the proverbial bag.

While the fair was an unmitigated disaster on virtually every business level, it did create some lasting positive effects. The Warehouse District, a darkly lit, creepy warren of vacant and decrepit warehouses, came to life in the decade following the fair, and is now one of the most highly sought after residential neighborhoods in the city. Some of the earliest condo conversions in the neighborhood were a direct result of the fair, and the rest were residual effects as the neighborhood gentrified over the ensuing years.

There was no Riverwalk Marketplace or Julia Street Arts District. The Contemporary Arts Center, though in business and a regular presenter of jazz shows in the late 1970s and early 1980s, was considerably smaller and was isolated on the mostly desolate streets. There were no hotels, club life or restaurants of any note in the area except a glorified skid row establishment called the Hummingbird Bar and Grill.

The abysmal failure of the Louisiana World's Exposition left an open sore on the business climate in New Orleans in general and the music scene specifically that in many ways has not healed completely. Jed's Lookout and Sheila's managed to stay in business for a while after the fair closed, but it was many years before the Warehouse District emerged as a trendy neighborhood.

The giant space occupied by the World's Fair remained pockmarked with blight for a decade as the financial debacle wove its way through the courts. The Riverwalk Marketplace was virtually the only bright spot in the area until new renovation added more condominiums to the area bringing upscale residents and the businesses that cater to them. However, the Riverwalk did not open until 1986.

The Wonderwall, an architectural and artistic marvel that was the whimsical heart of the fair, was dismantled and sold piecemeal at auction. Elements of its pastel-painted art deco design are still visible in some neighborhoods around New Orleans. The monorail and the M.A.R.T. (Mississippi Aerial River Transit) gondola were supposed to become part of the area's transportation infrastructure when the World's Fair closed. Needless to say, there is no monorail in the Warehouse District nor is there currently a gondola over the river. The temporary amphitheatre was torn down at the end of the fair's run. Ironically, the city is currently planning a giant open-air concert space to be located on the downriver side of the French Quarter.

The city of New Orleans, its Downtown Development District and the Arts Council of New Orleans tried gamely to keep the musicians employed with the continuation of the Brown Bag concerts at noontime in the Central Business District and the French Market concert series. But the population exodus that began with the oil bust continued virtually unabated and affected every aspect of the business community. One local publication described the year after the World's Fair, in succinct if a tad bit overblown terms, calling it, "the bleakest musical period since the Beatles single handedly destroyed the Crescent City's recording industry in 1964."

While those in the know were aware of the major problems facing the World's Fair even before the gates opened for the first time, much of the community was in the dark. No one wanted to dispel the giddy happiness and relentless optimism of hosting such a prestigious international event. There were even hints of new clubs on the horizon. In June, a press release announced that a new development would not only replace Tipitina's as the hippest musical hot spot in town, but would also raise the level of service and amenities to a level unseen in New Orleans except in the chic supper clubs of the downtown hotels. Of course, the planned location, right next to the police station at the corner of Magazine Street and Napoleon Avenue, had some tongues wagging.

Also in June, the opening of another new spot, the Carrollton Town Hall, was announced for the corner of Oak and Joliet right down the street from the Maple Leaf. That location made more sense since Tupelo's Tavern had changed hands again and was now a disco called Cats that eschewed live music. Reflecting the economy of the period, neither club was ever heard from again. The location on Magazine Street is now the gymnasium for St. George's Episcopal School. The location on Oak Street ran into zoning troubles with a nearby church and has been an auto repair shop and an antique store over the years.

More new live music spots entered into the local milieu that year as well, but none stood the test of time. Their inability to thrive was affected by similar zoning problems or other economic reasons. The New Storyville club, which opened in the fall of 1984 in the 1100 block of Decatur Street in the French Quarter, was poised to take the French Quarter by storm. Yet, like so many businesses in the bleak economic environment of the failed World's Fair and the oil bust, they clearly were hampered by unfettered optimism.

New Storyville opened with full-page ads promising an ambitious schedule including an "Invitational Jam Session" that would feature the cream of the crop of local talent playing "progressive jazz with blues overtones." This jam session was scheduled nightly, or rather every morning, from 4-7 AM. It followed a regular band lineup from midnight- 4 AM that followed full dinner service. The jam session lasted one month.

The Parkway Tavern on N. Carrollton Avenue in Mid City was a simple neighborhood bar whose owners decided after years of no entertainment that live music would be an incentive to get people to come out and drink. Their earliest schedules featured two acts that became well-known performers—Mason Ruffner, who began venturing outside of his regular gig at the Old Absinthe House as his fame grew, and the singer/harmonica player and bandleader J.D. Hill. The Parkway Tavern suffered a near lethal blow when it was inundated with the flooding following Hurricane Katrina, but they had already ceased presenting bands a decade or so earlier when neighborhood noise concerns forced the enforcement of an arbitrary bit of city zoning code.

Meanwhile at Tipitina's, competition from the Riverboat President coupled with shaky finances limited their booking agent's ability to attract national bands, although there were a few notable performances in early 1984. In January, the Radiators celebrated the club's seventh birthday with special guest Earl King. King was in fine form and tore through a blistering set of his classic tunes as the Rads simultaneously basked in the glow of their hero's outstanding performance and played ace backing band.

The great rock 'n' roll pioneer Bo Diddley performed in February with a band including his daughter, a slamming drummer. His set was inspiring primal rock 'n' roll, although his ego seemed to set the tone for much of the set. Less than a week later, the Brazilian husband and wife team, Flora Purim and Airto, performed at the uptown club. Airto's total mastery of a complex percussion set featuring a number of unusual hand drums was one of the highlights of their performance.

Tipitina's had an impressive schedule during Jazz Fest of 1984, and there wasn't even a hint to visiting music lovers of the club's eminent demise. The schedule mixed local favorites like the Neville

Brothers, the Radiators, the Dirty Dozen Brass Band, Marcia Ball, Little Queenie, Deacon John (with special guest Etta James and Earl King) and Clifton Chenier with reggae acts, Culture and the Gladiators, and another appearance by Bo Diddley. Tipitina's even hosted the first Battle of the Brass Bands that I recall with the Dirty Dozen pitted against the Pinstripe and the Chosen Few with Tuba Fats. Yet, the cracks in the façade at Tipitina's were expanding rapidly. With the kitchen and juice bar shuttered, the club started closing on Mondays beginning in April causing a whole legion of red beans and rice and veggie spaghetti eaters to seek out new dinner options.

The Monday closing became a trend in May, though they did open on that day during the Jazz Fest. In June, though the writing was clearly on the wall for the club's inner circle, they made one last ditch attempt at local relevance amidst the excitement of the opening of the World's Fair. The weekly closed day switched to Tuesdays, and a new group whose name became legendary was scheduled for an "exclusive premier engagement" on Mondays.

The Continental Drifters were supposed to be the saving grace for Tipitina's and bring Mondays back into glory. The members were all household names on the music scene in New Orleans—Tommy Malone, John Magnie and Johnny Allen along with Vernon Rome on bass, Kenny Blevins on drums and Eric Traub on saxophone. The first three musicians went on to form the subdudes. Incidentally, the Continental Drifters morphed at least two more times coalescing in Los Angeles around the drummer Carlo Nuccio and the singer/songwriter Vickie Peterson and then back in New Orleans centered on the husband and wife team of Susan Cowsill and Peter Holsapple.

Alas, it was not to be. Tipitina's closed its doors in late June. On August 12, there was a hastily arranged, poorly planned "rent party" in a last ditch effort to save the club. It was a Sunday afternoon, and no specific artists were advertised as appearing. Almost everyone in the music community, including many of the musicians who had donated their services over the years, was sick of the never-ending parade of benefit shows for air-conditioning and other ill-defined beneficiaries. No one I knew went.

Though the club would reopen eighteen months later to great fanfare with new ownership and a fantastic renovation, no one knew that at the time. The club was plagued by its complex ownership scheme, dire financial straits and in-fighting over the name and Professor Longhair's legacy. Few thought music would ever again emanate from the building at 501 Napoleon Avenue.

Amid the deep depression that hit the music community following the debacle of the World's Fair and the closing of Tipitina's, there were a few bright spots on the horizon. Benny's, a ramshackle bar on the corner of Camp and Valence Streets in uptown New Orleans, was still a neighborhood joint catering to working class blacks. However, for a short time in 1984, a new band called Endangered Species began playing at Benny's before they moved on to proper music clubs. The keyboardist Terry Manuel led the group featuring Cyril Neville on trap drums and Deacon John's brother, the bassist/guitarist Charles Moore. They called their sound "Booker-woogie" in tribute to the great New Orleans pianist.

Cyril Neville is ten years younger than his siblings in the family band. His musical influences are different. But more importantly, while his brothers experienced the overt discrimination of the Jim Crow 1950s, the timing of his youth placed him at the beginning of the tumultuous period of integration. He ultimately became known as the most politically active of the four brothers. His activism began to flourish during this period and would reach its peak with songs lamenting the state of blacks in South Africa, Haiti and across urban America such as "My Blood" and "Fear, Hate, Envy, Jealousy" that appeared on Neville Brothers' albums. Neville said at the time that the name of the band reflected the fact that, "neighborhood bars and neighborhood stars are endangered species."

Endangered Species could have referred to the band itself. They began playing the Monday night slot held down at the Maple Leaf by James Booker over the last eleven months of his life. Booker was moved from his longtime Tuesday night slot after missing the entire month of December 1983. But that gig didn't last long. Besides random shows at Benny's, they were no longer on the schedules of the Maple Leaf or any other club in town by the fall of 1984. Neville and Moore eventually joined forces again in the revamped Uptown Allstars. Manuel has played periodically around town since those days.

However, Endangered Species did reemerge as an opening act for Cyril Neville's new band, and they played a few gigs. Then the Endangered Species concept evolved into a non-profit entity that sought to help local musicians. The group was led by Neville and was eventually renamed "New Orleans Musicians Organized" (NOMO).

In early 1985, Benny's quietly began regularly presenting live music. Benny's was bare to the bone. The place was tiny with a short bar parallel to Magazine Street on the riverside of the building. The walls were not even covered in sheet rock, so the studs were fully exposed. Benny Jones and his brother ran the place, and they used the niches between the studs for concert posters and other memorabilia. There was no stage; the band simply set up at the uptown end of the small room. The space occupied by the bands was surrounded by framing studs, which made it appear that the band was playing in another room except that the walls were not yet built. Calling it surreal would be an understatement.

There was never a cover charge at Benny's even when it grew into the hippest late night music club in the city drawing Hollywood stars like Lisa Bonet and Mickey Rourke (when they were in town filming the voodoo noir thriller *Angel Heart*) and musicians known the world over. Passing the hat—actually a five-gallon plastic Kentwood water bottle—paid the band. One of the band members, a bar employee, a friend of the band or occasionally just a random fan would pass the bottle around the club, and people would jam bills through the narrow opening at the top. Money went in fairly easily, but it was difficult to get the bills out. But at least the tips were safe. While this seems like an inconvenient way for a band to get paid, the practice developed into a ritual, and each band had its own way of announcing that the set was coming to an end and it was time to tip the band. I remember many a night when that jug was filled to the top with bills. Eventually someone cut a special trap door in the side of the bottle to facilitate removing the cash.

The crowd hanging out at Benny's was about as diverse as at any club in town. In the beginning, it was purely a neighborhood joint frequented by working class blacks living in the area. But by the time Benny's peaked in popularity, the clientele was an equal mixture of black and white, middle and working class. Cyril Neville wrote a song about the joint that included the line, "Where the rainbow people and the rastas meet." The rest of the crowd included music freaks, slumming college students, out-of-town visitors, other musicians, late night drinkers and a fair share of drug sellers and users.

There was a carefree, easygoing vibe in Benny's that was only disrupted when the occasional street person or crack cocaine addict would bust through the front door. While it was a great place to hear music, the neighborhood was considerably rougher than it is today, and many a drunk got mugged leaving the bar in the wee-wee hours. In the end, it was the drugs that doomed the joint when employees were busted selling cocaine over the bar to undercover cops.

The regular gigs at Benny's began with Monday night blues shows, usually starring a great big bear of a man with a gold tooth who goes by the moniker, J Monque'D. In those days, he came across as a marginally talented singer and harmonica player with a gift for self-promotion and a knack for writing catchy blues tunes. While his musicianship was a bit questionable, he always surrounded himself with first-rate talent. His volunteer work as a deejay on WWOZ helped get the word out about live music at Benny's. Monque'D is now regarded as an elder statesman of New Orleans blues. He is also a member of the Creole Wild West Mardi Gras Indian tribe.

J.D. Hill also played occasionally in the first couple of months at Benny's with his band, the Jammers. The Jammers included Jack Cruz (a member of Walter "Wolfman" Washington's Roadmasters) on bass and a searing lead guitarist named George Sartin along with Dave Emilien on drums. They played an uptempo style of New Orleans-inflected blues and R&B. Hill is a monster harmonica player and a decent singer. He became one of the leaders of the scene at Benny's as it developed. Hill disappeared in the 1990s due to personal problems and only recently reemerged to play music again. He has been playing with Deacon John and has revived the Jammers with new personnel.

Among the other regular acts from the early days was the transplanted blues shouter Mighty Sam McClain (no relation to the bass player, Ramsey) with the talented, well-traveled Wayne Bennett on guitar. Before moving to New Orleans, Bennett had played with numerous A-list blues and R&B acts including Bobby "Blue" Bland, Otis Rush, Buddy Guy, Jimmy Rogers, Jimmy Reed, James Cotton, Jimmy McCracklin and John Lee Hooker. Locally, he recorded with Champion Jack Dupree and Johnny Adams. Bennett died in 1992 at the age of 58.

Another well-traveled blues guitarist, Eugene Ross, backed up Mighty Sam McClain when Bennett was not available. He also worked with Bobby "Blue" Bland as well as Ray Charles. Ross had a band called Blue Lunch that included the jazz guitarist Steve Masakowski (a member of Astral Project from its beginnings in the 1970s and now a highly regarded professor of music at the University of New Orleans). They were regulars at Benny's in that period.

By the time Benny's began hosting shows every night of the week in mid- 1986, Charmaine Neville and her new band, Real Feelings, were regulars on the lineup as was an energetic saxophonist named Paula Rangell who led a band called Paula and the Pontiacs. Both bands were composed entirely of men except the leaders.

Benny's quickly became *the* place to go when the music was over elsewhere. Once the renovated Tipitina's reopened in January 1986, it became a ritual to head over the Benny's when the music ended. Benny's was a late night place. A saying made the rounds, "There wouldn't be any, if wasn't for Benny." If you went to Benny's early, around 11 PM when the band started, the room would be nearly empty with just a couple of older cats sitting and drinking at the bar. But by three in the morning it was hard to find a parking place, and the sidewalk out front was teeming with late night revelers. The music rarely ended before 4 AM, and if enough people were feeding the Kentwood jug, the band would keep playing. Those early empty sets allowed Benny's to develop into a musical incubator. Bands would get a chance to work out new material and develop new arrangements without the pressure of a large audience.

While a lot of different bands played at Benny's over the years, two bands were defined by the place. When the Uptown Allstars first started, they were a vehicle for Gerald Tillman's radical rearrangements of songs from the Meters' catalog. The original band had Ivan Neville on keys, Renard Poché on guitar, Nick Daniels on bass and

Gerald Trinity on drums. But by the time the Uptown Allstars began playing regularly at Benny's, all that remained of the original band was the name and the new versions of the classic tunes. Cyril Neville took ownership of the group in 1985. Valence Street and the 13th Ward was the center of the Neville universe ever since the four brothers were children. Art Neville still lives on the street. So it was natural for Cyril to use Benny's as his personal playhouse when the family band was not on tour. All through 1985, the listed schedule for Benny's suggested that you call to see which band was playing because you never knew when Neville and his band would show up. This helped to create the aura that would define the place at the height of its popularity.

During this time, the Neville Brothers were experiencing unprecedented success. They retained the legendary Bill Graham of San Francisco, the greatest music impresario of the 1960s, as their manager, and a booking agency called Rosebud had the band touring the world and playing in bigger and bigger rooms. Graham also facilitated their connections with bands from his scene including the Grateful Dead for whom the Nevilles opened numerous high profile shows.

Touring the world broadened Cyril Neville's musical and cultural minds. He became considerably more politically outspoken when he was exposed to the differing ways blacks were treated across the globe. Afforded hero status and exemplary treatment in Europe and Asia, he became more conscious of the role of racism in the United States and how it affected musicians. Neville also became a big fan of reggae music following a powerful experience listening to the music of Bob Marley. His attraction to reggae was also influenced by time spent with Aashid Himmons, the leader of the Memphis band, Afrikan Dreamland.

Consciousness and the lilting beat of reggae became the touchstones of the Uptown Allstars. He branded their music "uptown reggae" and "second line reggae." The sound of the Uptown Allstars was a blend of Tillman's versions of the Meters' songs with original songs marked by a skittering reggae beat with lyrics reflecting positivist and political awareness. Neville viewed his new band as an extension of a long ago connection between the music of New Orleans and that of Jamaica. In the 1950s, Jamaicans were able to hear AM radio signals emanating from the radio studios of New Orleans. Musicologists suggest that some Jamaican music was influenced by New Orleans sounds.

Neville was joined in his side project by the new rhythm section for the Neville Brothers—Willie Green on drums and Daryl Johnson on bass along with Charles Moore and George Sartin on guitars. A great improvising saxophonist, Tim Green, and J.D. Hill were also regular contributors. Tillman was an occasional player in the band, but his habits were making him increasingly difficult and more irresponsible.

Daryl Johnson played the island rhythms with authority considering his long tenure with the Bahamian singer, Exuma. Green had the reggae beat down cold from the beginnings of the band. Behind the strong rhythm section of Green and Johnson, the groove developed in a loping syncopated style that reflected both the one-drop of reggae and the second line beat of New Orleans.

"Mean" Willie Green didn't get his nickname because of an attitude problem; he earned it in the trenches as a badass drummer. His kinetic playing allows him to completely drive a band. He is a masterful musician whose double time beats on the bass drum are created by using two bass drum pedals like a heavy metal drummer. When the Neville Brothers started being referred to as "the heartbeat of New Orleans," Green's fans started calling him "the beat of the heartbeat of New Orleans." Over the years he has been one of the most in-demand drummers who has played many different styles. He was a major influence on a whole new generation of musicians including most of the second wave of funk bands. With the exception of the four brothers, Green has been the only constant member of the Neville Brothers band since he joined the group. He is a monster player.

Charles Moore was trained as a classical guitarist and has been the bass player in various bands with his brother, Deacon John, for decades. As the guitarist with the Uptown Allstars, he played in a style that is also confounding—he holds the fingers on his fret hand like a bass player and plays without a pick in the style of a funk bassist. While Moore is no virtuoso on the electric guitar, after all it is his third instrument, he is an incredibly tasty player who conjures up the perfect lick every time he solos. His patient attack is part of what made the uptown reggae sound. By April 1986, the Uptown Allstars were playing regularly on Tuesdays at Benny's. The Uptown Allstars quickly became an institution. Neville had no competition for leadership of the band, and he grew into a charismatic front man singing and playing his congas while leading a truly exceptional band.

Several years later, when Benny's was peaking musically, a bassist and a guitarist from the Washington, D.C. area hooked up with a heavy metal drummer from New Orleans while in school at Loyola University. These three players, Robert Mercurio, Jeff Raines and Stanton Moore joined forces with the keyboardist Rich Vogel and the saxophonist Eric Jacobsen to form a college band called Galactic Prophylactic.

Shortly after realizing their name was juvenile, they shortened it to Galactic, and over the ensuing decade have become a formidable force on the national jam band scene constantly experimenting with their basic funky formula. When the band formed, they had a serious obsession with the Meters that culminated in a side project named the Ivanhoes after the Bourbon Street club where the Meters used to jam together.

Naturally, given the connection between Benny's and the uptown funk community, the members of the early version of the band were regulars at Benny's, and it was in that setting that they met the vocalist Theryl DeClouet. DeClouet was nearly twenty years older than the other musicians and was a veteran of the local scene. He played in vocal groups and soul bands throughout the 1970s including the a cappella outfit Hollygrove, named after the neighborhood in New Orleans where they grew up, and he fronted a great band called Reel Life that seemed to only play at the New Orleans Jazz and Heritage Festival. Listeners were immediately captivated by the singer's gritty, soulful sound.

DeClouet provided the band with much needed credibility. They were among the first of the second wave of New Orleans funk bands, and he was a charismatic lead singer. While he was with the band (he left in 2004), he wasn't on stage the entire set but would make a grand entrance decked out in matching bright suits like one of his heroes, Johnny Adams. He commanded the stage with such authority and was so well connected around town that the band needed him in the early days.

While the Benny's scene was heating up, business was not going as well for other clubs in town. Sheila's and Jed's Lookout, on the forlorn World's Fair site, managed to stay in business for a new more months. Jed's continued to book high profile national acts, including the Red Hot Chili Peppers and the Butthole Surfers, in addition to local bands like the Radiators and the Neville Brothers, but they were doomed by the out-of-the-way location and high rent. Sheila's closed in late January 1985. Jed's made it through March.

Three new clubs opened in 1985, and none were in business at the end of the year. Cheeky Chink's and the Town Hall Theater Pub opened at 1001 and 642 N. Rampart respectively. They were both small operations presenting low-key jazz acts in a cabaret setting. Cheeky Chink's hosted mostly black acts including the saxophonist Earl Turbinton, the bassist Walter Payton and a hot young guitarist named Carl LeBlanc and his band, Black Market. The Town Hall featured white acts like the Pfister Sisters and Little Queenie. In 1987, another club opened at 1001 N. Rampart Street called Bananas—it barely lasted six months. Try finding someone who set foot in either.

A more ambitious club opened its doors at 601 Tchoupitoulas near the old fair site. The club, which shared the same name as its address, opened in November 1985 with an impressive schedule that included touring acts like Asleep at the Wheel and the Allman Brothers' guitarist, Dickey Betts, with his own band along with local bands like the Continental Drifters, who now had Damon Shea playing drums, and the Radiators. Evidently they could also afford the increased fee the Neville Brothers were now commanding.

The club's owners were still spending freely in December 1985 with a schedule that included country-rock stylist Nicolette Larson, southern rocker Gregg Allman with his side project band and punk icons the Dead Kennedys. They closed at the end of the year promising the media they would reopen after renovations. In April 1986, new owners opened another short-lived bar at the location called Fandango's. They never even got around to presenting live music. Finally, in 1987 the spot at 601 Tchoupitoulas Street reopened after being shuttered for a year, but it was a disco (although the owners denied that designation) and rarely presented live music. Try finding someone who stepped foot in 601 Tchoupitoulas.

Madigan's, a small neighborhood bar in the Riverbend section of uptown, began quietly showcasing small bands and solo gigs. John Rankin was the first performer to play there regularly on alternating Sundays, but his early gigs were overshadowed by the long tenure of a young, white disciple of the blues great Son House who moved to New Orleans from upstate New York.

John Mooney immediately took the city by storm. While his early playing was eerily reminiscent of House, his mentor, it took on a New Orleans second line feel after he was living in the city for a while and started interacting with local musicians. He played a regular solo gig at Madigan's for years that was known for special guests dropping in to play a bit or just hang out. Mooney began playing around town more and more during this period. His earliest associations were with Jimmy Thackery, a fellow guitarist with the Nighthawks. The Nighthawks played regularly at Tipitina's and were a big draw.

As Mooney dug into the scene, he formed an important partnership with George Porter, Jr. and Johnny Vidacovich. They were the rhythm section for the first version of his band, Bluesiana, which played regularly at Tyler's Beer Garden. Mooney has now perfected his transition from an acolyte of the blues to an innovator in his own right. His stomping foot and screaming slide guitar generates the same tension and release of a New Orleans-style funk band. His trick was injecting the second line beat into the basic Delta blues style, and by doing so he created a new sub genre of the blues of which he is the only practitioner. Curiously, he considered himself a rock 'n' roll performer at the time.

* * *

While local bands were struggling mightily during this period, there were still a number of big stars playing in New Orleans, and one of the biggest was anticipated for February 1, 1985 in the Superdome. Touring on the strength of his monster hit, *Purple Rain*, Prince sold out the gigantic space.

The family of Professor Longhair had been having a rough time since his passing, but they received a major benefactor when the Windham Hill recording artist George Winston embraced his fellow pianist's work. Dancing Cat, a subsidiary of the label, released *Rock 'n' Roll Gumbo*—a lost session by Longhair—and Winston did a series of benefit concerts for the family including one at Tulane's McAlister Auditorium in late January 1985. While Winston is no Professor Longhair, the event had a feel-good vibe and Longhair's widow, Alice, and many of his various associates, running partners and musical compadres were in attendance.

Two new bands appeared on the scene in 1985. Java relocated to New Orleans for the winter from Wisconsin. They called their music "reggazzmafunk," and it was a highly danceable mixture of reggae, jazz and funk. They immediately generated a following. The group had an attractive lead singer and flute player, Lynnea Godfrieaux, adding yet another band of men fronted by a woman to the scene. While their music was actually rather light on the jazz, they had a wonderful horn-heavy sound and ended up spending a couple of winters in New Orleans to escape the brutal weather of the Midwest.

The guitarist Bruce Blaylock, who began playing around town as a Tulane law school student in a band called Oyster Legs, ended up amassing quite a resume before relocating to pursue his law career in Washington, D.C. He was in one of George Porter, Jr.'s early post Meters bands, the Funksters. He also did stints with the Nightriders and Gerald Tillman, and he was a member of Lenny Zenith's post RZA band, Pop Combo. After graduating from law school, Blaylock joined another new band, the Petries, that played catchy pop songs. They called their sound "tension pop." The leader of the group was the bassist and former member of the Cold, Vance Degeneres. But it was the keyboardist and vocalist, Lisa Mednick, who had everyone talking. She is a Washington, D.C. native who moved to New Orleans after a stint playing in hard rock bands in New York. She wrote some of the band's material and had a great stage presence. Though the Petries didn't last, Mednick went on to form one of the best bands to never make it out of New Orleans, the Songdogs.

With the addition of new bands and talent to the working musicians of New Orleans as well as the nascent scene developing at

Benny's, there was hope on the horizon for music lovers in New Orleans. The news that Tipitina's was definitely going to reopen in January 1986 had the entire music community energized.

The city of New Orleans was inundated with visitors on the last weekend in January 1986, but they were not all in town for the much anticipated grand reopening of Tipitina's. Superbowl XX, which Mike Ditka's Chicago Bears won over the New England Patriots, was scheduled for Sunday evening at the Louisiana Superdome. All of the stars were in town for a three-day extravaganza, and the renovated Tips was ready with three nights of great music. Friday night, Deacon John's New Orleans Rhythm and Blues Review hit the stage early, and the night didn't end until the wee-wee hours. The Dirty Dozen Brass Band opened the show.

Deacon John's great band backed an A-list parade of stars from the 1950s including Ernie K-Doe, Johnny Adams, Jean Knight, Jessie Hill, Barbara George and Earl King. After King's incendiary appearance, a jam session materialized. Art Neville took the stage and raised the intensity level through the roof with his spirited vocals and swelling organ. But the highlight of the early morning set had to be an unannounced appearance by Stephen Stills. He sang his classic, "Love the One You're With," to great applause from die-hards who refused to leave until the last note was played. Of course, I was in that number.

The locals in the sold-out crowd loved the club's new and improved layout. The two bars allowed for much quicker beverage service, and the bottleneck at the door simply ceased to exist. The bathrooms impressed everyone, but the balcony is what really got the tongues wagging. The club just seemed so much bigger, and the upstairs space provided respite from the crowds below.

Saturday night's act was the Radiators who were celebrating their eighth anniversary together. They tore through three sets of Fishhead music to the delight of many of the out-of-town visitors. The backstage was crawling with celebrities including Dennis Quaid and two members of the Superbowl's television broadcast team, Terry Bradshaw and Ken Stabler.

The final night of the weekend featured the Neville Brothers. They took the stage to a sold-out house of football fans celebrating the big game that had ended just a few hours earlier. The energy was palpable. A new era in New Orleans music had begun.

The best thing about the new and improved version of Tipitina's is that somehow, against the odds of encroaching commercialization and amid hints of modernity, the vibe in the place didn't change. The energy that was so profound in the first incarnation didn't flag one iota. It was the same place, only different. Part of the reason for the continuity was the doorman who controlled access to the second floor. The "fabulous fo'teen" always had huge guest lists, and Big Jeff made sure that the "right" people were still able to get onto the balcony.

Though the economy had been improving, Tipitina's went through a rough stretch in early 1988. The Jazz Fest, which was developing into the behemoth it has become, provided a shot in the arm in late April and early May. However, a partnership between Sonny Schneideau, the booking agent at Tipitina's, and a young writer at *Wavelength* who covered the burgeoning indie rock scene in the United States, impacted the focus of the club. James Lien was also the program director at WTUL, Tulane University's college radio station. Schneideau and Lien created the 'TUL Box—a Monday night series of concerts that were broadcast live on the station.

Tipitina's had presented national rock acts in its first incarnation and in the first two years under the new ownership, but the cornerstone of their schedule was local acts and bigger bands that drew from the same basic pool of R&B, blues and roots music. With the additional space created by opening up the balcony, the club was able to attract bigger bands from out-of-town. The partnership was a no-brainer from the start since the club was interested in generating more business from different demographics, and the live broadcasts were guaranteed positive publicity for both the club and for the bands.

The first broadcast in early May 1988 featured three local bands—NOBD, Oogum Boogum and a completely forgotten band called the Fuzzy Slippers from Hell. Ice-9 followed them a week later. Ice-9 was arguably the first of the second wave of funk bands that emerged following the breakup of the Meters, though they didn't last on the scene for too long. The band included some first rate young talent including the leader and guitarist, Doug Grean; James Cabarin, a stalwart drummer on the scene during this period; Ben Brecht, a super-funky bassist; and the great improvisational saxophonist, Tim Green.

Though most of the other new local bands were equally as forgettable as the Fuzzy Slippers from Hell, many of them had extremely peculiar names reflecting the new zeitgeist in New Orleans. Who knows whatever happened to Halcyon Daze, the Caterpillars, Suicidal Overdose, the Household Gods and Brewing Insanity?

The 'TUL Box took off as a concept, and within a month the first national act, Camper Van Beethoven, played the Monday night series with new local favorites, Tribe Nunzio, as the opening act. Within a year, Tipitina's was becoming well known among a whole new genre of nationally known musicians for its enthusiastic crowds, local flavor and late night ambiance.

Though some of these touring acts were better known than others at the time, nearly all have attained iconic status as originators of the indie rock concept. The list of bands playing there during the first years of the 'TUL Box reads like a who's who of seminal 1980s acts including Jane's Addiction, Violent Femmes, Pylon, Soul Asylum, They Might Be Giants, Poi Dog Pondering, the Mekons, Soundgarden, Scruffy the Cat, Billy Bragg, the Beat Farmers, the Indigo Girls and Peter Case. Bands from previous eras like the Ramones appeared on the 'TUL Box along with up and coming groups including two who went on to become major arena acts—Widespread Panic and Phish.

Within three years, the newly renovated Tipitina's achieved national fame. Stories began appearing in the out-of-town press, and the initial trickle of touring acts developed into a huge wave that eventually catapulted Tipitina's into the pantheon of the world's greatest clubs. Although local music lovers knew it since its humble beginnings as a venue for the great Professor Longhair and his contemporaries, now the word was out across the globe.

Chapter 8

THE JAZZ FEST GROWS INTO ITS NEW HOME

"They say that when you get within a hundred miles of New Orleans you begin to feel a little drunk on just the idea of New Orleans, and that with every turn of the wheel you get a little drunker, and then when you get here you're completely out of control—blotto on romance and sentiment and freedom—a spiritual binge."—Ernie Pyle

By 1984, the planning for the New Orleans Jazz and Heritage Festival had become a 12-month process as the organizers continued to fine-tune the layout at the New Orleans Fairgrounds. They added another intimate stage similar in concept to the Economy Hall Tent that had opened a year earlier. The Fais Do Do stage was originally planned as a home for Cajun and Zydeco bands, though it eventually became the go-to spot for a wider spectrum of music fans. To this day, it remains the one stage where a dancing crowd is expected.

Though it has been argued that Run DMC was the first rap act to appear at the Jazz Fest, Grandmaster Flash and his posse of rappers played in 1984 touring on the strength of his 1982 hit, "The Message." The song's ominous chorus still reverberates in the brains of music lovers, some of whom had already embraced hip-hop— "Don't push me 'cause I'm close to the edge/ I'm tryin' not to lose my head/ It's like a jungle sometimes/ makes me wonder how I keep from goin' under." Grandmaster Flash appeared after the Dirty Dozen Brass Band and before Irma Thomas making that day an early example of the intricate process that determines stage lineups at the Fairgrounds. Flash was a true innovator who invented some of the techniques turntablists still use today including cutting, back spinning and phasing. His set was short in length but left a long lingering legacy of curiosity among those who witnessed the performance.

The legendary South African pianist Abdullah Ibrahim also made his festival debut in 1984. Ibrahim, known as "Dollar Brand" before his conversion to Islam, is one of the greatest South African musicians. He weathered the years of apartheid in exile along with other musicians such as the trumpeter Hugh Masekela and the vocalist Meriam Makeba. Masekela, who had already graced the stages of the New Orleans Jazz and Heritage Festival, is an ebullient and effervescent trumpeter whose music often evokes the powerful strain of racial oppression engendered by apartheid. Yet his playing was filled with such joy that he seemed to have already transcended the pain of the era even though apartheid did not officially end for another decade.

Ibrahim's music, on the other hand, was moody and introspective. His tunes were more overtly colored with tension as if he had internalized the pain of racism. But like the work of Masekela and other musicians who have faced the tribulations of race, Ibrahim's music ultimately transcended those concerns and reached a heavenly grace.

Another musician who suffered the pains of racism and was still able to create a lasting body of work that belied the suffering of the Jim Crow era in America was Fats Domino. He was scheduled to close out the festival. Unfortunately, it was not to be. Along with Dr. John and the Neville Brothers, he had played two sets the night before on the Riverboat President, at 7:30 PM and midnight, and had to beg off the daytime show because his voice was shot. It was not the last time Domino was unable to perform at the Jazz Fest.

The ticket price rose yet again to six dollars. Despite the criticisms of some locals, the event kept adding bigger acts—Al Green also performed in 1984—and was developing into the world-class event that it is today.

Debate and discussion about the changes at the Jazz Fest was becoming a yearly ritual for fans of the event. Everything from the previous year was dissected though all the talk was mostly rampant gossip and speculation since the inner workings of the festival were not available to the public. However, after the festival in 1985, Bill Rouselle, the executive director of the New Orleans Jazz and Heritage Foundation, gave a free-ranging interview to a writer for *Wavelength* magazine. In the interview, he revealed a number of details of which the public was generally unaware. For example, he revealed that the festival was owned by a non-profit organization, the aforementioned foundation. That came as a bit of a shock to many people. Rouselle also discussed the many changes resulting from the festival's growth. He talked about the relationship between Quint Davis, the producer-director of the fest, and George Wein, the owner of Festival Productions, the company that puts on the Heritage Fair portion of the festival at the Fairgrounds, and the financial state of both organizations. The interview was groundbreaking with respect to how much was revealed to an otherwise ignorant public. While mundane concerns affecting attendees' personal experience (e.g. the cooler ban, higher admission and parking prices, and stage placement) dominated the interview, Rouselle admitted the festival barely broke even in 1984 and outlined a number of cuts to be enacted in hopes of getting the foundation back on solid financial footing.

Curiously, amid these cutbacks, the 1985 festival schedule was the most ambitious ever with a large number of big time acts appearing for the first time at the annual event. The list included jazz icons like Miles Davis, Sarah Vaughan and the World Saxophone Quartet, rap pioneers Run DMC and reggae greats Third World in addition to popular performers like Ry Cooder, Roy Ayers, and Stevie Ray Vaughan. Miles Davis was scheduled for an evening show at the Theater of the Performing Arts in Armstrong Park on a double bill with Wynton Marsalis. Marsalis, having left town in 1979 to attend college, rarely played in New Orleans (a fact still true today), so the concert was a homecoming and a major event.

Performances in New Orleans by the so-called "young lions" of jazz were few and far between because this media-created group, which also included other New Orleanians such as the trumpeter Terence Blanchard and the alto saxophonist Donald Harrison, was based out of New York. Marsalis was the media's darling even as he challenged writers about everything from jazz history to the role of the instrumentalist. Some considered him to be a jazz purist and a snob, but no one could argue with his prodigious technique and his achievements before he even turned 25. Some of his admirers even saw him as a savior rescuing acoustic jazz from fusion and electric instruments.

Davis was already an icon, arguably on the downside of his long career, but this show was one of the most highly anticipated in the history of the Jazz Fest. While Marsalis clearly admired the career of Davis, he was critical of the older trumpeter's forays into fusion and the use of electric instruments, synthesizers, and other electronic effects. Davis was no longer testing the limits of his audience as with his material from the *Bitches Brew* period. He arrived with a six-piece electric band featuring the guitarist John Scofield. Davis put on a decent performance, and the band played a wide range of styles including vamping reggae beats, churning Afro-funk rhythms, and delicate, understated bluesy ballads. But many of the younger fans in the audience, myself included, couldn't understand why he played almost the whole set with his back to the audience. Also, the inclusion of Cindy Lauper's pop hit, "Time After Time," had many in the crowd scratching their heads.

Marsalis had his classic band of the period with his brother, Branford, on saxophones, Kenny Kirkland on keys, Jeff "Tain" Watts on drums, and Charnett Moffett on bass. They played acoustically creating a stark contrast to the styles of the two trumpeters. While Davis' band appeared capable of roaring, they were content to let the leader set the tone with mostly whispery phrases and a tender approach.

Marsalis came prepared for an old fashioned cutting contest—an improvised battle between musicians who try to outplay each other while soloing and trading licks. He positively blew his head off. But thanks to his incredible technique, the performance never seemed like he was boasting or demonstrating his abilities for the sheer sake of showing off. There was a musical reason behind each phrase as he soloed, and his tone could go from hard-driving brusqueness to liquid lushness in a flash of understated brilliance.

Both leaders had their on-stage foils. For Davis it was Scofield. They played as if engaged in a heated conversation as they soloed back and forth. Scofield occasionally challenged the leader as if they were boxers training for a big fight. For Wynton, it was his brother Branford who swung hard during the moments of musical dialogue between the players. For all the seriousness Wynton projected, Branford provided the humor and looseness. The pianist Kenny Kirkland also added considerably to the inherent musicality of the performance. His unfortunate death in 1998 at the age of 43 deprived the world of years of his genius.

Ultimately, especially considering all the media hype leading up to the concert, it was a great event. There was no conflict evident between the two leaders, although a jam session never materialized. Davis had absolutely nothing to prove to anyone, least of all himself or his band. He went about his business in a professional manner not caring a bit about any judgment. Marsalis, on the other hand, exhibited all the brashness of youth exposing his deep talents both as a player and as a bandleader without coming across as an egotist. He played as if he had something to prove to the hometown audience, and prove it he did.

While there was no apparent friction within Marsalis' group on the stage, a few shorts months later Wynton would fire both Branford and Kenny Kirkland when they decided to take six months off to tour with the rock star Sting in the jazz-inflected band he put together following the breakup of the Police. It was the beginning of a long period of public disagreement and tension between the brothers.

Wynton may not have agreed with the reasons behind his brother's decision to tour with Sting even though money certainly played a role in the decision to take the job. They were young men playing jazz in New York City. They weren't making a lot of cash, and the tour represented a significant payday. But based on purely musical terms, there was some validity to the choice. Beside Kirkland and

Marsalis, the other members of Sting's new band included musicians with jazz credibility—Omar Hakim, a jazz fusion drummer who played with Weather Report, and Daryl Jones, a bassist who toured and recorded with Miles Davis.

By the end of the summer of 1985, the music community was buzzing with the news that Sting was bringing his new band to New Orleans. The show was scheduled for October 25 at the University of New Orleans' Lakefront Arena.

Branford Marsalis had already played a high visibility gig with Sting, albeit on television, when they appeared together at the Live Aid concert in London. Marsalis added some delicate saxophone work to a three-song acoustic set of songs from the songbook of the Police that also featured Phil Collins from the progressive rock band, Genesis.

The concert in New Orleans was planned in conjunction with the premiere of Michael Apted's movie, *Bring On the Night*, about the formation of Sting's new band. Hype about the tour and movie was relentless, and the feud between Branford and Wynton Marsalis reverberated across the nation. Branford spoke candidly to the media about the upcoming show. He was already thinking outside of the jazz box; he was interested in other sounds and felt musically adventurous. It wasn't a surprise to those following the arc of his career when he began sitting in with the Grateful Dead a few years later.

The comparison between Sting's "jazz" band and the Grateful Dead bears some discussion. For the duration of their long career, the central concept behind the Grateful Dead was improvisation, both individually and collectively. As in jazz, each member got his turn to solo, and some of the more compelling moments that occurred within each performance came about through collective improvisation. While no one would call the Grateful Dead a jazz band, over the years they attracted a fair number of jazz musicians who jammed with them. Branford Marsalis took a large measure of grief from his younger and stridently anti-pop brother, Wynton, as well as the jazz establishment for playing with "that hippie band." But Branford recognized that the music of the Dead was not about how many key changes or chords there are in a given song. It was not about how many tricky shifts in meter occurred, nor was it about any of the conventional ways music is categorized. He also knew the members of the band, particularly Jerry Garcia on lead guitar and Phil Lesh on electric bass, were masters of improvisation.

Communication between the members of a band that focuses on improvisation is the most important factor in producing a top-notch performance. Within the Grateful Dead, and within most working jazz bands, that communication often borders on the telepathic. Each musician is aware of what is happening as it happens, and they usually are able to anticipate what is going to come next within the particular musical framework in which they are operating. As in jazz, the feeling that this could go anywhere musically coupled with the idea that the music is not constrained by structure was paramount, and that must have been part of the attraction for Marsalis.

The give-and-take as the energy flows between the audience and the musicians (and among the musicians themselves) is most easily understood by concentrating on the sound itself and training the ear to hear the subtleties within the music. In order to really appreciate jazz, the listener has to pay close attention to the intricacies of the music each individual is producing as well as the collective efforts of the group. Otherwise, all that is heard is a generalized sound—a vague sense of tempo and rhythm amid an instrumental wash.

The same can be said for the music of the Grateful Dead. To truly enjoy a performance by the Dead, the listener has to stay focused and engaged. In essence, they have to try to become one with the band. Perhaps that is why they attracted so many fans who favored psychedelic drugs as an enhancement to their experience.

Another area of connection between the Grateful Dead and jazz concerns the role of the song. For the Dead and for most jazz musicians, the song is merely a vehicle used to achieve a certain level of musical expression. The song becomes the framework around which the musicians collectively express themselves. However, for the concept to work effectively, the framework cannot constrain the players as they make individual statements through soloing.

Jazz has its standards that include songs from other eras, great compositions from the pens of jazz's greats and songs from other genres such as Tin Pan Alley, the Great American Songbook and Broadway show tunes. Within jazz, there is no stigma attached to playing standards. Standards are the common language that allows jazz musicians to be instantly on the same page with each other.

Within pop music, the relationship between original songs and covers plays out differently. For a pop band to be great they have to write their own music, and a band that plays only covers is usually looked down upon and denigrated as "just a cover band." The Grateful Dead were able to avoid that stigma because of the way that they made each "cover" song their own. They also drew from a deep well of songs in a variety of American genres. Whether they were playing the blues standard, "Turn On Your Lovelight," the Johnny Cash classic, "Big River," or any other cover in their vast repertoire, each song functioned like a jazz standard; they were vehicles for personal expression through improvisation.

While the concerts with Sting's "jazz" band were not as free form with respect to song structure and set list as a concert by the Grateful Dead, those elements were part of what Sting was trying to accomplish as he left the confines of the Police—a rock 'n' roll trio. During the concert at Lakefront Arena, they performed a few songs from Sting's years with the Police that really got the crowd rocking. But the one thing I remember most was a sing-along with Sting singing a line and the crowd repeating it. He improvised each line like a scat singer, and he made each one progressively more difficult for the audience to mimic. The crowd kept up with the singer through several lines until he appeared confounded that this huge room was able to keep following him and could sing so well together. When it ended, he made a comment congratulating us on our musical skills and said that no other crowd had ever made it that far. It was a powerful moment that made a big statement about New Orleans crowds and the nature of jazz itself.

Back at the New Orleans Fairgrounds, it was evident that the organizers were still tweaking the set up in 1985. As the festival grew, there were some significant problems with sound bleeding between the stages, so adjustments were definitely needed. As usual, some longtime attendees complained about the changes in the layout, and others were irked by the growing list of sponsorships. But after the financial problems in 1984, sponsorships were inevitable.

However, the earliest stage sponsors were not connected to the main stages. In 1985, only three stages had sponsors—WWL-TV attached their name to the small Stage 4 now known as the Fais Do Do stage; WDSU and Pizza Hut got behind the Kids' Tent; and Rhodes Funeral Home and WYLD radio sponsored the gospel tent. A far cry from today's Jazz Fest with national sponsors covering the Fairgrounds, all of the sponsors in 1985 were local businesses with the exception of Pizza Hut which had a dedicated local franchise owner, Larry Lundy, behind the contribution.

The controversial booking in 1985 was the hardcore rap group, Run DMC. The band, which is now recognized as one of hip-hop's founding fathers, was hardly a household name as hip-hop was still in its infancy. Run DMC's groundbreaking collaboration with Aerosmith on the rock band's tune, "Walk This Way," that established the band in the mainstream of American music was still a year off. They didn't have a melodic feel like that of Grandmaster Flash from the previous year. But you have to give Quint Davis and the talent committee credit for taking a risk with such a contentious act.

By the time Jazz Fest rolled around in 1986, Ronald Reagan's vision of America was taking hold, and the long recession had faded into the distant past. The rough and tumble 1980s were in full swing. Though the festival lineup didn't hold any major surprises, the organizers added the second Friday making the festival a six-day event over two weekends. As the addition of new sponsors roiled through the minds of dedicated longtime festers, curmudgeons were convinced the end of an era was near. Actually, the era had already ended.

Stage 1 was sponsored by MCI, a new telecommunications company trying to break into a market dominated by BellSouth before the court-mandated breakup of the corporate giant, AT&T. Stage 2 bore the logo of local radio station WNOE, and Stage 4 was supported by WWL-TV. Rhodes Funeral Home and Pizza Hut retained their sponsorships of the Jazz and the Kids' Tents respectively.

In a decision laden with symbolism, Stage 3 was rechristened "the Fess Stage" in homage to the great pianist and spiritual father of the yearly event. A gigantic whimsical likeness of the great man graced the scaffolding over the stage. Though the Fess Stage eventually received sponsorships from Ray-Ban and the current sponsor, Acura, the image of Fess still looks down on the masses that crowd the infield.

As the festival continued its trajectory of growth, it began to attract a much larger out-of-town following that descended on the city each spring. Flights into the city were now in high demand and were usually oversold resulting in missed flights for many fans of the annual event. Rental cars streamed in from airports in nearby cities. New Orleans culture was looming large in the country with the breakaway success of the Cajun chef Paul Prudhomme (he actually relocated his entire restaurant, staff included, to New York City for a few months in the summer of 1985) and the many New Orleans musicians making in-roads on the national and international stage.

The growth of the festival had a powerful economic effect on the city, and it began to rival Carnival as the number one revenue-generating event in the increasingly tourist-focused economy of the mid-1980s. Area businesses of every variety looked forward to the festival to stake themselves financially before the always-slow summer. It wasn't just the casual music fan who became enamored with the Jazz Fest. Celebrities of the music, television and film worlds were attracted to the laidback charms of the city and the musical smorgasbord of the festival. Under hats and behind shades, David Byrne of Talking Heads, John Fogerty of Credence Clearwater Revival and Paul Simon wandered the Fairgrounds in 1986.

Stevie Ray Vaughan had been a regular visitor to New Orleans for several years playing gigs at Tipitina's and other venues as well as befriending a number of local musicians. His debut at the Jazz Fest was anti-climatic for me because I was already bored with his blues-rock style. But for blues lovers, his set with his band, Double Trouble, was one of the highlights of 1986.

Veteran festival photographer Michael P. Smith photographed Vaughn a number of times including shots of the guitarist posing wearing a Mardi Gras Indian's elaborate feathered crown and laughing with New Orleans musical icons, Earl King and Dave Bartholomew. Vaughn's face in the photos perfectly captures the ebullient energy at the Jazz Fest in the mid-1980s.

While the Jazz Fest was undoubtedly growing, the years before 1986 never had an epic crowd like the one that showed up at Stage 1 (because sponsors have changed numerous times over the years, I will continue using the old stage numbers for continuity) on the first Saturday for a set by the '60s singer and political figure, Joan Baez.

I was curious about her performance, and when I rounded the track approaching the side of the stage, I was shocked to see thousands of people overflowing the grass track on the outside edge of the infield. Though it is a common enough scene in the modern era of the festival, the sheer number of people forced hundreds to simply lay their blankets down on the dirt track. With such a large turnout, the festival's organizers immediately began making plans to tweak the layout yet again leading to such modern amenities as giant video screens and remote speakers. Eventually, the Fess stage (stage 3) became the only "big" stage hosting most of the national touring acts. In 2007, Stage 1's layout was tweaked again in an attempt to return it to near-equal status with the Fess stage.

In April 1987, the New Orleans Jazz and Heritage Foundation took control of WWOZ's F.C.C. license. Though it took a few years, the station eventually became solvent under the guidance of the non-profit foundation's board and a new management team. With its problems gradually being left behind, the new team opened the door for the station to become a much more significant part of the fabric of the city. But more significantly, it set the stage for the music at the Jazz Fest to be broadcast live over the airwaves.

The station also moved into Armstrong Park from the station's original home above Tipitina's and began to settle into a groove. However, an ill-advised plan to turn Armstrong Park into a European-style theme park based on the design of Tivoli Gardens in Copenhagen, Denmark, was a threat. The plan, an insult to African-American culture, showed a grave lack of respect for the Tremé neighborhood's history. It never got off the drawing board, although members of then-Mayor Sidney Bartholomew's office did travel to Denmark to investigate the idea.

New Orleans continued to fuel the national imagination as the film "The Big Easy" was released in 1987. Though much maligned for bad accents and other transgressions against the culture of Louisiana, the vehicle starring Dennis Quaid exposed a healthy segment of the American public to the music of Cajun and Zydeco stars Beausoleil, Dewey Balfa and Terrence Simien, and reintroduced Irma Thomas to the nation.

The vibe at the Fairgrounds in 1987 was tinged with regret. Alan Jaffe, the founder of Preservation Hall and one of the leaders of the effort to bring traditional jazz back to the French Quarter, passed away.

That same year, two exciting new players on the national scene played at the Theater of the Performing Arts as part of the Jazz Fest's evening concert series. Wynton Marsalis headlined the bill. Stanley Jordan had performed at Tipitina's a year earlier, and his approach to the guitar was seriously impressing virtually every person who saw him perform. He developed a style using a hammering technique to tap out notes on the fretboard rather than picking or strumming. This was an innovative approach for a jazz guitarist, though heavy metal players had used it.

The inventive vocalist Bobby McFerrin was also on the bill. It was a brilliant match up because he was doing for jazz vocals what Jordan was doing for jazz guitar. McFerrin was still a year away from his smash hit "Don't Worry, Be Happy," but he was already highly acclaimed for releasing the first jazz vocal album with no instruments or overdubs. McFerrin had actually spent a fair amount of time in New Orleans before he broke out nationally. He sang with Astral Project in the early years of the band.

The concert was a stunning display of individual virtuosity. Both McFerrin and Jordan played solo. They just stood on the edge of the stage and performed for the large, highly appreciative crowd. Marsalis' set was almost anti-climactic after witnessing such genius.

For the first time in its history, the Jazz Fest commissioned Scott Ray and Associates to survey its patrons in an attempt to assess the spending of locals and visitors alike. The results of the effort indicated that the Jazz Fest had truly become an economic force in the city. The numbers were no surprise to regular attendees. An estimated 300,000 people attended the festival in 1987, the biggest number thus far, and the growth again affected change.

In 1988, the Fairgrounds relented and allowed the festival to expand onto the grass track at the very outside perimeter of the infield. With the music tents moved as far back as possible, there was considerably more room on the infield.

The Jazz Fest program debuted a design innovation that became a standard in publications across town. The "cubes," as they are known today, showed the schedule in a grid layout with the stages along one axis and the times along the other. It quickly became the only truly effective way to plan a day at the Fairgrounds.

The Koindu stage was renamed Congo Square. It retained all of the same elements of Africana while the new name was more in keeping with the "heritage" portion of the Jazz and Heritage Festival. The Congo Square stage was the site of one of the most amazing performances ever to occur at the Jazz Fest.

Malavoi of Martinique played a style of music that few had ever heard. The band was essentially a string ensemble with four violins, a cello, upright bass, electric piano, drum kit, congas and three singers. Their music was decidedly Caribbean, but it had an old school flavor that seemed European to many listeners. Gene Scaramuzzo wrote about the group a month earlier in *Wavelength* magazine. Their repertoire had elements of early Caribbean genres like the beguine, but they mixed in songs from the European dance tradition of quadrilles and waltzes.

Malavoi's sound had a heavy rhythmic balance, courtesy of the drummer and the percussionist, while the strings created an ethereal feeling like being wrapped up in a cloud. The music was unfamiliar but clearly authentic. It was easy to imagine them playing at a wedding on a Caribbean beach a hundred years ago until the electric keyboard punched up the sound into the modern day. The crowd in front of the stage that day included numerous local musicians and two who were internationally known—David Byrne of Talking Heads and Paul Simon. No one in attendance would ever forget the incredible performance that afternoon. It also clearly affected Byrne and Simon who went on to become huge champions of the sounds of the diaspora.

There were numerous other highlights at the 1988 Jazz Fest. The great jazz pianist Dave Brubeck played to a huge, adoring outdoor crowd on Stage 1. Taj Mahal made an appearance backed by George Porter Jr.'s latest band, the Funksters. George had reformatted the membership of his band once again with the journeyman guitarist Bruce Blaylock along with the pianist Phil Parnell and the drummer Kenny Blevins. The biggest difference in his sound was the addition of the vocalist Leslie Smith. Smith only lasted a short period, and Nora Wixted, a French Quarter cabaret-style singer with whom Porter had also been working, replaced her.

With the addition of a vocalist, Porter's repertoire opened up considerably. New songs entered into the set list, and Porter earned a new generation of fans by performing several shows on Tulane's campus and concentrating his bookings at the surrounding bars. Just like Joyride before them, the Funksters did not last. Cracks were beginning to appear in Porter's funky facade as the years of drug use were beginning to take a toll. A tragic death became one of the catalysts for Porter to kick the habits that were holding him back.

On August 30, 1988, the great and innovative New Orleans drummer James Black died of a drug overdose. Besides being an explosive drummer, Black also played trumpet and piano. He was a first-rate composer whose works are still being performed by another generation of musicians. Black played with most of the modern jazz players in New Orleans and also toured and recorded with a number of national acts during a sojourn to New York City. He played with Lionel Hampton, Horace Silver and Yusef Lateef among others. In New Orleans, he recorded one album with Nat Adderly and two with Ellis Marsalis. He appeared on *Fathers and Sons*, an underrated concept album featuring Chico and Von Freeman on one side and Ellis Marsalis with his young sons, Wynton and Branford, on the flip side, and *Tropical Breeze* with a group of New Orleans musicians called Jasmine. A very young Cassandra Wilson was the vocalist in the group led by the harpist Patrice Fisher.

Black was a major influence on Johnny Vidacovich and, by turn, a whole slew of other younger musicians including Stanton Moore of Galactic. He was also an important figure in the musical life of his slightly younger contemporaries like Ellis Marsalis and Germaine

Bazzle. Considering his major role in modern jazz in New Orleans, it's a shame he only recorded sporadically and never released an album under his own name.

James Black and George Porter, Jr. were running partners, and Black's death was an awakening for Porter. He entered rehabilitation for his own drug problems soon after Black's death, and his career took off for the second time after he emerged clean and sober.

Black's death also set the stage for the ascension of one of the greatest drummers to emerge from the Crescent City in the modern era. David Russell Batiste, known to all as Russell, is from a well-known New Orleans musical family. His father was a member of the Gladiators, contemporaries of the Meters and popular around town in the 1960s. Batiste plays numerous instruments, is a serious composer and was a child prodigy. He began playing with the Batiste Brothers Band, a group featuring his father and uncles as well as other family members, when he was seven years old.

Batiste first began performing regularly in the late 1980s when he was a member of Charmaine Neville's band. He was just out of high school, and his playing was as mature as drummers who were ten years older. He had serious chops, incredible power on the kick drum and an exquisite sense of rhythm honed by his years with the acclaimed St. Augustine High School marching band. He began a long-term musical relationship with George Porter, Jr., and the door opened for the formation of Porter's most successful solo band, the Runnin' Pardners (perhaps named in deference to his relationship with James Black) and the Funky Meters, a group that has existed for longer than the original configuration.

The first Sunday lineup on the Fess Stage in 1988 was very impressive. Bourbon Street stalwart, Gary Brown, opened the day followed by Walter "Wolfman" Washington and the Roadmasters; Calypso star, the Mighty Sparrow, was up next followed by the Godfather of Soul, James Brown. New Orleans' own Queen of Soul, Irma Thomas, and an intriguing African performer named Samite of Uganda were at the end of the day.

In those days, the stage times at Jazz Fest were so punctual that you really didn't need a watch to know what time it was. If a band was set to start at 12:15, they started at 12:15—not a second sooner or later. However, James Brown clearly did not get the memo. He was at the height of his drug consumption, and the show was delayed time and time again. His tardiness was infuriating, and many people abandoned the area after fuming for at least an hour. Irma Thomas was reportedly very gracious about losing most of her allotted slot.

The second Saturday had an equally impressive lineup on the Fess Stage (Stage 3) with West Coast pianist Charles Brown opening the day followed by the Radiators, Los Lobos and Little Feat. Unfortunately, torrential rains that began on Friday afternoon almost caused the festival staff to cancel the day. They ended up opening the gates in the late afternoon and the schedule had to be shuffled around. All the tents were up and running, but only Congo Square and Stage 1 had live music. The Radiators, Queen Ida (the zydeco star) and five other acts were cancelled. Still, the *Times-Picayune* reported that 35,000 people slogged through the mud and endured a light drizzle. The sun finally came out on the last day of the fest when an estimated 65,000 people baked along with all that caked mud. The total for the six-day event in 1988 reached 305,000 and set a new record despite the rainy weather. Inexplicably, the Rebirth Brass Band was not scheduled on a stage as they had been in 1987 for their inaugural performance at the Jazz Fest. They were scheduled for a parade around the Fairgrounds instead.

There was one other significant club show during Jazz Fest that year. Blacktop Records put on a showcase at Tipitina's that became a tradition and spawned an acclaimed series of live albums. The first year was simply called "Blacktop Night," but it soon became known as the Blacktop Blues-A-Rama. In 1988, the performers included Anson and Rockets, Sam Myers, Nappy Brown, James "Thunderbird" Davis, Ron Levy, Mighty Sam McClain and the inimitable Earl King.

The Jazz Fest still had many of the elements that made it so attractive to the first wave of festers, but it continued to change slowly and insidiously. There was now a whole contingent of out-of-towners who considered themselves to be experts on all things local. The influx of knowledgeable out-of-towners was a mixed blessing since they certainly brought plenty of money to spend in local restaurants and clubs. However, they began trying to assert themselves and their out-of-town values over the locals usually by trying to tell us where and when we could dance. Of course, this has become commonplace now. The Jazz Fest organizers finally recognized there was a problem with a group I named "the chair people." They created "no chair" zones at the big stages in 2007.

Another big change happened after the 1988 festival. The Riverboat President left town, and the loss was downright tragic for long time fans of the annual event. Music lovers were unanimous—the Riverboat President was an amazing venue for Jazz Fest concerts. The ambiance of cruising on the Mississippi combined with the guilty pleasure of being a captive audience was not easily replicated.

In 1989, the organizers scrambled to find an adequate replacement that would duplicate the wonderful ambiance of hearing live music on the Mississippi River. The solution was a huge outdoor tent dubbed the "River Tent" set up just upriver of Spanish Plaza on a dock outside the Convention Center. The River Tent was a substandard alternative, but the technology that allowed for such a huge, temporary venue was regarded as cutting edge.

Reflecting the ambitions of a festival that was growing at an incredible pace, the River Tent had an amazing lineup of performers scheduled. On the opening night of Jazz Fest, the first show featured Santana and the Neville Brothers. Saturday night, Dr. John and his New Island Social and Pleasure Club opened for Jimmy Buffett and his Coral Reefer Band.

No shows were scheduled at the River Tent for Sunday and Monday nights, but concerts were scheduled from Tuesday night through Saturday night of the second weekend. Tuesday was a reprise of the Miles Davis and Wynton Marsalis double bill. Wednesday night was "La Noche Latina," and Thursday night was Robert Cray, the great Senegalese singer, Youssou N'Dour, and Ivan Neville. George Benson and Spyro Gyra were set for Friday, and Van Morrison, the Fabulous Thunderbirds and Allen Toussaint were scheduled for the final night's blow out.

I was at Thursday night's concert at the River Tent. Ivan Neville was at one of the many peaks in his career. He had recently released a solo record, *If My Ancestors Could See Me Now*, and was recording and touring with Keith Richards of the Rolling Stones as well as Robbie Robertson and Bonnie Raitt. He was also living in Los Angeles at the time, so the show was a homecoming as well. He put on an impressive set with his mostly L.A. based band, the Room.

Youssou N'Dour blew the crowd away with his incredible voice and the calm-in-the-middle-of-a-storm patrician demeanor of his great band. Cray was anti-climatic.

A few short hours after the concert ended, the River Tent was destroyed as 75 mile an hour winds and a reported tornado tore through the city. Had the storm arrived earlier, deaths would have occurred since the tent had a capacity of over 2000 people. The tents at the Fairgrounds were also destroyed, and for the first time in the fest's history a day had to be cancelled.

When the River Tent was destroyed, the festival's organizers had to scramble yet again in order to accommodate the other scheduled shows. The solution was to move the two remaining concerts to the Municipal Auditorium. I also attended the Saturday night concert with Van Morrison, the Fabulous Thunderbirds and Allen Toussaint. The show was sold out. The evening was a nightmare of epic proportions for fans used to the laid back attitude at the Jazz Fest and local clubs. The set-up was not very well thought out with twenty feet of empty space between the stage and front row where no one was allowed to stand, never mind dance.

The security team of New Orleans police officers was unrelenting. They didn't want dancing in the aisles; they wanted everyone in a seat. Numerous people who wanted to be up close spent all of Morrison's set roaming around trying to avoid the cops. His performance was uninspired. He was probably not feeling it from the crowd considering the nature of the set-up, and the whole experience felt like a waste of time and money. Weeks later, a local publication suggested that the official Jazz Fest night shows might be an endangered species. It was a few years before they became extinct.

Because the storm destroyed much of the temporary infrastructure at the Fairgrounds, the schedule for the second weekend had to be rearranged. Despite the lost day, the overall attendance at the 1989 Jazz Fest was higher than the year before.

While the festival staff was working out the problems associated with the loss of the Riverboat President, the clubs in town were gearing up for the biggest Jazz Fest ever. Tipitina's pulled out all the stops with an incredible lineup for Piano Night since the great expatriate blues pianist, "Champion" Jack Dupree, was in town. Dupree was a legend among pianists in town, but since he was living in Europe, visits to his hometown were rare. Every single piano player in town wanted to be on that bill. Unfortunately, Dupree, who was 79 years old at the time, cancelled at the last minute. However, Ed Volker, Dr. John and a whole cast of piano players graced the stage until the wee-wee hours.

Since the grand reopening of Tipitina's three years earlier, the club's cachet kept increasing with memorable performances and wonderful vibes. The corner at Tchoupitoulas and Napoleon in uptown New Orleans became a magnet for stars large and small. At one point, Bonnie Raitt pulled up on the back of someone's motorcycle. Robert Cray, Boz Scaggs and Ivan Neville were trading notes besides a telephone pole. George Porter, Jr. and Leo Nocentelli showed up. There was no question—the Jazz Fest was the center of the musical universe.

Chapter 9

A NEW GENERATION OF MUSICIANS AND BANDS

"Each night seems like a thousand years, I just can't lose these young boy blues"—Doc Pomus/Phil Spector

Allison Young, late of the Distractions, joined the keyboardist and vocalist Lisa Mednick in forming the Songdogs and, along with a group of first-rate players, they became a New Orleans supergroup of sorts. The band also included Bruce McDonald and Red Priest on guitars, Tom Marron on fiddle and vocals, Lenny Jenkins on bass and a young drummer named Paul Santopadre. Jenkins was recruited from the jazz world for this idiosyncratic danceable rock band. Santopadre was in his early twenties, and at times in their nascent period he seemed like he was overwhelmed with the other personalities in the band. But he quickly became an integral part of the team.

McDonald picked out sterling lines, and Priest, who had logged thousands of miles with the band Satisfaction, played mostly rhythm guitar. Priest's most recent gig had been with bluesman J Monque'D, and his connection with Benny's Bar provided a venue for the band right as they were forming. McDonald and Priest were the grizzled veterans joining forces with two strong-willed women. Mednick brought plenty of fresh ideas to the band, and her musicianship was superb. She was the least familiar with the musical styles of New Orleans, but the others allowed her plenty of space and relished in her totally original pop songs.

Marron was the wild card, and he became a goofy front man even as he contributed songwriting to their all-original repertoire. He would add tasty fiddle licks inspired by his fascination with Celtic music. When not soloing or adding vocals, he would often spin a basketball on the tips of his fingers contributing to the carnival atmosphere of the highly energetic band of seven musicians.

Young reluctantly shared the spotlight at center stage with Marron. She was the only non-instrumentalist in a band loaded with great players and equally gifted songwriters. Yet her vivacious, sexy stage persona and powerhouse vocals kept most of the eyes in the audience on her compact curvy frame.

The Songdogs played their first show in early 1986 at Tipitina's as an opening act for the Continental Drifters who recently added Holden Miller on vocals. Before the summer ended, the Songdogs were the talk of the town. Within a few months, they would captivate much of the music community with their strong musicianship, tight interplay and original songs. They began playing every Tuesday at the Maple Leaf in September, and the shows were nearly always packed with people coming out to see the next big thing out of New Orleans.

By they end of the year, they had switched places with the Continental Drifters and were now the headliners at Tipitina's. A&R (artists and repertoire) scouts for out-of-town record labels were interested in the band. They recorded a live album at Tipitina's and seemed poised to break out nationally. They had everything in place to become a national sensation. But it was not to be. With seven members, the band struggled to coalesce around everyone's individual schedules. They experienced the high-low dichotomy of coming very close to signing a national record deal several times. Jenkins and Marron quit the band and were replaced by Paul Clement and Nancy Buchan respectively.

On December 13, 1989, a Wednesday, New Orleans' latest best hope for pop stardom, the Songdogs, played their farewell show at Tipitina's. Some of the members of the Songdogs had already debuted a new band, the Hooligans, as a back up group for the singer/songwriter Shad Weathersby. At that point, they had lost hope and were just another band eaten up by the music business machine. It was over before it was over. Of course, that's just my opinion.

The Continental Drifters had been gigging around town fairly regularly beginning in 1984 and lasting through 1987. But the lineup of the band was constantly in flux, and though they had some good songs, the group never completely jelled. A critical comment they constantly heard—and it wasn't exactly a compliment for the fledgling band—was that they were too loud. An over reliance on volume helped mask the less than stellar musicianship of some of the players who moved through the band. But more importantly, the constant criticism about the volume led to the three principals' next project, the subdudes.

On March 3, 1987, Tommy Malone, John Magnie and Johnny Ray Allen, along with the percussionist Steve Amadee, who was childhood friends with Malone and Allen, gave the many critics what they wanted and performed acoustically at Tipitina's. The "subduded" presentation led to the group's name.

While Magnie mostly played piano and electric keyboards prior to the advent of the subdudes, he gravitated to the accordion in the early days of the band. The acoustic setting was perfect for the instrument, and before too long Magnie's stage persona began to evolve into a willowy sage who leaned in close for vocal harmonies with his bandmates.

The other major instrumental change that evolved as the subdudes grew into a well-honed national act was Amadee's percussion work. He perfected a unique style of play that involved using pressure on the head of a tambourine to change the pitch of the instrument. He would play the tambourine with a drumstick while holding the head with his thumb. By varying the pressure on the head, he was able to modulate the pitch to generate a much wider range of sound. The technique was not unlike that of a talking drum player. It was groundbreaking in a sense, and drummers and percussionists flocked to see this new technique and to marvel about how he could sound like a bass drum and a snare drum at the same time.

Drawn by Malone's good looks and the feel-good disposition of the group, many of the new band's fans were women. The band developed a strong local following in the first few months of its existence playing as "John Magnie and the subdudes." They headlined at Tipitina's in June, played a couple of Tuesdays at the Maple Leaf in July, and headlined at Tips again in August before disappearing from the city completely. Competition from other bands was one of the reasons, but the subdudes moved to Colorado just as they were taking off in New Orleans.

Though the subdudes were one of the more important bands during this period, much of their growth as a unit occurred beyond the eyes of their original New Orleans fans. This proved to be beneficial because each homecoming became an occasion, and the ephemeral nature of the group allowed them to begin drawing big crowds whenever they returned to the Crescent City

When the members of the subdudes realized the viability of the new project, the Continental Drifters simply faded away. Carlo Nuccio, the last in a series of drummers who played with the group, moved to Los Angeles and took the band's name with him. Eventually, a new version of the Continental Drifters coalesced in the City of Angels around Nuccio and another expatriate New Orleanian, the bassist Ray Ganucheau.

In Los Angeles, the group started playing regularly and attracted a number of other musicians interested in their loose approach to songwriting and the New Orleans vibe. Before long, the new version of the group added some famous names and became another supergroup of sorts. Mark Walton, who had logged time with the Dream Syndicate; Susan Cowsill, of the Cowsill musical family (the inspiration for TV's Partridge Family); Vickie Peterson, formerly of the Bangles; and Peter Holsapple, a journeyman musician who was a member of the dB's and a side musician for R.E.M., joined the group. The guitarist Robert Maché was added when Ganucheau quit.

The story of the band is considerably more complicated than my brief description. Suffice it to say, however, that after several years in Los Angeles and numerous personnel changes, the group moved to New Orleans and quickly became the latest sensation.

In the fall of 1988, the subdudes made their first return to New Orleans since they began their long sojourn in Colorado. The group had jelled completely, and they had composed a new raft of great songs. They were on the verge of signing with a major label, Atlantic Records, and the show was packed to the gills. Everyone wanted to see the hometown boys at their homecoming.

Steve Amadee had perfected his unique percussion style on the tambourine. Tommy Malone was coming into his own as a song-writer, and the new songs, plus a great cover of Al Green's, "Tired of Being Alone," showcased his sterling high register vocals. The bassist Johnny Ray Allen was all smiles as John Magnie danced around the stage like a pied piper wearing a red and white accordion.

The crowd greeted them like conquering heroes. It was obvious this band had something special—born in the clubs of New Orleans, and honed in the small college town of Fort Collins, Colorado. They returned fully formed; locked, loaded, and poised to take on the world.

Over the course of the next eight years, the subdudes did just that. They released four critically acclaimed albums and helped usher a new style, Americana, into the national mainstream. But as with so many successful bands, they were having substance abuse and interpersonal problems.

In the summer of 1996, the subdudes began one of the more bizarre chapters in the history of New Orleans music. They announced they were breaking up, but rather than simply fading away like so many bands that lose the ability to make music together, they scheduled a farewell tour that included four shows in New Orleans.

In late September, the Tremé community buried one of the icons of the 1950s R&B era in New Orleans. Jessie Hill was James and Troy "Trombone Shorty" Andrews' grandfather, and the two young musi-cians led a young group that performed at the jazz funeral. Among the mourners was the great bluesman, Taj Mahal, who was in town for a concert later that day.

It was an outdoor show at the "Fly" facing the Mississippi River behind the Audubon Zoo. The subdudes were the closing act. Taj Mahal and Little Feat were opening for them. The finale of Mahal's set that afternoon was a raucous version of Hill's biggest hit, "Ooh

Poo Pah Doo." Most of the members of Little Feat were on stage singing the chorus. It was an awesome moment and a real tribute to one of the kings of the music community

Despite the high energy set by Mahal, the subdudes' closing performance was downright lackadaisical, and since their plans to break up were already well known, the decision to go on a farewell tour stunk of contrivance. Tommy Malone was as pale as a ghost, and Johnny Ray Allen looked like he'd rather be anywhere else. I wrote in my journal, "Why not just break up now?"

On October 31, 1996, they played at the House of Blues, and the following two nights they held forth at Tipitina's. The wonderful chemistry, spirited harmony vocals and musical interplay that were hallmarks of the band's sound was barely evident as the members were reportedly unable to even talk to one another.

With the breakup of the subdudes, John Magnie and Steve Amadee moved back to Colorado, so Tommy Malone and Johnny Allen needed another outlet for their considerable talents. They formed yet another supergroup of sorts, modeled on Ry Cooder's Little Village, and named the band Tiny Town. The group was centered on the acclaimed Nashville based singer/songwriter Pat McLaughlin. The drummer was the great session man and New Orleans club veteran, Kenny Blevins. Tiny Town had an instant buzz because of the personnel involved, but the group, which in retrospect was little more than a vehicle for McLaughlin rather than a genuine collaboration, didn't last long.

But like the proverbial phoenix rising from the ashes, the subdudes began performing and recording again eight years later. The bassist and songwriter, Johnny Ray Allen, was gone from the group, and two new members joined the original trio that initially brought that "subduded" sound to the stages of New Orleans. They continue to thrive mostly as a touring act.

One of the most significant of the new arrivals to begin impacting the music scene during the 1980s was a guitar player and successful bandleader from England who was fascinated by the deep well of New Orleans R&B. Jon Cleary had an uncle who turned him on to Professor Longhair and other musicians from the golden age of R&B in New Orleans.

As fate would have it, Cleary landed smack in the middle of a lively music scene at the Maple Leaf Bar on Oak Street when he first arrived in the city. Before he began gigging around town, he worked painting the old building that houses the club in exchange for admission and beverages. He gradually learned to play the piano in the raucous two-fisted style of the New Orleans greats from Champion Jack Dupree on down to the Maple Leaf's own James Booker. The impetus for learning a new instrument was the simple fact that there was a piano in the house where he was living at the time. He absorbed the styles of Professor Longhair and Dr. John as well.

By April 1986, he began playing solo piano gigs around town billed as Jon "King" Kleary. Naturally, the first place he regularly played was the Maple Leaf where he took over James Booker's old slot on Tuesday nights. Piano Night was resurrected at the new and improved Tipitina's, and Cleary began playing there on Monday nights as well. His compelling story and capable playing began opening doors with other musicians.

By early winter, he was a member of Walter "Wolfman" Washington's new band, the Roadmasters. Beginning in early 1987, he was also playing in an R&B band led by the saxophonist Ken "Snakebite" Jacobs called the Ninth Ward Millionaires and on selected gigs with Snooks Eaglin. Besides maintaining a busy performance schedule, Cleary became an in-demand session player appearing on albums by local artists such as Washington, John Mooney, Guitar Slim, Jr., and Johnny Adams. By the 1990s, Cleary had graduated to the national level while still maintaining his local connections with his solo act, the Absolute Monster Gentlemen.

Taj Mahal recorded some of Cleary's songs, and Cleary played for a time in the modern day bluesman's band before moving on to a successful collaboration with Bonnie Raitt for whom he still records and plays. He also recorded with B.B. King and Eric Burdon among others.

In his early days in New Orleans, his act consisted of a small number of originals, tunes from the pen of Dr. John and Professor Longhair as well as a number of songs from the local R&B canon. He proved to be a quick study and got the New Orleans piano style down pat while he accompanied himself with a strong singing voice that showed no trace of his British roots. Over the years, Cleary could always be counted on to play at various benefits and tribute shows connected to the piano tradition of New Orleans. While clearly enamored with the legends of the city, he eventually developed his own voice. Since the formation of his own band, his solo act has focused on original tunes long steeped in the traditions.

Cleary was part of a whole cohort of piano players who migrated to the Crescent City around the same time. Amasa Miller has made a career providing tasteful piano support for a wide range of female vocalists. He was an in-demand sideman for singers like Charmaine Neville, the Pfister Sisters and Leigh Harris (Little Queenie). He is also a student of international styles and plays the accordion. Tom McDermott, an erudite player and writer from St. Louis who is now one of the leading players on the scene, also arrived in town during this period. One of his early gigs was with the Dukes of Dixieland playing for tourists on the Steamboat Natchez. They joined the veteran, John Magnie, who arrived in 1976.

By 1987, the piano scene in New Orleans was greatly enhanced by the return of Henry Butler. He is a New Orleans native who left town for greener pastures as a younger man. Though today he is widely known as a blues and funk player, during this period he was completely devoted to jazz. He played with an A-list of musicians including the bassist Charlie Haden and the drummer Billy Higgins. Though he didn't move home for a couple more years, he appeared regularly in New Orleans during this period at the Jazz Fest and at Snug Harbor.

Once he moved home, Butler was everywhere and began transitioning his musical focus to R&B and funk. He sat in with Kermit Ruffins and Snooks Eaglin on a regular basis and even played a number of full shows with the Barbecue Swingers. He sat in anywhere and everywhere typically upstaging the best players in the band. However, as a guest performer, he was never egotistical; he is just that good.

One instance in particular sticks out. Butler showed up at Muddy Waters to sit in with George Porter, Jr.'s band. He had the whole club mesmerized with his version of "Baby What You Want Me to Do." Then, as if to top himself, he played a long improvisational instrumental passage on "Fever" so jazzy that the rest of the band was left in the dust. Even Porter was amazed. Rather than try and outdo Butler, Porter followed Butler's tour-de-force guest turn with something no one in the crowd had heard before—a new hip-hop-inspired version of the Meters' classic, "Funkify Your Life."

After moving back to New Orleans, Butler's band included a young jazz bassist, Chris Severin, who is now one of the first call bassists in town adept on both the acoustic upright and the electric and versed in every genre. Herman Jackson was the drummer. Jackson and Butler have played together since their college days, and the band could play anything. Every time they played together, they just ripped through a mixed bag of jazz and funk. Severin was a monster, leaning into his upright and plucking fat notes that seemed to slide through the ether and connect directly with Butler's rollicking left hand. Jackson had near telepathic rapport with Butler as well.

Butler was a college professor in Indiana before moving back to New Orleans. His early gigs as a resident of the city had a strong educational component, and some people on the scene began calling him Professor Henry. At a gig at the Old U.S. Mint, he demonstrated improvisation by playing and singing two very different versions of "Amazing Grace." He was positively bubbling with energy and talked effusively about the music as another young bassist, David Pulphus, looked on with rapt attention and his old buddy, Herman Jackson, observed the mostly tourist crowd with studied indifference. But the jazz fans in the crowd were astonished.

Another piano player who deserves mention at this point is Harry Connick, Jr. He was a child prodigy who recorded his first album as a pre-teen after spending time under the tutelage of James Booker. By 1988, when he released *20*, his first breakthrough recording as an adult, he was on his way to mega-stardom in music, film and theater. But before he left New Orleans for fame and fortune, he earned a prestigious gig—he was one of the first players to ever appear solo at Snug Harbor.

By the mid-1980s, African and Caribbean music began making serious inroads in New Orleans as local promoters were emboldened to give more of the music a chance in the clubs. The root of this widespread fascination with the music of the African diaspora can be traced to a performance by the Nigerian ju ju music legend, King Sunny Adé, at The Dream Palace during Carnival of 1982.

I recall never seeing such a large band or hearing such incredible music. The band had five guitars including Adé (one musician was on pedal steel—an instrument more commonly found in American country music), an electric bass player and trap set drummer along with singers and percussionists. Their sound was clearly organized and well honed, but it was nearly impossible to tell what was happening on the stage—there were just too many instruments and too much sound. What stands out the most for me, besides the incredibly maniacal dancing that began the minute the show began and didn't stop until it was over, were the talking drum players. A talking drum is a small instrument shaped like an hourglass and bound with a set of strings that allow the player to modulate the pitch of the drum. Placed under one arm, the musician squeezes the strings to change the pitch. The drum is played with a curved stick that has a rounded tip. The instrument is revered in West Africa where it was used in the days before modern communication to converse over long distances.

All this is academic, however, when compared to hearing a talking drum played by the masters in King Sunny Adé's band. Though the changing pitch of the drum is said to mirror some of the elements of various West African languages, it seemed as if the musicians were speaking English loud and clear through their drums. The band had three talking drummers, and though one was definitely the leader, they each took turns wowing the crowd with their virtuoso prowess. Meanwhile the African members of the audience were paying homage to the great musician from the Motherland. They approached the stage with cash money, not just ones but also fives and tens and twenties, and showed their appreciation by plastering the bills on the leader's forehead using his sweat as glue.

That night in 1982, the band played until dawn, and the exhausted revelers spilled out onto Frenchmen Street on Mardi Gras morning. The power of King Sunny Adé's performance immediately began spreading among the musical cognoscenti like a myth. If everyone who claimed to have been there were actually in attendance, Frenchmen Street would have overflowed into the French Quarter.

Over the ensuing decade or so, dozens of top name African and Caribbean bands would appear in New Orleans. Tipitina's led the way by booking most of the acts. The Killer Bees were a great reggae band from Texas that included the future Papa Mali on guitar. They played in town many times during this period, and their original songs introduced many local listeners to a new genre, world beat, that mixed up various styles of African derivation.

In November 1986, O.J. Ekomode and the Nigerian Allstars played at Tipitina's for the first time. Though from Nigeria, Ekomode lived in the United States and spoke fluent, though heavily accented English. Because he sang some of his songs in English, his music was more accessible and many more fans were introduced to the beat of the talking drums. He probably played more times in New Orleans than any other African artist.

The Jazz Fest also continued to support the sounds of the Motherland and the diaspora. Chief Commander Ebenezer Obey and his Interformers Band and Olatunji and his Drums of Passion were booked at the 1986 Jazz Fest. Obey played Nigerian ju ju music in a more traditional style than King Sunny Adé. He had the crowd in the palm of his hand as his band tore straight through an amazing set on the Koindu (Congo Square) stage. Olatunji's set was like a drum circle except that each and every one of the players was a monster musician. The sheer power of his drummers, who played with such muscularity and precision, cannot be explained—it must be experienced. Wave after wave of rhythm washes over the listeners inundating them like organized cacophony and compelling them to move.

The widespread support developed by touring reggae bands aided in opening the doors for more adventurous musical bookings. Touring acts often hired local reggae bands including the Shepard Band and the Elements that had built-in followings. But another often overlooked factor in discussions of what eventually became a golden period for fans of the music of the African diaspora was the presence of the writer Gene Scaramuzzo at *Wavelength* magazine. He literally paved the way for many readers.

When Scaramuzzo first starting writing his column he focused on reggae, but like many of his readers, he quickly began exploring other sounds. By the end of his tenure at the magazine, he had turned on his readers and his listeners on WWOZ's "Caribbean Show" to the South African music of Hugh Masekela and Abdullah Ibrahim, the protest funky soul of Fela Kuti and other Nigerian musicians, Caribbean sounds including the Carnival anthems of Trinidad and Tobago and the zouk of Martinique and all their antecedents. Scaramuzzo was like a walking, talking and writing encyclopedia of the diaspora. He was also a drummer well versed in the techniques required to perform the various styles.

A third factor that helped create this surge in music of the African diaspora was the opening of Tower Records' local franchise on Decatur Street in the French Quarter at the end of 1987. The national chain's presence immediately impacted other local record stores, which viewed Tower Records as yet another example of the homogenization of New Orleans. But no one could argue with the depth of the store's stock, especially in the African and Caribbean sections.

The surge of interest in the music of the African diaspora was not limited to New Orleans. David Byrne's band, Talking Heads, mined the territory in the late 1970s. His solo album, *Rei Momo*, strongly influenced by Brazilian music, was released in 1989. His first Brazil Classics release, *Beleza Tropical*, was also released that year.

Bands all across the country were being impacted by the influence of the sounds of the diaspora, and many of them found their way to the lively, dancing musical scene in New Orleans. The Bonedaddys, an incredible world beat band from Los Angeles, burst on the scene in July 1988 with a half page advertisement in *Wavelength* demonstrating the difference between music business in New Orleans and in one of the major music capitals of the country. They were an unknown entity in New Orleans, and they were actually spending money to advance a show and promote their debut recording!

The ad, with a blurb taken from a review in the *College Music Journal*, stated unequivocally, "Looking like natives of Gilligan's Island, this ready-for-carnival ensemble rocks the world beat like never before. Crazier than the Crazy-8's, funkier than Fishbone, as colorful as Kid Creole and the Coconuts, and as flavorful as anything in banana leaves, the Bonedaddys hit you with LA pop/rock/funk, Afro disco, English Beat-ish ska, American R&B and freaky French

Caribbean junkanoo that'll heat up any kind of luau. Yo, Holmes, this bone's for you!" The *New York Times* weighed in as well, "First exposure to the Bonedaddys is like losing your virginity—you know it's a good time, but you're not really sure what it is yet…so you do it again—as many times as you can stand it!" Their motto was, "In the beginning was the bone, and the bone was good."

Though their ad didn't mention it, the Bonedaddys were also huge fans of New Orleans music and covered songs from the pens of the Meters and Allen Toussaint. By their third visit to New Orleans, they had endeared themselves to huge segments of the music community. A couple of sit-in performances by "Mean" Willie Green of the Neville Brothers band helped as well.

Also in 1988, another world beat act, an enigma named Dan Del Santo said to have coined the name for the genre, made his first New Orleans appearance at the Storyville club on Decatur Street. He was an irascible character who smoked pot on stage and sang songs about the revolution that was coming when the First World collapsed. Whether he actually coined the name of the genre back in 1983 has never been clearly established, but Del Santo, a Texas radio deejay, was a serious scholar of all of the genres of music from the diaspora. He introduced each song with a description of the style he was playing, and then his band just ripped it up. It was dance music with a lesson. He eventually returned to New Orleans a number of times and became a real favorite.

Sadly, smoking marijuana on stage was not his only vice. He was also selling it, and when he got busted for conspiracy to distribute in 1992, he skipped bail and fled to Mexico. He died there in 2001 at the age of 50 when he was unable to get adequate medical care for esophageal bleeding. For nearly ten years, the world beat and African music fans in New Orleans were left wondering what had happened to the great proselytizer and bandleader until word of his passing reached the city.

Also in 1988, just as the Jazz Fest ended and the summer doldrums began to set in, local music lovers were enlivened by the news that a new festival was making its debut in June in City Park. The Reggae Riddums Festival took over the old driving range on Marconi Drive and attempted to create a Jamaican vibe in the northernmost city of the Caribbean. That first year's lineup was impressive. The one-day event included local reggae acts along with three greats from the genre—Yellowman, Toots and the Maytals and Pato Banton.

Reggae Riddums became an early summer tradition in New Orleans and joined the Internationale Festival de Louisiane, started in 1986 in Lafayette to celebrate the francophone heritage of Louisiana, as another festival celebrating world music. The organizers brought in bands from all over the world and further exposed music lovers in South Louisiana to the styles of French Africa and the Caribbean.

Tipitina's was now on a serious roll presenting African and Caribbean acts. King Sunny Adé returned for two nights in June 1988. The great Brazilian troubadour Milton Nascimento played the club in August. On September 1, the Bhundu Boys appeared and world music lovers in the city were exposed to a whole new style of African music. The Bhundu Boys were from Zimbabwe, and they played a high energy, guitar-oriented African style like rock stars. Though their music was closely related to the soukous of neighboring Zaire, they called their music "jit." They hit the stage in matching native-inspired costumes. The music was highly danceable, and the crowd ate up the lead guitarist's shimmering lines and the rhythm section's relentless groove.

Another Nigerian band, Chief Twins Seven Seven who played the older highlife style, appeared in November, and the great South African vocal group, Ladysmith Black Mambazo, graced the stage with their heavenly vocals at the end of the month.

In late August 1989, the great Nigerian musician/activist Fela Kuti was scheduled to appear two nights in a row at Tipitina's with his band, Egypt 80. The whole contingent of world music lovers in town was totally jazzed at the chance to hear this legend, but the first night was a giant let down from all the hype leading up to the show. Despite the fact that he had over thirty musicians and dancers on stage, the show was lackadaisical, lacking any energy at all. Fela appeared tired, bored and/or a little stoned. He stopped the show numerous times for long-winded, self-focused speeches that destroyed the flow of the set.

The second night, however, was a different story. Fela appeared rested and energized, and the whole show reflected his renewed vigor. However, he played the exact same show, right down to the same gestures and language in the speeches.

The next night, the mighty soca star, Arrow, played at Tipitina's. Arrow, a prodigious composer with hundreds of songs to his name, has only covered one song in his illustrious career—the Meters' classic, "Hey Pocky Way." His band, National Force, played an opening set with such intensity that the crowd went crazy before the singer even hit the stage. Arrow made his entrance like he was James Brown, and many in the crowd were treating him as if he were God himself. Over the course of a two-hour set, the band rocked Tipitina's like it had never been rocked before.

By the early 1990s, it was impossible to deny—there was an incredible amount of music from the African diaspora being performed in and around New Orleans. The city government and its agencies also got into the act. In late May and early June 1991, the French Market hosted a festival celebrating the music and culture of Martinique, and fans of the diaspora were exposed to yet another musical element of the diaspora. For several days, three bands of vastly different styles from the Caribbean island inundated the French Quarter and the Le Meridien Hotel on Canal Street.

A manic group, the Plastic System Band, which had percussion equipment made of plastic drums of all sizes, paraded through the French Quarter. Despite their unusual instrumentation, they fit perfectly into the New Orleans vibe.

African music predominated at Tipitina's all summer long. Diblo Dibala, Kanda Bongo Man's guitarist, and his band, Matchacha, put on a great show, and members of the audience were up on stage dancing with his dancers. A month later, Les Têtes Brulées appeared at the uptown club. They played super high-energy soukous, and the tunes had weird, Zappa-like overtones. Their look complemented the unusual music. They wore torn shirts with strange little backpacks, and their faces were painted with wild, white stripes. In early September, I.K. Dairo and the Blue Spots played at Tipitina's. Dairo was considered the grandfather of Nigerian ju ju music. He played the accordion and guitar, and like many of the West African bands that came through New Orleans, he had an awesome talking drummer.

The sounds of the diaspora match perfectly with the music of New Orleans as both musical traditions share certain characteristics: the music is incredibly compelling and overwhelmingly infectious, it is relentless and highly danceable, and most importantly, the vibe is rich and intense.

Upon further analysis, however, there is clearly more at play than just the interplay between the crowd and the musicians. Something else makes African music that much more compelling. The attraction is connected to the polyrhythms of the music shared by only a few other musical cultures outside of Africa including New Orleans, the Caribbean and Brazil. It is no coincidence that each of these locales forms part of the vast African diaspora that emerged in the years after the slave trade began.

While the rhythms themselves may vary slightly and the music can range from the jazz of New Orleans to the samba of Brazil, from the rhumba of Cuba to the compas of Haiti, from the zouk of Martinique to the reggae of Jamaica, there exists an inherent compassion in this music that belies the often horrid conditions of those who first created it. Out of the despicable practices of the North Atlantic slave trade came some of the most amazing music on our planet. Coaxing such joy from indescribable pain defines our humanity, and I regard that accomplishment as one of the greatest collective achievements of mankind.

Some of the shows occurred in the most unusual places and attracted an entirely different crowd. The Trinidadian soca star Baron appeared at a random hall across the Mississippi River in Gretna. Baron had a full band including a horn section, and they played until 5 AM to a crowd of Caribbean expatriates and a few slightly rumpled revelers from uptown.

In the summer of 1991, Diblo Dibala appeared at Tipitina's with his new band, Loketo. The group featured another great vocalist, Aurlus Mabele. Soukous music had taken over New Orleans and the club was packed with frenetic dancers.

A month later, Club Kilimanjaro featured Sam Fan Thomas and his Makassi Band, a hot African group from Cameroon. Club Kilimanjaro was a short-lived venture located on the corner of Louisiana Avenue and Carondelet Street in uptown at the storied location that housed the Nitecap. The original version of the Meters played there regularly in the late 1960s.

Flora Purim and Airto appeared again at Tipitina's in August. Dan Del Santo returned to the uptown club in September, and the New Orleans saxophonist Earl Turbinton played the whole three-set show with the world beat star. Johnny Clegg, a poppy South African singer/songwriter, appeared with his band, Savuka, at Tipitina's in October.

The new wave era was over in New Orleans music, and new acts were forming in the wake of this unprecedented exposure to music of the African diaspora. Curtis Pierre started Casa Samba, his long-running Brazilian dance and drum band, and a group of local percussionists including Luther Gray, Kenyatta Simon and Kufaru Mouton formed Percussion, Inc. These two are among the longest standing and most respected drum troupes in the city.

In the wake of the dissolution of the Continental Drifters, another new band, Tribe Nunzio, appeared on the scene and began riding this wave of percussion-heavy dance outfits. The members of the band were all veterans of other local bands. Vernon Rome and Damon Shea played bass and drums, respectively; Jeff Treffinger was on guitar; and the inimitable Holden Miller fronted the band. Her crazy outfits and stage antics set the tone for this group of quality players. They would eventually become a very popular act on the scene.

New bands from the diaspora were appearing every month or so, and old favorites returned regularly as they developed a fan base in New Orleans. The shows always left the audience feeling elated and ecstatic. For a large group of like-minded music freaks, it was full immersion in the golden age of African and Caribbean music in New Orleans.

Chapter 10

THE NEW BRASS BAND GENERATION

"Without this guy, the world would still be square"—Hugh Masekela on
Louis Armstrong

By 1989 the Rebirth Brass Band was still going strong on Thursday nights at the Glass House when a new brass band jam session
that laid out the groundwork for the beginnings of Kermit Ruffins'
solo career started at Sidney's Saloon on St. Bernard Avenue. "Uncle"
Lionel Batiste, the irrepressible bass drummer and vocalist, was at
the center of this new downtown scene. Ruffins has credited Batiste
with teaching him many of the old time tunes that make up his solo
repertoire. At Sidney's, the songs came quickly amid the carrying on
of a fun-loving group of musicians that included members of the
Tremé, Rebirth, Olympia and Dirty Dozen Brass Bands.

The band included Benny Jones, the dignified leader of the
Tremé Brass Band. He held the line on his snare drum while a young
white kid from uptown named Davis Rogan was doing his best on
the keys. His capable presence on a makeshift bandstand in a tiny
bar in Tremé was a big surprise. It was the beginning of his long
career as a musician in New Orleans.

Derrick "Khabukey" Shezbie, a child prodigy on trumpet who
began playing with the Rebirth when he was ten years old, was

now a veteran at fourteen, and he was on the bandstand as well. Khabukey provided some moments of levity when he performed with Rebirth due primarily to his young age.

One particular instance deserves mentioning here. The Rebirth played at a private party at an apartment complex on Tchoupitoulas Street in 1989 (full disclosure—I booked the band). The group of musicians set up on the patio near the pool, and several hundred revelers got to see them up close and personal for the first time. The set up was rather genteel with folks lolling about eating barbecue and drinking beer. For effect, they had moved a sailboat into the pool, as it was too late in the season for swimming. Between sets, Shezbie jumped from the tiled edge of the pool onto the deck of the sailboat with his trumpet in hand. It was only a short distance, but he was a little kid, and when he landed on the thin bow of the boat he raised his trumpet over his head in triumph. After attracting a small crowd with his stunt, he tried several times to jump back across the expanse of cold pool water, but he didn't anticipate the inertia of the boat. Each time he started to jump, the boat moved in the opposite direction. The rest of the band and much of the crowd was in stitches by the time he finally figured out how to get off the boat without drowning his beloved trumpet.

The scene at Sidney's was much mellower with an older crowd than at the Glass House. At one point, Ruffins and Batiste shared the single, tinny-sounding microphone. The song they chose was "What a Wonderful World," and the whole place quieted down for the spellbinding duet. Yet they still managed a short second line parade at the end of the second set. At this point, nearly fifteen musicians packed into the room along with assorted customers sitting at tables, on the pool table and at the bar.

The entire place emptied out—at least four trumpets, three trombones, a clarinet, various saxophonists and the rhythm section spontaneously took to the street. They finished the song standing in a circle on the corner while the whole bar, including the bartender, danced around them. The exuberance these musicians exhibited for nothing more than the contents of the tip jar, the pleasure of the jam session and the gentle camaraderie of this subculture was very endearing. Clearly, hearing traditional jazz played in tiny back o' town clubs in sketchy neighborhoods was one of the best ways to experience the true culture of New Orleans.

Ruffins and many of the musicians in his developing orbit regularly frequented these small clubs. They interacted musically and personally with the older generation, and the music and culture was transmitted via these informal gatherings. A new club began presenting live music in the Tremé on Sunday evenings in 1989. Located on the corner of St. Philip and N. Villere Streets, the Petroleum Lounge, a large open room, was popular with an older Tremé crowd.

Special guests were part of the experience of seeing live music in the Tremé as many of the brass band and traditional jazz musicians gravitated to the area if they didn't actually live in the neighborhood. One particular show at the Petroleum Lounge that stands out was the Easter Dance featuring the Tremé Brass Band. It was a family affair that evening with a communal attitude about performing. Musicians came and went, sitting in for as long as they felt like it. Kermit Ruffins played the bass drum while his partner, Philip Frazier, played his usual tuba. The great traditional jazz trumpeter, Gregg Stafford, was there along with Milton Batiste, the patriarch of the Olympia Brass Band. John "Prince" Gilbert played his usual tenor saxophone and even played soprano on one tune.

While the Petroleum Lounge was only open for a short period, a Sunday night ritual developed amid the inviting vibe of the close-knit Tremé community. There was never a guarantee concerning talent, but you could count on witnessing numerous younger musicians soaking up inspiration and repertoire from their elders.

On August 7, 1990, the Rebirth Brass Band played for the first time at the Maple Leaf Bar. It was a Tuesday night, and the gig was a fill-in on the schedule since the club didn't have anyone else available to play during the dog days of summer. By the end of September, the Rebirth was playing every Tuesday night. They are still at it over twenty years later, and it is the longest running regular gig by any band in town.

The presence of the Rebirth *Jazz* Band (as they were still being billed at most gigs) changed the demographics of the Maple Leaf almost instantly. Though the club hosted numerous black bands over the years, the audience for those bands was predominantly white. The Rebirth brought with them a whole contingent of fans that turned the club into a further-uptown version of the Glass House for one night a week. The regulars at the Maple Leaf couldn't believe their eyes when they first got a look at the crowd of dancers.

While the Maple Leaf's patrons had seen its fair share of wild dancing at shows by the Radiators, Walter "Wolfman" Washington and others, nothing could prepare them for the full-on house shaking that accompanied every Rebirth gig. The crowd was always thick and the energy was out of control.

The band played, as they did at the Glass House and other clubs in the 'hood, without the benefit of microphones. Some of the members liked to unscrew the bare light bulbs hanging over the stage and play in semi-darkness. With a band featuring eight, sometimes, nine musicians, the tiny stage was packed.

The dance floor directly in front of the stage was ground zero for the dancers. They came in all shapes and sizes with the one constant being that they were all quite young. This was a new style of dancing that coupled the old traditional second line steps with newer moves combining elements of break dancing and hip-hop. The dance floor was an opportunity to cut loose, and there was an informal pecking order based on who had the best moves.

Jerry Anderson, a drummer playing with Danny Barker at the time who eventually became the first drummer for Kermit Ruffins and the Barbecue Swingers, was one of the leaders. His style was hyper-kinetic—he would spin like a ballet dancer, do splits, jump up and then step so quickly that his feet were a blur.

Sometimes, the dancers would get into cutting contests and a circle would open up in the middle of the dance floor. The two combatants would be in the middle of the circle, and the crowd would gather around and egg each of them on higher and higher while the horns screamed. The informal winner would usually be the dancer with the most stamina. This style of dancing is often referred to as "buck jumping."

One of the most interesting aspects of the early days of the Rebirth at the Maple Leaf was the nearly constant presence of a group of young, mostly underage black musicians standing nearly motionless either at the very front or just off to the side of the stage. They weren't drinking or partying in any way. They were studying.

At this point, the Rebirth had been together for over seven years. The Dirty Dozen wasn't playing very many hometown gigs as they were constantly touring the world. The Rebirth was *the* band, and the youngsters watching devotedly were the next generation soaking up the music and learning by observing the new masters.

Milton Batiste had a group under his tutelage called the Olympia Brass Band, Jr. They eventually changed their name to the New Birth Brass Band when they decided to step out of the traditional style and began playing the hot new style being popularized by the Rebirth.

Philip and Keith Frazier's brother, Kerwin "Fat" James, was one of the regulars studying the band at the Leaf. He became the tuba player for the New Birth. James suffered a stroke in Houston during his Hurricane Katrina exile and never recovered. He died in New Orleans in 2007. Tanio Hingle and Kerry "Fat Man" Hunter were the drummers, bass drum and snare drum respectively. They are still stalwarts on the local scene. James Andrews, the trumpet player who eventually became known as "the Satchmo of the Ghetto" and led his own band of youngsters in Jackson Square, was a regular as well. He watched Kermit Ruffins like a hawk.

Solidifying a steady, good-paying gig at the Maple Leaf wasn't the only positive thing happening for the Rebirth. They were developing a bigger local fan base outside of the Tremé and the brass band community; they began regularly opening shows at Tipitina's for the Neville Brothers and earned their first shot at headlining in 1990.

Their first album on Rounder Records, *Feel Like Funkin' It Up*, was creating a sensation, and the single, "Do Whatcha Wanna," was being played on two local commercial radio stations, WYLD and WQUE. The song was a huge smash locally, and it was the first time in decades that a New Orleans musical act was getting regular airplay on local commercial radio. The label actually sent all of their remaining stock of *Feel Like Funkin' It Up* to New Orleans to satisfy the local demand.

"Do Whatcha Wanna" was so infectious that other musicians began covering it. Cyril Neville played it to open his second set at a show at Tipitina's, and Snooks Eaglin, the human jukebox, could never resist the chance to cover a local hit.

Every year at Thanksgiving, New Orleans hosts the Bayou Classic, a college football game between rivals Grambling and Southern. While the game is important for the players and football fans, the halftime show pitting the two colleges' marching bands against one another, is a huge draw especially for musicians. Philip Frazier and Kermit Ruffins were in the audience at the Superdome that year when both marching bands closed their shows with newly arranged versions of "Do Whatcha Wanna," the new anthem of New Orleans. It was the proudest moment in the young band's history.

Ron Levy, the producer of *Feel Like Funkin' It Up*, knew he had a hot band on his hands. But he also knew that the studio recording paled next to the real thing—the Rebirth performing live in their own element. He scheduled two nights of live recording at the Glass House that was released the following year as, *Rebirth: Kickin' It Live*. Though the album was billed in the media and on the label's press materials (as well as on plenty of sources to this day) as a Mardi Gras recording, it was actually recorded on Ash Wednesday and the following night.

The recordings were crazy affairs, and I have to give massive amounts of credit to Levy for pulling it off. I was there both nights and Wednesday, given that it was the day after Carnival, was considerably more laid-back. The band, which had marched in Zulu's parade Mardi Gras morning and then played an impromptu second line in the streets of Tremé after the parade, was exhausted. So were all the patrons. I would be surprised if any of the music from Wednesday night made it onto the final record. It was really just a dress rehearsal and a chance for the engineers and producer to get the sound right. Thursday night was a different story. It was their regular night at the Central City bar, and the usual crowd showed up.

Whenever the Rebirth plays at a second line there is usually a dedicated group of amateur musicians equipped with cowbells, tambourines or just beer bottles right behind the rhythm section. These freelance percussionists add considerably to the sound created by the band as they march through the city. Rebirth brought in two of these players, Morris Brothers on tambourine and Solomon Shabazz on bells, to augment the sound and create a second line vibe.

I still marvel at how the production team was able to get microphones, both for the band to use for vocals and to make the actual recording, into the tiny bar. The result was a great recording that captured the vibe of the place perfectly. Nearly ten years later, the Rebirth recorded another live album—this time at their new home—the Maple Leaf Bar.

One week to the day before the recording at the Glass House, at the height of the Carnival celebrations around town, the Rebirth played at Tipitina's with Bo Dollis and the Wild Magnolias to celebrate the revered Mardi Gras Indian big chief's first new recording in over fifteen years. His disc, which was released on Rounder Records, was called *I'm Back... at Carnival Time*. It featured the Rebirth on several tracks.

For the show at Tipitina's, the Rebirth opened with a set of their own and the Wild Magnolias, Dollis' longtime tribe, followed them. At this point in time, Mardi Gras Indians performing on stage was still a rare experience. The set was transcendent and Big Chief Monk Boudreaux was a big part of the reason. Their act, with the two big chiefs standing side by side on stage, was very effective because Boudreaux's calm, almost spooky spirituality contrasted brilliantly with Dollis' feel-good party persona.

The night ended with the Rebirth back on stage with the Indians. They reprised three of the songs that appeared on Dollis' album: "Big Chief," "Tipitina," and "Shallow Water." The show was the beginning of a long partnership between the two groups. Two years later, Rounder released another album, *Super Sunday Showdown*, which featured both acts.

By 1991, Kermit Ruffins was getting itchy with his role in the Rebirth; he wanted to sing more. So, he began putting together jam sessions that eventually morphed into his solo act. Though he was not old enough to be a member of the Fairview Baptist Church band that had nurtured many of the musicians in town, he was paying close attention to the work of Danny Barker.

On April 6, 1991, the two musicians appeared together at the Contemporary Arts Center. The occasion was a tribute to Louis

Armstrong. They both sang songs associated with Armstrong including a great version of "Black and Blue." The band featured Walter Payton on bass, Shannon Powell on drums, and Lucien Barbarin, a distant relative of Barker's, on trombone. Barker played banjo and guitar. Powell is a son of the Tremé and an inventive musician who spent years touring with Harry Connick, Jr. He is now a mainstay at Preservation Hall and pops up repeatedly throughout this tale. This was the band that eventually backed up Ruffins on his first solo album, *World on a String*. Incidentally, while Ruffins was developing his solo act, he wasn't always able to hire such first class talent, so the jam sessions that he hosted featured younger musicians who were willing to work for tips in order to gain experience.

A week after the gig at the Contemporary Arts Center, Danny Barker appeared at the French Quarter Festival with his own group featuring Jerry Anderson on drums, Walter Lewis on piano, and Frank Naundorf on trombone. Ruffins sat in the entire show, playing solos on the trumpet and soaking up his lessons from the old jazzmen.

The first time I saw what was then being billed as the Kermit Ruffins Project (or the Kermit Ruffins Experience) was at a tiny bar on Barracks Street in the lower Tremé called Junior's. The bar changed hands shortly after my first visit and was christened the Little People's Place. After they renamed it and Ruffins' mother-in-law began running the business, it became his de facto hang out.

It was two days after the big show at the Contemporary Arts Center, and the vibe was considerably more down home. The place was so small that the band set up in the corner right next to the front door. Every time the door opened, another musician walked in. Ruffins immediately greeted the newcomer and checked to see if he had brought his instrument. The only non-musicians in the joint were the neighborhood folks and a handful of Ruffins' fans who had heard about the gig directly from one of the musicians. It was not advertised at all.

Shannon Powell was drumming, but Ruffins took over the kit after a while followed by Ajay Mallory, the ace snare drummer for the Rebirth. Most of the other members of the Rebirth and other young brass band musicians were hanging out. Davis Rogan and

Arthur Kastler played the whole night on piano and upright bass respectively.

The vibe was as relaxed as a jam session in Kermit's living room. Musicians came up onto the bandstand and played when they felt like it. Everyone was taking turns and switching instruments. Keith "Wolf" Anderson, the trombonist with Rebirth, tried out the trumpet and ripped a solo. Allison Miner, the Rebirth's new manager and one of the creators of the Jazz Fest, sang a song in a beguiling alto.

Everyone, with the exception of Rogan and Kastler, was cutting up and cutting loose. The young white guys were too nervous among such talent. The band took long breaks between songs and between sets, and there was more laughter and good times than imaginable. But, in retrospect, it is clear that Ruffins was finding his new direction though few knew it at the time. The same musical scene was repeated numerous times over the next couple of years as Ruffins honed his solo act. He also brought the jam to other bars in the area including Sidney's Saloon and Café Brasil on Frenchmen Street.

Ruffins continued to play and record with the Rebirth, but he began missing smaller, less consequential gigs as he developed his solo act. Other changes were in the air as well. There were a number of new brass bands emerging such as the Little Rascals, the Soul Rebels and the New Birth. The personnel in the Rebirth and the Dirty Dozen Brass Bands were changing as well.

Roderick Paulin, a saxophonist from the legendary Paulin musical family, began playing with the Rebirth on a regular basis before becoming a full time member. Paulin's father, Ernest "Doc" Paulin, was one of the last links to the earliest brass bands in New Orleans. He died in 2007 at the age of 100. Though his group, which at the time included Roderick and a number of his siblings, didn't perform too often in nightclubs, they were regulars at the Jazz Fest. Paulin brought a schooled musical ability to the Rebirth and quickly established himself as a strong soloist, dedicated ensemble player, and most importantly, a top-notch composer. Though he was playing with the band at the time their second studio album for Rounder Records, *Take It To the Street*, was released, he didn't appear on it.

But by the time *Rollin'* arrived in stores in 1992, Paulin was an integral part of the group primarily for his songwriting. He wrote two of the songs, "You Move You Lose" and "Whop!," and shared writing credits with Philip Frazier on two others, "Thousand Island," and the title cut. He brought a different energy to the band on stage as well. While John "Prince" Gilbert, the first saxophonist, was a fine player, he liked to cut up on stage and loved a good time after the show was over. Gilbert and Paulin played together numerous times during this period. They were perfect foils for each other on stage because the difference in their personalities was reflected in their playing. Each musician brought his own sensibility and intensity to the proceedings.

Intensely focused on the music, Paulin was a serious young man. Most nights at the Maple Leaf, the majority of the band's members spent the breaks drinking beer, cutting up and partying. But Paulin and Keith Frazier were both in college at the time, and late arrivals to Oak Street were often greeted with an unusual sight—two members of Rebirth studying with their books propped open on the hood of a car.

Roderick Paulin eventually left the band and began developing his own solo project. In 1993, he debuted the Hitmen at the New Orleans Jazz and Heritage Festival. In keeping with his high musical standards, he recruited the great pianist Ed Frank for his intergenerational band. He also had the drum phenom Brian Blade, Jamil Sharif on trumpet, and Julius "Jap" McKee on upright bass, rather than his main instrument, the sousaphone. Paulin's good friend Robert Taylor sang an incredibly bittersweet version of the jazz standard, "Skylark," at the Fairgrounds.

Derek "Dirt" Wiley also left the Rebirth to pursue a higher calling—he became a preacher. Glen Andrews, a member of the same Tremé family that produced James Andrews, Revert Andrews and Troy "Trombone Shorty" Andrews among others, joined the group on trumpet. Around this same time, Stafford Agee joined the group on trombone, and there were a number of Rebirth shows during this period featuring three trombones—Agee, Reginald Steward and Keith "Wolf" Anderson. However, Anderson was close to leaving the group.

During a tour of Europe in the summer of 1991, Kirk Joseph and his trombone-playing brother, Charles, had some difficulties that resulted in their exit from the Dirty Dozen Brass Band. Evidently in a hurry to solidify their lineup, the Dozen hired Keith "Wolf" Anderson to play tuba. Revert "Peanut" Anderson became the trombonist for the Dozen.

I learned the news that Anderson was leaving the band on September 24, 1991 at Rebirth's regular show at the Maple Leaf. My only comment in my journal was, "Oh, my God!" Anderson was one of the most important members of the group, and I had a hard time imagining how they would go on without his charismatic stage presence. Little did anyone know at the time, but Kermit Ruffins was on his way out as well.

Four days later, Anderson performed with the Dirty Dozen for the first time at a street festival in the Tremé. He handled the gig, but the band sorely missed Joseph. Anderson stayed in the Dirty Dozen through the year, but was eventually replaced by an actual tuba player, Julius "Jap" McKee. He never re-joined Rebirth. After a long stretch playing in the French Quarter and with pick-up bands, Anderson joined the Hot 8 Brass Band.

While Joseph's sudden departure from the Dirty Dozen, a group whose sound he helped define, was surely a blow, he quickly began developing his solo career. He formed a brass band, the Frappe, that was active during Carnival, and he began playing modern jazz gigs with the cream of the crop of New Orleans jazzmen. Within a couple of years, he became part of two groundbreaking ensembles that profoundly affected the direction of the city's music scene.

In late November 1991, Joseph appeared at Snug Harbor with a group including the guitarist Carl LeBlanc, the drummer Jason Marsalis and the saxophonists Reggie Houston and Tim Green. Joseph's father, Waldron "Frog" Joseph, a veteran trombonist, also played. As is fitting for a musician of his caliber, the first set was funk, and the second set was jazz improvisation.

LeBlanc was clearly a jazz guy, playing long, clean lines on a hollow bodied six-string, but he had an adventurous, avant-garde side as well as the ability to play some serious funk.

One particularly memorable show featuring Carl LeBlanc occurred the night after Halloween at Nikki's Dockside, a black neighborhood joint on Chartres Street in the Bywater. The bar was set up with tables almost all the way to the stage, and there were only a handful of people in the place. LeBlanc had Donald Ramsey on bass and Tony Dillon on drums. Both of his sidemen are sympathetic musicians who can play any style of music depending on the occasion. They were on fire. LeBlanc was cooking, playing sinuous solos and comping jazz chords while the rhythm section was in full bore funk mode.

On the break we headed outside to get some air, and when we returned the jukebox was blaring some soul classic at top volume. A woman in a skimpy tank top and ratty blue jeans was literally grinding against the wall by the side of the stage, lost in the reverie of the song. The band got back up on the bandstand, but all the eyes in the place were on the woman who was dancing as if to save her life—alone, eyes shut, in pure rapture and oblivious to the attention. The band didn't want to break the spell, but they also needed to start playing. So, they just started playing along to the song on the jukebox. When it finally ended, the bartender cut the jukebox and the band just continued playing the same groove before segueing into the next number.

While the Rebirth was going through the various personnel changes, they were also confronted with the fact that the Glass House was out of business following a drug bust after Jazz Fest in 1991. Their last few shows there were epic four-set affairs that were packed to the rafters. Nearly every night, the band would march out into the street with the entire crowd second lining behind them. The scene on the street was as raucous as inside—sweaty dancers were buck jumping on the neighbors' stoops, strutting their stuff up and down the block, and climbing on the roofs of parked cars to bust a move. The closing of the Glass House was the end of an era although the band quickly moved the Thursday night gig to another bar in the same Central City neighborhood. Kemp's was located just off the corner of Lasalle and Washington Streets right across the street from Shakespeare Park. It was a bigger place on a bigger street and the crowds just grew and grew. Kemp's was also a favorite of the uptown Mardi Gras Indians and was a prime stop on the second line routes. Occasionally during Rebirth's show, a number of Indians from the Black Eagles tribe were in attendance. They often took over the dance floor with their wildly kinetic dancing and their mysterious rituals. The band just dug down deeper and let the Indians do their thing.

At the end of 1991, the music community became aware of a development that had been building for some time. Kermit Ruffins had signed a solo deal with Justice Records opening the door for his exit from the Rebirth Brass Band. He continued to develop his solo act over the course of the next few years while still performing with the Rebirth, but it was the beginning of the end of one of the most musically scintillating collaborations in modern New Orleans music.

Ruffins took a big chance by choosing to position his solo act in the traditional jazz genre. He was the first young player to prove a living could be made playing age-old sounds and singing venerable old chestnuts. The move, while clearly not eagerly anticipated by fans of the Rebirth, eventually created a demand for traditional jazz that continues to develop well into the 21st century. There are currently over a dozen neo-trad acts playing in New Orleans and a whole slew of new players mining the same musical territory.

With the early success of Kermit Ruffins' solo career, another brass band trumpeter began experimenting with leading a traditional New Orleans jazz band. Mervin Campbell was the trumpeter for the Soul Rebels when he began booking gigs as Kid Merv and All That Jazz. Like Ruffins, he tested the waters with low-key, neighborhood gigs at joints like the Little People's Place. He often hired Jerry Anderson on drums. He was mining the same basic territory as Ruffins and was doing so with his own elegant style. Campbell had a lighter, breathier tone than Ruffins and a better singing voice. He quickly became a welcome new addition to the growing ranks of young men playing traditional jazz.

On June 23, 1993, The Rebirth Brass Band celebrated their tenth anniversary with a parade through the Tremé. As one of the hardest working bands in the city, they decided not to play at their own party. The Little Rascals and the New Birth Brass Bands provided the entertainment, and Kermit Ruffins drove his pickup the entire length of the parade while friends and family danced in the bed of the truck.

Later that summer, Ruffins began a regular Monday night gig at Russell's Cool Spot, the old Petroleum Lounge. On July 12, his current bassist, Kevin Morris, performed with Ruffins for the first time. The venerable bassist Richard Payne, who had been playing occasionally with Ruffins, was on the gig, but everyone noticed the instant rapport between Morris, Ruffins and the drummer Jerry Anderson. The trombonist Corey Henry, who was leading the Little Rascals Brass Band at the time, sat in as did the trombonist Eddie Boh and James Andrews. Morris, Anderson and Henry eventually formed the core of Ruffins' solo act, the Barbecue Swingers.

Most of the small clubs where Ruffins was playing at the time did not have a piano, but when one was available, Thaddeus Richard, a veteran player, or Dwight Fitch, a young up-and-coming musician, typically played. His longtime pianist, Emile Vignette, was active on the jazz scene, and when he joined the band the first incarnation of Kermit Ruffins and the Barbecue Swingers was established.

In November 1993, the Tremé Music Hall, a new venue located catty-corner from Joe's Cozy Corner at the intersection of N. Robertson and Ursulines, hosted Kermit Ruffins and his solo project. The place was unlike anything the neighborhood had seen in many years. The pristine building was completely renovated. Ruffins encouraged me to check it out at a Rebirth gig by saying, "The bathrooms are so clean you could eat off the floor."

However, it didn't stay that way. During the club's short existence, it hosted numerous shows by Ruffins, Shannon Powell (when he was not touring with Harry Connick, Jr.) and the Rebirth (the photograph on the album cover for Rebirth's last Rounder recording, *Rollin,'* was shot there). It was a pristine oasis in the middle of the ghetto, but hooligans soon began defacing the club, destroying the new fixtures in the bathrooms and essentially running it into the ground. The Tremé Music Hall closed after a police raid netted dozens of handguns and drugs.

As Ruffins was digging deeper and deeper into traditional jazz, his change in musical direction began affecting his fans. The crowd at the recently opened Palm Court Jazz Café on Decatur

Street in the French Quarter began changing to reflect a younger and more local clientele. One of the best bands playing there regularly during this period was the Humphrey Brothers, Percy on trumpet and Willie on clarinet. The old cats sure could play. The inherent musicality in their playing and their near-telepathic rapport was clearly something younger musicians sought to emulate.

One particular evening in November 1993, Ruffins closed down an evening at the Palm Court that began with the Humphrey Brothers. It was the best showing thus far of his fledgling solo career. He had Shannon Powell, Richard Payne, and Thaddeus Richard in the band, but the highlight was the inclusion of Danny Barker on the set. He sang four songs while playing guitar and then played banjo for the rest of the show.

In January 1993, Kermit Ruffins played a one-off gig at a ramshackle joint called Vaughan's deep in the Bywater neighborhood. Within the year, he was playing there every Thursday night—a tradition that continues to this day.

Current visitors to the city and newer residents would have a hard time imagining the bar as it was configured in the early days of Ruffins' tenure. The band still sets up in the same basic spot, but the space has more than doubled in size after an extensive renovation during which they knocked down a wall and moved the bar to the far edge of the building.

In those early days, the dance floor was a long narrow corridor alongside the bar. The only spot where you could really see the band, since they were not set up on a stage, was right smack in front of them or in a tiny corner at the near end of the bar. But the lack of adequate space didn't deter Ruffins' fans, and the place quickly became an underground hot spot. Due to neighborhood concerns, they rarely advertised the gigs. It was another major scene that literally developed on a need-to-know basis. The bar was just too small to handle any significant crowds.

Despite all the factors that would seemingly be against its success, Thursday nights at Vaughan's became a must-see event for locals and visitors alike. And considering Ruffins' success since those early days, it's certainly a testament to his skills as an entertainer and to the acumen of Cindy Wood and Big Chris, the proprietors, that little about the vibe as changed.

There has been a cover charge since 1996, and the music no longer starts well after 11 PM. However, Ruffins still cooks outside on his grill, and Big Chris still serves free beans on the break, but most importantly, the freewheeling musical attitude that defines Ruffins' career remains fully intact. Musicians have always felt welcome at the bar, and Ruffins is never one to suggest that someone may not have the skills to sit in with his crack band. Over the years, young up-and-coming musicians from the brass band and modern jazz scenes have tested their chops in cutting contests with Ruffins and the members of his band.

Dozens of high profile guests have also made appearances at the tiny club. Harry Connick, Jr., at the height of his fame, showed up with a couple of the guys from his band right as the Barbecue Swingers were about to take a break. Connick took over the piano, and his bassist spelled Kevin Morris. They played for a good twenty minutes while Ruffins watched with a bemused look on his face. Meanwhile Big Chris Songy, who couldn't care less about big stars, put out his pots as scheduled. It was rather incongruous to see the regulars chowing down on beans and rice oblivious to the star turn that was occurring. Connick, having been schooled as a young piano phenom by James Booker, is just as down home as Ruffins. On the break, he helped himself to a piece of chicken off of Ruffins' grill and stood halfway in the middle of Dauphine Street sucking the meat off the bone.

Chuck Badie, the venerable bassist, lived in the Ninth Ward before Hurricane Katrina. Vaughan's was on his way home from his regular Thursday night gig, and he would invariably stop in for a nightcap and a brief sit-in. Sometimes, when he was in the mood, he would literally take over the band calling tunes and directing solos. One particular night after the show had technically ended, he performed a vocal duet with Ruffins on James Moody's "Moody's Mood for Love" as Jerry Anderson was packing up his drums. Though not really a singer, Badie cracked up the remaining regulars, including Ruffins who nearly busted a gut, with his gruff vocals and well placed asides.

In January 1998, another venerable elder of the New Orleans community made an appearance at Vaughan's. Big Chief Donald Harrison's love of jazz was instilled in his son, Donald, Jr., from an early age and the elder Harrison helped develop his son's unique jazz-Mardi Gras Indian hybrid. His appearance on the corner of Dauphine and Lesseps caused quite a stir.

Before the show began, Ruffins, Shannon Powell and Jerry Anderson gathered outside the club and led a large group who sang backup for the big chief on his signature tune, "Shallow Water." Though no one had a tambourine much less a microphone, the group clapped and drummed Indian beats on the outside of the backstage door while Harrison beamed with pride and pleasure.

Harrison hung out all night and witnessed one of Ruffins' classic musical free-for-alls. There were four trombones on the tiny bandstand most of the night. The traditional jazz trumpeter, Leroy Jones, and the madcap German saxophonist, Martin Krusche, sat in. Chuck Badie sang scat vocals as if possessed by the spirit of Satchmo. Big Chief Donald Harrison, still glowing, reprised his performance in front of the full audience. They ate it up and cheered lustily for the old chief.

Henri Smith, a deejay on WWOZ, began doing introductions of the band, and eventually he was singing with them as well. He honed his talent playing in front of the crowd at Vaughan's and became a performer in his own right. Smith was hardly the first or last performer who got a career assist from performing with the Barbecue Swingers at Vaughan's. Among the young musicians who were beginning to appear on the scene was a vivacious vocalist named Samirah Evans who hailed from the Midwest.

By the spring of 1994 she started playing gigs of her own. She performed on April 8th at the Dragon's Den with another musician relatively new to town. Matt Perrine played upright bass with the guitarist Anthony Brown, but he soon became an in-demand player on the sousaphone. He is now one of the stalwarts of the local scene. Evans left town some months after Hurricane Katrina.

Numerous stars including Wynton Marsalis and the trombonist Greg Boyer from George Clinton's various aggregations have sat in at the Bywater club. Local players like the drummers Shannon Powell and Herlin Riley, the trombonist Delfeayo Marsalis, and the trumpeter Irvin Mayfield were all regulars in the later years. For a period, a Jewish rabbi who played a tiny horn called a pocket trumpet was a welcome guest.

In April 1999 Vaughan's reopened with a full renovation. The capacity of the dance floor increased, but so did the size of the audience as more and more people discovered the hidden Ninth Ward gem and crowded up close to the band.

Thursday nights at Vaughan's became part of the itinerary of the savvy music tourist. The down home scene and winning vibe was being celebrated all across the international media. The music was classic New Orleans, and there were ample opportunities for photographers to capture the irrepressible Ruffins manning his barbecue pit and playing his horn.

In November 1999 the acclaimed director Bob Mugge was in town shooting a documentary to be titled, "Rhythm 'N' Bayous: A Road Map to Louisiana Music." Vaughan's was one of the chosen locations for a performance by Kermit Ruffins and the Barbecue Swingers. But Mugge and his crew seemed to think that the singular vibe in Vaughan's needed tweaking. He tried to change the atmosphere of the evening by altering the set up in the club. After waiting until just before the band hit the stage to bring out the release forms for them to sign, one of his lackeys attempted to put a rope in front of the dance floor to keep people away from the band and to facilitate the shoot. Another big delay ensued as Ruffins and many in the crowd objected to this imposition of external values. It was hard to understand how this well-regarded director and chronicler of roots music would even consider attempting to change one of the most salient features of a performance by the Barbecue Swingers at Vaughan's—the crowd is practically on top of the band and everyone likes it that way. Some outsiders, even an ethnomusicologist as well respected as Mugge, just don't get it.

It's been said that nothing stays the same. Incredibly, more than ten years later, Vaughan's remains a New Orleans icon. The cover charge has gone up; the personnel in Ruffins' band have changed. Emile Vignette never returned to New Orleans after Hurricane Katrina and passed away in December 2011. Richard Knox eventually took over the piano bench. Corey Henry now plays trombone with the Rebirth Brass Band. But the wonderfully inviting vibe, laid-back attitude, and even the free food still help tourists understand just how special New Orleans really is.

As late as 1993 Ruffins was still playing most of the high profile gigs with the Rebirth Brass Band, and one particular show at the Jazz Fest warrants recounting. The second weekend of the Jazz Fest in 1993 was a wet one, which pleased the die-hards to no end because it kept the rookies and tourists away. There was mud everywhere and a whole slew of shows had to be cut short when a massive lightning storm hit the area on Saturday.

The organizers of the festival still didn't know on which stage to put the hot sound of the Rebirth. Inexplicably, they were scheduled to close the usually sit-down jazz tent on Saturday. A young percussionist from New Orleans, Scott Messersmith, was helping to drive the band with his searing conga playing along with the snare drummer, Ajay Mallory. They were tearing the roof off the proverbial sucker. The drums had the crowd going wild, and the ushers had given up trying to keep people from dancing in the aisles when the sound was suddenly cut. No one in the tent, including the members of the band, knew how bad the storm was raging outside, and a riot nearly broke out since the sound was cut long before the set was scheduled to end. Of course, the Rebirth doesn't need a sound system, and they just kept playing to the crowd's delight until they were actually ordered off the stage. It was later confirmed that the authorities were trying to empty the entire Fairgrounds before someone got hit by lightning.

Messersmith was all over the Fairgrounds and in various clubs all week long. He sat in with a couple of Mardi Gras Indian tribes in addition to performing with the Rebirth. He returns from his home in Colorado nearly every Jazz Fest to play with his local favorites.

When the Rebirth Brass Band played at the New Orleans Jazz and Heritage Festival in 1994, it was the first time without their irrepressible co-leader, Kermit Ruffins. He was slowly easing his way out of the band, and in August he announced his official departure from the group. Kenneth Terry, a trumpeter with the New Birth, took over fronting the band. With Ruffins officially out of the band, he needed to generate more income with his solo act. That meant more gigs.

Toward the end of 1994, a chef from Chicago and schoolteacher from Florida opened Donna's Bar and Grill on Rampart Street just across the street from the entrance to Armstrong Park. In the early days, they served Charlie Sims' fabulous food to small crowds being entertained by young musicians who usually played on the streets of the French Quarter. That group of players included at least one, the modern day bluesman Corey Harris, who has become a nationally known recording artist and received a coveted McArthur Foundation "genius" grant in 2007.

Harris was just beginning his transition from street performer to stage act. His time in New Orleans was critical to his musical development, and each local performance seemed to add depth presaging his widespread critical acclaim, particularly when he began experimenting with the lap steel guitar and Caribbean rhythms.

Donna's didn't really find its niche until they began hosting performances by the growing coterie of brass bands in the city. Donna's made the transition into the informal "brass band headquarters" when Sims, Donna's partner in business and life, was working his day job as a chef for Amtrak on the "City of New Orleans" train between Chicago and the Crescent City. He met the members of the Tremé Brass Band on the train and invited them to sample his fabulous cuisine at Donna's, which was then fashioned as more of a restaurant than a nightclub.

When Kermit Ruffins and the Barbecue Swingers began a long-standing Monday night gig at Donna's a year later, the club was officially on the map. On May 1, between Jazz Fest weekends in 1995, Ruffins played his first Monday night at the friendly club on the cusp of the Tremé and the French Quarter.

Because of the laid-back vibe and inviting atmosphere of Donna's, many elder statesmen of the brass band community gravitated to the intimate club. Ruffins gave them stage time and continued to develop strong relationships that further influenced his new career direction. Primary among them was "Uncle" Lionel Batiste. Batiste is a wisp of a man who plays bass drum for the Tremé Brass Band and is an irrepressible personality with a penchant for dark glasses at night and dapper suits that recall an earlier era. His nickname comes from the fact that everyone knows him, and since he can't possibly remember all the names, he simply calls his many younger friends "nephew" or "niece."

Batiste became a regular, entertaining everyone with tall tales of gentlemanly conquest and *sotto voce* fables of life in the old Tremé. During the second set of Ruffins' first show at the club, he decided it was time to perform, but without his bass drum he was forced to improvise. Batiste headed into the kitchen and came out with a stack of pots and pans, which he painstakingly assembled on the floor in front of the band. After getting his set up just right, he pulled a pair of spoons from some hidden pocket and began playing this makeshift percussion kit while on his knees. Everyone in the place began cracking up at what initially appeared to be part of a comedy routine. However, Batiste is a talented percussionist, and after a minute or so the band realized he was serious. Without the aid of a microphone, he proceeded to take an amazing solo on the pots and pans. After a song or two, he picked up the kitchen equipment, took a small bow and headed back to his beer at the bar. He performed the same musical stunt a few more times at both Donna's and Vaughan's, and it was never reduced to shtick. It was just the fun-loving, musical nature of the man on display.

Another veteran from another genre, the legendary R&B shouter Ernie K-Doe, also appeared several times at Donna's during Ruffins' regular Monday night shows. One particular performance stands out. K-Doe was known during his prime as one of the most charismatic performers supposedly rivaling James Brown, but it had been decades since he hit such heights of personality. He had become a parody of himself given to verbose claims of greatness and haranguing his audiences with shouts of, "Let me hear you say K-Doe" over and over. However, once he got sober his career took another turn.

It was late in the evening during the third set, and there couldn't have been more than ten patrons in the bar when K-Doe strolled through the door. The stars must have been completely aligned on this night because K-Doe sang three songs and perfectly channeled his youthful self. I remember thinking to myself, so that's what he was like as a young man. It was an over-the-top performance with not a hint of self-consciousness—he felt it as well, and the tiny crowd rewarded him with a huge ovation.

It wasn't just veterans who were regular guests at Donna's on Monday nights. Delfeayo Marsalis played many nights on trombone (he was also a regular at Vaughan's) especially before Corey Henry had solidified his role as Ruffins' on-stage foil. One particular Saturday night in March 1994, before Ruffins began the regular Monday night gig, Delfeayo had in tow his younger brother, Jason, who was still in high school. Jason played drums on a couple of songs before Delfeayo took him home on the break. It was clear even then that Jason was going to become a musical force to be reckoned with. Delfeayo turned right around and made it back for the second set.

After Jason Marsalis graduated from high school, he began gigging much more around town while studying jazz at Loyola and Southern Universities. He played regularly with Ruffins and also showed up occasionally just to jam. At a show in February 1997 at the Dragon's Den, he arrived towards the end of the night after playing another gig. He joined Derrick Freeman, the regular drummer that night, on an amazing two-man drum solo that lasted for close to 40 minutes. They played together on the single drum kit by repeatedly trading seats and sticks. They must have switched places at least four times without missing a beat. Ruffins was long gone and the whole duet took place while Kevin Morris and Emile Vignette carefully packed up their equipment. The two drummers were still at it when the bassist and pianist eventually walked out the door and down the winding staircase to Esplanade Avenue. A handful of people stuck around just to watch the two young musicians experimenting with the music.

Irvin Mayfield was another high schooler who began sitting in with Ruffins at Donna's. He was making impressive progress on the trumpet, and they held good-natured cutting contests every time Mayfield showed up at the club. Their friendly rivalry peaked once Mayfield had his own band, and the two trumpeters began staging battles between the two bands.

A Ruffins gig in those days meant any number of players sitting in. Anthony "Tuba Fats" Lacen, an icon among French Quarter street musicians, played regularly on his namesake instrument. Leonard Blair, a stylish saxophonist who relocated to Europe in the late 1990s, could be counted on to play and sing the standard, "Don't Get Around Much Anymore." A Japanese banjoist named Hiro, a regular with Tuba Fats in Jackson Square, sat in fairly regularly as well. Members of the Dirty Dozen, Little Rascals and the Rebirth were usually in close proximity as were older musicians such as the two brilliant saxophonists, Elliot "Stackman" Callier and Frederick "Shep" Shepard.

Shepard and Callier were the saxophonists in the Tremé Brass Band. They were also veterans of Fats Domino's band. The Tremé Brass Band released a great record in 1996 with both James Andrews and Kermit Ruffins taking star turns on the traditional material as well as the now-classic title cut, "Gimme My Money Back."

In the summer, Vaughan's got a piano, opening the door for Emile Vignette to join the Barbecue Swingers. But for the time being, various piano players sat in including Henry Butler, when he was in town, and Willie Metcalf as well as Ruffins' regular pianists at clubs with a piano, the aforementioned Thaddeus Richard and Dwight Fitch.

Gigs at Donna's were some of the most laid back in the city. Jam sessions and guest musicians were always welcome. Before they moved the stage, the band set up in the back of the room, and the free-for-all atmosphere was clearly impacted because you literally had to walk through the band to get to the facilities. Free food on the break added to the family vibe.

One night in particular illustrates the wonderful camaraderie and *joie de vivre* evident at nearly every one of Ruffins' gigs at Donna's. Irvin Mayfield played piano the whole night. Late in the second set, everybody switched instruments. Ruffins played the drums while the drummer played the piano. Corey Henry handed his trombone to Kevin Morris who gave up his bass to Mayfield. Mayfield even took a shot on the trombone. Amazingly, they sounded fairly decent, and the packed house ate it up.

Another local luminary who popped into Donna's regularly was the renegade Mardi Gras Indian, Tyrone Miller. He is widely known as "the baddest Indian who never sewed a suit." Miller is immortalized in Ruffins' song, "What Is New Orleans?" When Miller arrived at

Donna's, the place was very likely to turn into an informal Indian practice. Miller would take over the bandstand and sing lead on various Mardi Gras Indian songs. His gravelly voice was entirely captivating, and he could cast a spell over both the audience and the band. Everyone would sing the refrains while Corey Henry or one of the other musicians used the kitchen's service bell as added percussion.

While Monday nights at Donna's became a regular gig for Ruffins, he still spent plenty of time performing at other clubs. In April 1995 a young drummer from Texas who was studying music in New Orleans made his first appearance with Ruffins' at Little People's Place. Derrick Freeman eventually became Ruffins' regular drummer. He didn't swing in the old school style like Jerry Anderson, but he played with a powerful sense of groove and his good-natured personality fit quite well with the rest of the band.

Halfway through Freeman's first gig, Ruffins disappeared briefly and then returned with one of the most humorous props to grace any stage, anywhere. The song "If You're a Viper" was a standard part of his solo repertoire, and as he sang the first line of the song, "Dream about a reefer five foot long…," he pulled a five-foot long joint from behind his back. Everyone in the place nearly busted a gut laughing, and Ruffins got the same response when he pulled the same stunt a month later in front of thousands of people at the Jazz Fest.

The Little People's Place continued to be Ruffins' main base of operations during this period. It's where he hung out and held court with his many friends and where he first conceived of his solo project. But the same insidious forces of gentrification that had doomed other neighborhood joints threatened the tiny bar. As incredulous as it seems, outsiders moved onto a thriving block in the middle of one of the most vibrant musical communities in the world and then decided that the bar, which had been in business since the 1940s, had to cease all live music operations.

With the help of some pro bono work on the part of a lawyer named Billy Geary, the club was able to slow down the shifting demographic in the neighborhood. Several stories chronicling the case were featured on the cover of the *Louisiana Weekly* (full disclosure—written by me), and stories also appeared in other local publications. After a bitter battle complete with police actions and restraining orders, the bar was able to continue business, but Ruffins stopped playing there regularly as soon as his solo career began to take off. The place was just too small. Today, it opens periodically as a stop for second line parades in the Tremé.

By the mid-1990s, Ruffins was fully settled into his solo career. He had steady gigs, but he still yearned for more fun and for more musical exploration—the two hallmarks of his personality. Besides being strongly influenced by Louis Armstrong, the trumpeter began digging heavily into the work of Cab Calloway, and he regularly watched videos of the two jazz icons. What first just seemed to be a lot of talk became a reality when Ruffins debuted his big band on a Sunday afternoon at the 1993 Jazz Fest.

On February 11, 1996, Ruffins performed with his big band at the House of Blues for the first time. The band included the cream of the crop of young Tremé talent including Corey Henry and Charles Taylor. The pianist Willie Metcalf and the guitarist Bert Cotton were also in the band. The trumpeter Irvin Mayfield, who was developing into a formidable talent, took the podium and conducted his own arrangements, and Ruffins' wife at the time even added to the fun with a sweet, if a bit giggly, backing vocal on "Moody's Mood For Love".

Ruffins' big band experiment was a brilliant idea, and the band itself was very different from both the Rebirth and his solo project, the Barbecue Swingers. The loose, laid back vibe was put on the back shelf, except for the leader's effervescent personality, in favor of strong arrangements (many by the great maestro, Wardell Quezergue), well-articulated solos and great ensemble work. The big band went through numerous personnel changes and played on and off for a few years. But sadly, like so many big bands, it was doomed by economics. It just isn't feasible to earn enough to pay fifteen or more musicians in a band that only works sporadically.

For about six months in 1996, the vacant lot on the corner of St. Philip and N. Robertson Streets in the Tremé neighborhood became a part of the Ruffins experience. He would invite the crowd at Donna's on Monday night to join him the following afternoon. He brought his barbecue rig (conveniently mounted in the bed of his pickup truck) and his horn to "the lot" on Tuesdays, and an informal jam session would materialize out of the musical ether of the Tremé.

Though the scene with Ruffins didn't last long, "the lot" has remained a geographic touchstone in the Tremé. In the first decade of the 21st century a neighborhood group purchased it with the expressed purpose of preserving the space from development. It is called "Tuba Square" in honor of the great Anthony "Tuba Fats" Lacen—one of the stalwarts of the traditional jazz community.

In 1997, Joe Glaser of Joe's Cozy Corner, which was only a block from "the lot," started presenting more live music. Kermit Ruffins began experimenting again by collaborating with different musicians at the Tremé club. He formed a progressive jazz band with Michael Ward (the violinist, not the percussionist), Chris Severin, Henry Butler, Shannon Powell, and Percy Williams, his uncle, on congas and flugelhorn. The band was amazing. Ward, who later started playing smooth jazz, screamed out lines on his violin as Butler and Powell roared away. The music wasn't progressive jazz per se. For example, they played Stevie Wonder's "Isn't She Lovely." But it was definitely not the Barbecue Swingers. The progressive jazz band played a few more times before Ruffins abandoned the experiment.

On New Year's Eve in 1997, Tipitina's opened a location in the French Quarter. Ruffins began playing the Sunday jazz brunch, and the management began trying to lure him into playing a weekly nighttime gig. The effort paid off, and on June 29, 1998, he played his final Monday date at Donna's.

It was a bittersweet night. Despite all of the raucous behavior, over-the-top special guests and incredible musicianship that occurred over the course of four years of Mondays, the night was uneventful. It was as if Ruffins and his band, all of the regulars as well as Donna and Charlie Sims knew that a move of some sort was inevitable given Ruffins' rising star as a solo act and personality. The good times on Rampart Street had passed us by as if in a dream.

The following Monday, July 6, Kermit Ruffins and the Barbecue Swingers made their debut at Tipitina's French Quarter. Ruffins had Delfeayo Marsalis on trombone since Corey Henry was out of town with another band. The show began with his usual opening songs, "Chicken and Dumplings" and "Monday Date," and Shannon Powell sat in on one tune. They tried in vain to recreate the singular atmosphere at Donna's, but as I noted in my journal at the time, "(It was) a good time, but a far cry from Donna's."

The decision by Ruffins to abandon his longtime Monday night gig at Donna's in favor of Tipitina's was one he must have briefly regretted. By the beginning of December, his Monday night tenure at Tipitina's French Quarter was over. It lasted less than six months. In a strange twist of fate for the trumpet-playing marijuana advocate, the district attorney, a vocalist named Harry Connick, Sr., replaced him.

Without the Monday night gig, Ruffins began looking for new places to play. A long-standing Wednesday night gig at Le Bon Temp Roule in uptown New Orleans began after a one-off gig at the bar in 1999. Le Bon Temp Roule attracted a different crowd than either of the two downtown clubs, Donna's and Vaughan's, where Ruffins performed regularly. A whole new generation of uptown students from both Tulane and Loyola were exposed to the swinging version of jazz Ruffins had perfected. The nights on Magazine Street were the setting for some of the most compelling performances from a group clearly hitting its stride.

During the first Mardi Gras show at the new spot, Ruffins and company played "The Mardi Gras Mambo" three times on one night including a fascinating instrumental version of the classic Carnival song. In April, the trumpeter Irvin Mayfield, who had released his first solo disc the previous year on Basin Street Records, showed up at Le Bon Temp Roule. As his career heated up, he was no longer a regular guest at Ruffins' shows, so the appearance was surprising. However, Ruffins and Mayfield had something else in mind. They staged a brawl for a hired photographer with the intent of hyping an upcoming Battle of the Bands between the two trumpeters' outfits. Though the staged fight was designed as a public relations ploy, the Battle of the Bands was a great concept. The two bands set up on stage at the same time and alternated tunes.

Ruffins' tenure at Le Bon Temp Roule extended for nearly four years, and over that period a scene connected directly to his other longstanding gigs at Donna's and Vaughan's gradually emerged. There was a steady parade of special guests and a regular crowd.

A new trend emerged in early 2000. At the end of each set, Ruffins encouraged the young women in the crowd to get up on the bar and dance. It was yet another example of the trumpeter's ability to interact with his audience and helped cement his reputation as the leader of the neo-traditional jazz scene in New Orleans.

While Ruffins was cultivating an audience geared more towards having a good time, dancing and partying, many of the musicians in his orbit were serious young players intent on developing their talents in a setting distinctly different from the classroom or sit-down jazz clubs like Snug Harbor or Sweet Lorraine's. With Ruffins laid back approach to special guests, he never told *anyone* they couldn't sit in, and with the less-than-rapt attention of his dancing audience, shows at Le Bon Temp Roule and Vaughan's were the perfect setting for young musicians to test their chops. Over the years, many of them have carved out careers for themselves both in New Orleans and across the country.

There have been some personnel changes in the Barbecue Swingers since those heady days at the start of the new century. Kevin Morris has played an electric bass since Hurricane Katrina. There are new songs in the repertoire and new faces in the crowd. But for the most part, going to a performance by Kermit Ruffins and the Barbecue Swingers remains exactly what it was when he first became a solo artist—a singular, quintessential New Orleans experience that hasn't changed very much at all. He has become a world-renowned ambassador without sacrificing an iota of his personality, musical style or street credibility.

Chapter 11

THE RISE OF FRENCHMEN STREET

"After silence that which comes nearest to expressing the inexpressible is music."—Aldous Huxley

Sometime in the early weeks of 1986, after Tipitina's grand reopening, another club with less lofty ambitions quietly opened on the corner of Frenchmen and Chartres Streets in the Faubourg Marigny. Café Brasil began as a space sporadically presenting "art, music, theater and espresso."

One of the first high profile gigs held at the new club was a Carnival ball performance by the Samba Devils, though curiously it was held the week after Mardi Gras in 1986. That was the beginning of a long string of Brazilian and Brazilian-inspired bands to appear at the club. By the end of the year, Curtis Pierre had started his longstanding group, Casa Samba, and Café Brasil became a significant part of a burgeoning scene on Frenchmen Street.

Café Brasil built up its business and significance organically. The Brazilian owner, Ade, spent little time on issues like schedules or listings and booked his friends and neighbors to perform. The club became popular because of its location amid a neighborhood of similarly minded musicians.

Occasionally, Café Brasil hosted high profile gigs including a benefit show for WWOZ on December 27, 1991. The modern jazz saxophonist and New Orleans Center for Creative Arts graduate Donald Harrison, Jr. had been making waves all over the country

189

along with the other young lions, a group including Wynton and Branford Marsalis among others. He played with Art Blakey and the Jazz Messengers, had an acclaimed band with the trumpeter Terence Blanchard and was developing his own conceptualization of jazz.

His father, Donald Harrison, Sr., was a well-respected Mardi Gras Indian chief who, after stints in other tribes, began leading his own gang, the Guardians of the Flame. Harrison, Jr. began forging a synthesis between modern jazz and the music of the Mardi Gras Indians. The two men and their distinctive musical styles came together that evening. The Indian tribe performed first, and Harrison, Jr. played his alto horn over the ancient rhythms of the Mardi Gras Indians. Then James Singleton and Johnny Vidacovich, the rhythm section for Astral Project, backed up Harrison, Jr. on a jazz set. Finally, Kermit Ruffins, Nicholas Payton, and the Marsalis brothers, Delfeayo and Jason, joined in for a spirited second set.

Harrison, Jr. codified his new musical concept in a landmark album, *Indian Blues*, which was released that year. It featured his father on vocals and a great modern jazz band including Carl Allen on drums and Cyrus Chestnut on piano. Dr. John added his voice, piano and star power to a couple of tracks. The recently reissued record is a must-have for anyone interested in understanding this fascinating blend of genres that could only have been born in New Orleans.

However, during this early period most of the shows at Café Brasil were decidedly low key. After a set at Snug Harbor in 1992, I stumbled upon a very informal jam session that eventually morphed into one of the longest running bands to get its start in the early days of this new scene on Frenchmen Street. A trio was playing Yiddish folk songs to a small crowd. It was Jonathan Freilich on guitar, Arthur Kastler on bass and Ben Schenck on clarinet, and I was witnessing the earliest incarnation of the New Orleans Klezmer Allstars who were billing themselves as the Allstar Klezmer Band. Schenck and Freilich moved to New Orleans in 1988 and 1989 respectively. Kastler is a local.

When I saw them a few months later, they had augmented the band with an accordion player and a saxophonist, and they were playing at Tipitina's. I thought it was a quick ascent to the top of the club heap for a brand new band, and then I noticed "Mean" Willie Green playing drums. His playing, honed over the years laying down the beat for the Neville Brothers, allowed the Klezmer Allstars to blend a variety of sounds into a musical mélange. I have often argued that the Klezmers are really a jazz band playing folk music, and once the multi-reedist Robert Wagner replaced Schenck in the band, it became a truism among jazz music lovers. Wagner put aside his swaggering, muscular style on saxophone replacing it with intricately winding clarinet lines when he performed with the Yiddish band. My feeling is you can dance the hora all night long, but those are jazz solos on every tune.

By the beginning of 1993, the new band was quickly becoming the talk of the town. Their inspired set later that year at the Jazz Fest, again with Green on drums, solidified their standing as the hottest new act in town. Their set was on the Fais Do Do stage in the middle of the day on the second Friday. The grass out front was overwhelmingly crowded as people streamed in from other parts of the Fairgrounds drawn by Green's relentless beat and the pied piper clarinet work of Ben Schenck. They were mentioned in nearly every publication as the "find" of the fest. By the end of the year, the Klezmer Allstars were drawing huge crowds attracted to their danceable grooves, good time attitude and jazzy solos.

In early June, the Klezmer Allstars played to a sparse crowd on a hot Saturday night at Tipitina's. The place was mostly empty with just a handful of fans of the young band. A large group of people entered the bar and headed straight for the dance floor. It was the actress Julia Roberts and her entourage. They easily doubled the number of people in the bar.

Though most of the intimate crowd of friends of the band recognized her as she had been in town for some time shooting "The Pelican Brief," everyone ignored her in true New Orleans style and allowed her the elusive freedom of feigned anonymity. After a few songs, her entire group was sweating profusely and dancing vigorously to the infectious sounds of the Klezmers. A song or two later, she sent one of her flacks towards the front to ask me a question— who is that awesome drummer? When I passed on the word that he plays with the Neville Brothers, they doubled the intensity of the dance.

The group lasted about an hour until, nearing the end of the set, a young woman in the crowd broke the spell by walking up to Roberts and asking for an autograph. Literally dripping with sweat, she scowled, turned away and within seconds they were gone. I found out later that Roberts had heard the Klezmers the night before at Café Brasil where they had been playing a 7 PM early gig, and she decided to come back for more. She also met Lyle Lovett that night and began her short-lived love affair with the odd-looking country star.

Due to the success of the early gig at Café Brasil, which helped launch the New Orleans Klezmer Allstars, Ade began adding other early shows most of which featured young jazz players studying at the local universities. Musicians such as the bassist Neal Caine and the saxophonist Ian McPhail were regulars, so the musical stew heating up on Frenchmen Street gained fresh ingredients.

Across the street from Café Brasil, the Dream Palace, which had gone through numerous ownership and management changes along with dark periods, emerged as Café Istanbul in April 1991. The new ownership began booking bands including a talented New Orleanian, Blake Amos, who had spent some time in Brazil and was writing and playing music that mined both locales for inspiration. He quickly became a favorite on the scene because of his ability to intuitively connect the two places. He often had the great improvisational saxophonist Tim Green in his band.

When Checkpoint Charlie opened on the corner of Decatur and Esplanade, there were four clubs presenting live music in close proximity and the Frenchmen Street scene was now booming. The new downtown nexus for the next generation of hep cats was completed when Kaldi's, a coffee shop with a decidedly bohemian vibe, opened on Decatur and Ursulines Street in the lower French Quarter and the Dragon's Den opened above a Thai restaurant on Esplanade Avenue.

Ben Schenck began playing at Kaldi's on a regular basis at the end of 1991. He was also playing with Kermit Ruffins at the Little People's Place. Kaldi's became a crucial hangout and venue for a whole new group of young musicians including the alto saxophonist Wes Anderson and the gypsy jazz guitarist Tony Green. It's important to note at this point that there were very few clarinetists working outside of the traditional jazz scene in New Orleans. Though most of the brass bands throughout the history of the genre featured the keening sound of the clarinet, neither the Dirty Dozen, the Rebirth nor any of the younger bands included the instrument. Schenck, with his impossibly tall frame and pied-piper persona, affected everyone on the nascent scene's perception of the instrument. Within a short period, the New Orleans Klezmer Allstars began playing steady gigs as a trio at Kaldi's.

Kaldi's was also a spot to catch up-and-coming jazz musicians from UNO and other universities as well as younger players in a variety of styles. Modern jazz musicians like the adventurous multi-reed man Rob Wagner, who eventually replaced Schenck in the Klezmer Allstars, and the saxophonist Brice Winston, who has forged a successful career performing with Terence Blanchard, gigged there. The bassist and the guitarist of the gospel band the Friendly Travelers, Cornell Williams and Derwin "Big D" Perkins, were regulars too. They became the rhythm section of Jon Cleary's Absolute Monster Gentlemen.

Nicholas Payton, a trumpet prodigy with a serious New Orleans pedigree, began showing up at Kaldi's instantly boosting the coffee shop's profile among the young jazz players. His father, Walter, was a highly regarded bassist before his passing in October 2010. Nicholas would often play piano, amazing the older patrons and players with his chops on his *second* instrument. Everyone already knew he was a great trumpeter. Payton released his major label debut, *From This Moment*, on Verve Records, in 1994. That same year, Payton teamed up with the octogenarian trumpeter Doc Cheatham on a sweetly swinging album, *Doc Cheatham and Nicholas Payton,* which also came out on Verve.

Curiously, despite a long career in jazz, Cheatham hadn't been back to New Orleans since he played with Cab Calloway as a young man. He was a gentle soul who was quickly welcomed into the jazz scene in New Orleans. He performed numerous times in New Orleans with local backing bands and was a regular at a series of benefits for the school band at Lafayette Elementary School.

The first incarnation of the Storyville Club on Decatur Street didn't attract many local music lovers. But when new owners took over in 1992 the booking policy changed dramatically, and it became a new hot spot adding to the musical allure of the neighborhood. It is now the location of Jimmy Buffett's Margaritaville. One of the first shows presented by the new management that helped put the Storyville Club on the local radar was Little Village, a supergroup featuring Ry Cooder, John Hiatt, Nick Lowe, and Jim Keltner. The subdudes and a new band, the Observers, led by Rickie Castrillo (the Master of Ceremonies at Tipitina's), were the opening acts. Four years later, Tommy Malone of the subdudes fronted another band that paid homage to Little Village. They were called Tiny Town.

On the walk between Kaldi's and Frenchmen Street all styles of music could be heard emanating from Checkpoint Charlie. In 1992 a new band, Irene and the Mikes, began tearing it up at the 24-hour club. The group's sound featured songs from the 1960s as well as blues standards. Irene Sage was a compelling presence with a ballsy voice. For a time she was the heir-apparent of roots-rockin' New Orleans bands fronted by women. Unfortunately, Irene and the Mikes were never able to achieve long term cohesiveness and they eventually disbanded after numerous personnel changes. Sage and Mike Darby, the band's guitarist, still perform occasionally as solo acts and supporting players.

There were so many great shows and musical interactions during this period in the lower French Quarter and along Frenchmen Street that it would be impossible to relate them all. However, one night illustrating the connection between these clubs and the musicians, stands out. The subdudes were playing the Krewe of MOMs Halloween Ball at Storyville. On the set break, all four members of the band walked down into the Marigny, jumped on stage and played two tunes with Tribe Nunzio at Café Brasil. Of course, a small group of fans followed them.

The scene on Frenchmen Street was positively electric with hundreds of people milling around in extravagant costumes. It's been said that New Orleans is the ultimate adult destination for Halloween, but it wasn't always that way. That night back in 1992 was the beginning of a new era with respect to adult costuming and revelry on Halloween.

After the subdudes jammed with the Tribe, we followed them back to Storyville where the party was in full swing, and no one could believe the jam we had just witnessed at Café Brasil. It was just another example of the wonderful musical cross-pollination that occurs in the clubs of New Orleans. The best thing about it was that the musicians were totally nonchalant as if to reinforce the notion that this happens all the time around here.

To continue the saga of the development of Frenchmen Street into the arts district it is today, I need to introduce some new characters. The nouveau funk outfit Smilin' Myron began gigging around town in the fall of 1989, and I saw them for the first time in March at the TGIF Party on Tulane's campus. The band's guitarist was Sam Hotchkiss and the drummer was Andreas Argenti. Both are still active on the scene today. An early component of the second wave of New Orleans funk bands, their sound clearly demonstrated they were direct musical descendents of the Meters. Smilin' Myron also featured Kirk Branch, a funky bassist in the mode of George Porter, Jr. and Tim Guarisco on second guitar. In my estimation, the only problem was their percussion player who was clearly the weakest musician on stage that afternoon. I found out later that his name was Michael Skinkus. He is now one of the most respected percussionists in the city and has appeared with the best musicians playing in a mind-bending array of bands in every style imaginable.

Two Swedes, the guitarist/singer/songwriter Anders Osborne and the violinist/ singer/songwriter Theresa Andersson, relocated to New Orleans while they were still teenagers. After a period in the trenches, they began playing together around town. As luck would have it, two new clubs opened in 1991: Checkpoint Charlie (on the corner of Esplanade Avenue and Frenchmen Street at the edge of the French Quarter and the Faubourg Marigny) and Vic's Kangaroo Café (located on Tchoupitoulas Street in the Warehouse District). The couple became regulars at the two clubs in late 1991. They played an early evening gig on Sundays at Vic's' and a regular hours gig on Tuesdays at Checkpoint Charlie. They quickly earned a small but dedicated following because of Osborne's incredible ability to write songs that sounded like they were written by a Southern rocker rather than a blond-haired Swede.

His searing slide guitar work along with Andersson's fetching good looks and ethereal backing vocals were also part of the appeal. The fact that they were lovers created a wonderful vibe on stage. Once she pulled out the violin, all the music freaks in town were astounded by the inherent musicality of the duo.

Osborne's career took off early in 1992 when he won two contests, WWL-TV's Jazz Search and the Abita Beer/*Offbeat* magazine's open blues jam. The Jazz Search victory earned him his first slot at the Jazz Fest. He also released his first album credited to the Anders Osborne Orchestra, *Doin' Fine*, which came out on the local Rabadash label. Over the course of the rest of the decade, Osborne's life resembled the proverbial rollercoaster. He had some well-documented battles with substance abuse, and his relationship with Andersson ended.

Osborne drastically changed the sound of his band when he enlisted the sousaphonist Kirk Joseph, the drummer Kevin O'Day and the saxophonist Tim Green, along with an adventurous trombonist and composer named Mark McGrain who had moved to town from Boston. Osborne's songwriting skills were always among the best, but his music became considerably more jazz-oriented with long, winding solos and a much sharper edge to the sound. McGrain began playing around town with a wide range of players. Ed Volker, the Radiators keyboardist, entered into another prolific period of solo gigs, and he hired McGrain and Michael Skinkus to flesh out some of his tunes that didn't fit with the Radiators' repertoire. McGrain also began picking up jazz gigs with his band, Plunge, and also as the Mark McGrain Ensemble. He hired the cream of the local jazz scene including Johnny Vidacovich, James Singleton and Charlie Miller for gigs at Snug Harbor. The songs were dynamic with super strong soloing throughout the set.

One night at the Mermaid Lounge, McGrain, Kirk Joseph, Michael Skinkus and a tabla player named Andrew McLean played a mesmerizing purely improvised show. The four musicians had no set list and no actual songs, yet they were able to create a broad palette of sound highlighting their disparate and varied musical interests

In more recent years, Anders Osborne has become one of the most acclaimed songwriters of his generation. His work has been recorded by major country acts including "Watch the Wind Blow By" that was a huge hit for Tim McGraw.

Andersson has also prospered since their breakup, although it took her longer to find her direction. She began playing mostly jazz on her solo gigs, and she hired first class talent from the young cohort of jazz players emerging on the scene. She also began playing in the rock setting with members of the downtown scene at Checkpoint Charlie. She played with a band billed as the New Orleans Supergroup that included Mike Darby, the guitarist from Irene and the Mikes, Dee J, the singer for the Flavor Kings, Alex McMurray, Carlo Nuccio, and a trumpeter/singer named Boo Lacrosse.

On one particular night, they jammed until the wee-wee hours. Andersson began the evening playing acoustic guitar, then she strapped on Darby's Stratocaster and ripped on the electric guitar late in the show. Up until that point, she had not played much guitar on stage, although the instrument is a standard part of her arsenal today. Her style continued to evolve through different musical phases before settling into her current act. A fascinating solo performer, Andersson plays every musical part—guitar, fiddle, voices and percussion—and builds up a song by using multiple effects she manipulates with her feet.

Mike Ward was a percussionist and raconteur who played with a wide range of acts culminating in the biggest stages in the world when he went on tour with Harry Connick, Jr. His first advertised gigs in New Orleans were with Charmaine Neville and Ron Cuccia's jazz-poetry ensemble. But he also played with a number of other local acts including the Rebirth Brass Band and John Mooney. His powerful conga playing and natural rapport with Russell Batiste defined his work with Neville at Snug Harbor and at Benny's. Ward had a charismatic personality. He was charming and people naturally gravitated to him. When Daryl Johnson lost his gig with the Neville Brothers, and his two short-lived bands, Trouble and Sahib, disappeared, he hooked up with Ward to form Mike Ward and Reward.

The first time I saw the band perform was at Tipitina's in January 1991. The group included Oliver "Lee Lee" Alcorn on drums and the vocalist Theryl DeClouet, mostly known at that time for his band,

Reel Life, who always turned in high energy sets at the Jazz Fest. The band's songs were tight, modern-day funk reflecting the hard times of New Orleans' ghetto living with titles like "Pocket Change," as in, "I ain't got no…" and "Ain't No Yachts in the Ghetto."

Mike Ward and Reward became a proving ground and incubator of young talent, and a number of first-rate players matriculated through Ward's band including the guitarists Alex McMurray, Jonathan Freilich and Mike Napolitano as well as the bassist Jimmy Ives. Though Ward is recognized for his role in the music community during this period, the gigs were often slapdash affairs as the personnel in the band were constantly in flux. The best way to hear the great music of Reward is on DeClouet's first solo album, *The Houseman Cometh*.

The band played a prominent role in what is arguably one of the wildest, longest days and nights of music I have ever seen. The concert, which took place late in 1992 at the Storyville Club, was billed as the Funk-A-Thon. It was an all-day, all-night affair and featured an incredible array of talent as a benefit for the then-fledgling NO AIDS Task Force. The Contenders with the TKO Horns—a group including members of Walter "Wolfman" Washington's horn section, followed a couple of opening acts that I missed. Next came some brilliant sets by Washington and his band, Carl LeBlanc, the Observers, Smilin' Myron and the legendary producer Daniel Lanois, with Daryl Johnson on bass and congas, before the main act hit the stage. Robbie Robertson, the leader of The Band, had recently recorded his *Storyville* album in New Orleans with local musicians, and he appeared with Mike Ward and Reward as his backing band. Jonathan Freilich was playing guitar. Big Chiefs Monk Boudreaux and Bo Dollis joined them in full Indian suits. Leo Nocentelli played a little guitar before retreating. The whole set ended with a massive Mardi Gras Indian jam. The night itself ended after Renard Poché's new band, Poché, tried gamely to keep the energy going. But it was 3:30 in the morning and most everyone was worn out from thirteen straight hours of hard New Orleans funk.

The Vince Berman Trio was the first local band for the guitarist Alex McMurray, the rakish singer-songwriter who later formed Royal Fingerbowl and has been a stalwart on the scene since his first forays into the musical waters while he was still a student at Tulane. Perhaps it was an early example of McMurray's wry and sardonic sense of humor, but the group wasn't a trio and there was no one named Vince Berman in the band. McMurray had also worked in a reggae band, Crucial Roots, and other groups including the afore-mentioned Reward. He has a wicked sense of humor and an equally wicked technique on the electric guitar

Davis Rogan, one of the musicians who first began working with Kermit Ruffins on his solo act, began putting together a project of his own in 1995. He had been working diligently on his piano play-ing and was developing some skill on the Hammond B-3 organ. He was also progressing as a songwriter. Rogan assembled a first class group of musicians including McMurray who had moved on from the Vince Berman Trio. He also recruited Kirk Joseph, late of the Dirty Dozen, Keith "Wolf" Anderson, late of both the Rebirth and the Dirty Dozen, Brice Miller, a talented trumpeter from another New Orleans musical family and the leader of the Mahogany Brass Band and Kevin O'Day, a young drummer still studying with Johnny Vidacovich at Loyola University. I first saw All That perform at Café Brasil on April 4, 1995.

Sitting in that night with Rogan and company was a young saxo-phonist, Ben Ellman who, having played with the little Rascals Brass Band as well as other downtown musicians including early versions of the New Orleans Klezmer Allstars, eventually joined Galactic. The group had great potential, and Rogan's ability to recruit such first class talent, particularly Joseph, a musician with a growing legend among the cognoscenti, was impressive.

All That mixed up genres. Rogan's love of hip-hop and his liter-ate sense of word play combined with an acerbic wit formed the foundation of their lyrics. The music was straight from the Sixth Ward with a fat dose of Meters-esque funk. The horn section got even fatter when they added Doug Miller on baritone saxophone. The band resembled the Dirty Dozen with Joseph's percolating sou-saphone providing a strong bottom end buttressed by Miller's sax work, which resembled that of Roger Lewis in the Dozen. But that is where any and all comparisons end. All That was truly original and represented a new direction in New Orleans music.

In the rockin' setting of All That, McMurray perfected the role of the screaming lead guitarist that worked so well with Reward and other funk bands. His pyrotechnics mirrored the work of Leo Nocentelli and other funk guitarists with stunning runs designed to keep the crowd moving. His histrionics matched the frenzy of the rest of the band.

At the 1996 WTUL Rock On Survival Marathon, Tulane University's sorely missed fundraising concert weekend, McMurray's over-the-top performance was a defining moment in All That's career. At the conclusion of an amazing set featuring members of the Rebirth as guest rappers, McMurray stripped down to his boxer shorts and proceeded to jump off the four-foot high stage while still playing his guitar. With the rest of the band laughing hysterically at his antics, he took a wicked solo in the front of the stage, threw his guitar on the ground and then theatrically bowed to his instrument as it lay on the grass feeding back through the massive PA system.

Because of a variety of factors, including myriad personnel changes over the years, All That existed for a relatively short span. Rogan's difficulties managing such a large and diverse group of musicians were reflected in his songs. One notes that 58 musicians played in All That, and another includes a hilarious mix of answering machine messages during which various musicians explain why they can or cannot make a specific gig. All That released three albums including their tour-de-force, *The Whop Bam Boom*, which appeared on Rounder Records and was produced by the prolific Scott Billington. Though short-lived, the band successfully changed the face of New Orleans music and opened the door for other like-minded groups blending brass, funk and hip-hop.

Two members of the local music cognoscenti, David Kunian and Patricia Gorman, came up with the rather interesting concept that all of the young musicians in the fertile downtown scene were actually members of one very large band that simply broke up into smaller groups for nightly gigs. Though the concept was likely just Kunian's and Gorman's humorous take on the ever-shifting personnel in All That, there was a grain of truth to the idea as dozens of extremely talented musicians, all friends and in many cases interchangeable within the individual groups, were now performing in a huge range of genres. For example, the New Orleans Klezmer Allstars included Glenn Hartman, on accordion, who played with McMurray in the Vince Berman Trio. Hartman eventually joined Anders Osborne's band on keys. Stanton Moore, Galactic's drummer, played regularly with the Klezmer Allstars. Ben Ellman, who eventually joined Galactic, also played in the Klezmer Allstars. He was an old friend of the guitarist Jonathan Freilich who led the Klezmers but also played in a considerably more avant-garde style with his groups, Naked on the Floor and Mutiny.

Incidentally, in the late 1990s Freilich began branching out and extending his creative vision. He formed the first avant-garde big band in the modern history of New Orleans. The Naked Orchestra featured nineteen musicians including most of the stalwarts of the downtown scene. Their music, complete with written parts and Jimbo Walsh conducting, set a new standard for composing and exposed hardy listeners to a compelling personal conceptualization of music.

The clarinetist Ben Schenck formed his own band, the Panorama Jazz Band. They continue to play on Frenchmen Street to this day and have greatly expanded their repertoire to include folk music from across the globe.

An older percussionist from Cuba named Hector Gallardo was an influential figure to the band. Many forays onto Frenchmen Street during this period would find Gallardo and Michael Skinkus playing hand drums on the sidewalk in front of Café Brasil. Having played with virtually everyone on the fertile Frenchmen Street scene from jazz artists like James Singleton and Steve Masakowski to more traditional Latin bands, Gallardo's influence on the New Orleans music scene cannot be underestimated.

When the great Cuban bassist, Israel "Cachao" Lopez, was scheduled to perform twice in New Orleans in June 1995, world music fans all over town were atwitter. Along with Skinkus, Gallardo and his regular band members, Lopez performed at the Hyatt Regency to a rather staid crowd. The following Sunday was an entirely different experience when he performed at the Reggae Riddums Festival in City Park. He played the same basic set, but at the outdoor festival the energy was intensified. The band was tighter and hundreds of people danced to the compelling Cuban rhythms. The visit by Cachao set the stage in New Orleans for a Cuban music craze that continued for many years.

Mas Mamones was another new band that formed around this time. They featured a much-improved Michael Skinkus on percussion, Jonathan Freilich on guitar, Kufaru Mouton, a percussionist of some renown who played trap drums in this band, a singer named Manny Lander, as well as Robert Wagner. A flutist and saxophonist named Hart McNee, who was a mentor to the younger musicians, was also in the band. Mas Mamones was playing Cuban music primarily focusing on the mambos, cha-cha-chas and boogaloos of Havana in the 1940s and 1950s.

For many of the musicians on the scene, playing in multiple bands helped their pocketbooks and their chops. Mas Mamones remained a minor act on the scene, but their bassist, Andy Wolf, and O'Day of All That joined forces around this time with McMurray to form his own band, Royal Fingerbowl. McMurray played two disparate roles in both All That and Royal Fingerbowl. With the Fingerbowl, his work as a bandleader and songwriter was more stripped down and led to comparisons to Tom Waits. However, he was never afraid to let a guitar solo rip even in the trio setting of Royal Fingerbowl.

McMurray played sitting down with Royal Fingerbowl, and he developed a guitar technique that resembled no one as much as Snooks Eaglin. He played chords and then quickly let loose a lead run before going back to a more rhythmic style to accompany his gruff, matter-of-fact vocals. Wolf and O'Day were the perfect rhythm section. They could veer into jazz territory often creating a tin pan alley-style musical palette that matched McMurray's fleshed out vision of his songs. With the Fingerbowl, all of the music served the songs, and all three musicians regularly modulated the tempo and the tension/release dynamic with gifted aplomb.

McMurray's songs ranged from darkly colored ballads to weirdly orchestrated rave-ups. O'Day brought a jazz sensibility tempered with big rock fills to the proceedings while Wolf exuded confident, yet brooding sensuality. They were an awesome band from the moment they began playing together. Royal Fingerbowl actually played a lot of covers in the early days, but they were often unusual choices reflecting the band's collective sense of humor; e.g. Wolf taking a vocal turn on Merle Travis' 1947 comic gem, "Smoke! Smoke! Smoke! (That Cigarette)," or McMurray turning the gender sensibility of Madonna's "Like A Virgin" inside out.

I had a piece on Royal Fingerbowl published in Tower Records' *Pulse!* magazine saying, in part, "Royal Fingerbowl pushes the twin envelopes of genre and farce. McMurray's songs are vignettes peopled with characters that would be unsettling in the bleakest film noir or in the fiction of Raymond Carver or Henry Miller… they are laden with forthright pathos and tempered with mundane sophistication."

Royal Fingerbowl played nearly a year of early afternoon gigs at Margaritaville, but the Dragon's Den was their home base and a scene quickly developed around the new band. Two young women paraded around with antique cigarette trays suspended around their waists and gave away butts. McMurray threw cigarettes to the crowd. Every show featured an "interpretive dance contest" with the band wailing away on the most aggressive jazz-rock riffs while encouraging members of the audience to hit the dance floor like maniacs.

As the band's popularity developed, so did their twisted sense of humor. Though known for their late night performances, Royal Fingerbowl was booked at 11:15 AM on the second Saturday of the 1997 New Orleans Jazz and Heritage Festival. Looking like they had barely gotten any sleep, they launched into a twisted version of "Oh What A Beautiful Morning" to start the set. They also played a new song listing all of the problems with the bathrooms in the downtown bars with the refrain, "Hey Man, It's Time to Start Dealing With Your Can."

A music fanatic named "Beatle" Bob Matonis, a festival regular who dresses like the early Beatles, was dancing his bizarre, herky-jerky style on stage during their set. He revels in his ability to get back stage and eventually on stage, and his ubiquity at the Fairgrounds left many in the audience bewildered about his growing celebrity. He was even featured in an article in *USA Today*. At the time, the crowds seemed to be evenly divided between those who loved his antics and those who despised his presence.

So a year later, Royal Fingerbowl decided to push the envelope of farce even further. Unbeknownst to all in the audience, they formed an alliance with the odd-dancing, retro-dressed super fan and set up one of the most humorous incidents to ever occur on a stage at the Jazz Fest. During an interview on WWOZ that aired in the days leading up to the Jazz Fest, the band suggested there existed an anti-Beatle Bob contingent and that his life might be in danger. At the conclusion of their performance, they orchestrated the assassination of Beatle Bob.

The scene was played out with some delicious details. Andy Wolf, the bassist, confronted Beatle Bob, who was on the side of the stage, over the microphone and accused him of distracting the audience with his ridiculous dancing. Wolf then pulled out a mock pistol and fired three shots. Beatle Bob fell onto the stage, and a team of "medics" rushed to his rescue, loaded him onto a gurney and carried him off stage. Meanwhile, a "police officer" "arrested" Wolf and even cuffed him on stage. Diehard fans of the Fingerbowl were practically falling over with laughter. Unbelievably, some people in the audience didn't realize that the scene was an elaborate joke playing off both the band's penchant for erudite humor and Beatle Bob's rapidly developing cult of personality.

McMurray's wonderfully twisted songs led Royal Fingerbowl on a meteoric rise, but their descent was just as swift. In the fall of 1996, Royal Fingerbowl announced that a major label, TVT Records, had signed them. The band was absolutely on fire at the time playing crazy, late night sets to small, but adoring crowds. The musical creativity was peaking, and the group even joined forces with members of the Klezmer Allstars and All That to perform a version of "Willie Wonka and the Chocolate Factory" complete with actual dialogue from the film. There was hope in the air for breakout success for a band that had barely made a mark locally. After the deal was announced, the group embarked on one of the most brutal tours ever devised playing 24 shows all over the East Coast in 26 days. It was simultaneously the beginning of the end and the end of the beginning for Royal Fingerbowl. The trio suffered through nearly a month of being paid poorly to play poorly attended gigs in dive bars while sleeping in fleabag motels far from home.

Kevin O'Day played his last gig with the band at the Dragon's Den on January 9, 1998. It was a crazy, whacked out gig from the first notes. During the interpretive dance contest, as the band wailed away on "Oh What a Beautiful Morning," one of the dancers crashed into Alex McMurray's guitar. Perhaps in reference to O'Day's eminent exit from the band, they did a bizarre cover version of Sonny Bono's "The Beat Goes On." Royal Fingerbowl roared through three sets until 3:45 AM when O'Day went into Keith Moon mode. He ripped his drum kit apart, kicked the bass drum over and had to be restrained from breaking the mirror behind the bandstand when he started swinging his high hat stand over his head.

Although O'Day insisted to the media that he simply wanted to devote his time to other musical interests, the display was clearly the result of two years of pent up frustration that saw the band on the brink of national stardom only to have the whole affair come crashing down like a fledgling chick too soon from the nest. Carlo Nuccio replaced O'Day in the band, and Wolf quit soon after and was replaced by Matt Perrine. After two albums that sold poorly (the label had no idea how to market McMurray's mad genius) and the defection of O'Day and Wolf, the band was finished.

Curiously, O'Day continued to regularly sit in with the group, and each instance reminded me of what might have been. While Nuccio is an accomplished musician who also plays guitar and writes his own quirky originals, his drum work never had the nuance necessary to recreate the Fingerbowl's jazz sensibility. He sounded fine on the rocking numbers but left large holes in the ballads. The second version of the group has reunited occasionally.

In 1994, another great scene materialized at Café Brasil. A great Brazilian band called Banda Logun played nearly every Thursday at the Frenchmen Street club. Banda Logun's membership continuously fluctuated, and regulars in the Marigny neighborhood such as Manny Landers and Kenny Claiborne often joined in with the Brazilian percussion section. But the main draw of Banda Logun was a beguiling singer and guitarist named Angela Patua. She played frenetically on acoustic guitar and sang wonderful songs in Portuguese. She left the city, and the magical nights at Café Brasil were left to other performers.

In December 1995, another new band that garnered great attention for their blend of hip-hop, rock and avant-garde jazz made their debut. Iris May Tango was named after a newspaper headline referencing the possible convergence of two tropical storms in the Atlantic. The metaphor perfectly suited the band's conflagration of styles.

Two singer/rappers with hard to decipher nicknames, Yours Truly Chaddy-1-P.U.S. and Keng, fronted the band. Keng had a crazy three-foot hairdo, and Chaddy had a muscular, imposing physique that belied his gentle singing style. They had a decidedly hip-hop stage presence as they sang and rapped quirky songs including one called "Hairdo" that became a cult hit around town.

The band represented the cream of the crop of the next generation of downtown hipsters playing music without regard to any expectations. Kevin O'Day and Andy Wolf were the rhythm section. Robert Wagner played keyboards and saxophones, sometimes at the same time. An edgy guitarist named Rene Duffourc rounded out the group.

Shows by Iris May Tango were free-for-alls. When they played at the Dragon's Den, Wolf, showing a different side of his musical personality as an electric bassist, sometimes climbed the railing surrounding the smallish band space and played atop a two-by-four. The rappers occasionally confronted the audience with faux machismo, a different approach from the usual laid-back style of rapport in New Orleans, and the crowds loved it. Iris May Tango quickly became the latest sensation.

In the late 1970s and early 1980s, there were two clubs in what the city calls the Frenchmen Street Arts and Cultural District. Now, even on a slow night in the middle of the week, the four-block stretch teems with energy and music that rivals Bourbon Street in its 1950s heyday. Though the street is no longer a musical incubator—the hipster elite bemoans the economic gentrification and musical stultification—it is a must-see destination for music-savvy visitors to New Orleans. But during the 1990s, a new generation of downtown musicians centered on Frenchmen Street, nearly all of them members of the "one band that breaks up into smaller bands on a nightly basis," was driving the direction of New Orleans music.

Chapter 12

JAZZ STUDIES AND STREET SMARTS

"Music and thinking are so much alike. In fact you could say music is another way of thinking, or maybe thinking is another kind of music."—
Ursula K. Le Guin

❦

The success of the Neville Brothers throughout the 1980s was driving national and international interest in New Orleans funk and soul. The new music on Frenchmen Street remained a best-kept secret for locals and insiders as visitors flocked to Tipitina's to bow down at the altar of the patron saint, Professor Longhair, whose bust graced the entrance of the uptown club.

However, in New York and in the jazz press, acoustic New Orleans jazz was coming into focus again after years of jazz fusion and smooth jazz dominating the market. The young lions of jazz, led by Wynton and Branford Marsalis, Terence Blanchard and Donald Harrison, Jr. were raising the profile of the city on the national scene with intriguing music and the occasional brash statement. By the early 1990s, the four were settling into their own careers, and any visit home was a significant occasion. Wynton and Harrison, Jr. also began embracing the deep well of New Orleans music and the street culture of the city.

Donald Harrison, Jr. released *Indian Blues*, his landmark synthesis of modern jazz, Mardi Gras Indian percussion and call-and-response vocals that featured his father, the revered Mardi Gras Indian big chief.

Marsalis hired Herlin Riley, a drummer with deep roots in the Lastie family of New Orleans traditional jazz players, to replace Jeff "Tain" Watts. Riley is four years older than Wynton and had already been a member of Ahmad Jamal's trio from 1984 through 1987 when he joined Marsalis' group. His rhythmic gifts rooted in gospel music and the streets of New Orleans added another dimension to Wynton's sound especially on the three-volume series, *Soul Gestures in Southern Blue,* and his defining effort, *Majesty of the Blues.*

When Marsalis returned to New Orleans in the fall of 1991, it was his first date in the city with Herlin Riley on drums. They played at Tulane University's McAlister Auditorium. The performance was a tour-de-force due in part to Riley's amazing ability to synthesize musical styles. After starting the set with the modern jazz that defined the earliest part of his career, Marsalis and the band cut loose on the blues. At the end of the performance, they dipped into the *Soul Gestures in Southern Blue* catalog. Riley started "Uptown Ruler," the title cut of Vol. 2, with a Mardi Gras Indian war cry and a shot to his tambourine. The song and the show ended with the entire septet chanting "Hey Pocky Way" until the song faded out accompanied only by Riley's solo tambourine. It was a powerful, mesmerizing display of musical genius that continued to be a part of Marsalis' act until he disbanded that particular group in 1994.

Despite the success of the young lions and the steady stream of talent matriculating through the New Orleans Center for the Creative Arts (NOCCA), the New Orleans Public Schools system's crown jewel program, many people were still dissatisfied with the state of education in the city. Ellis Marsalis, the patriarch of the family as well as one of the city's most important music educators, gave an interview before he left the city in 1986 for a one-year fellowship at Virginia Commonwealth University. He felt the public schools were failing the children. One year away stretched into two, and his decision to leave New Orleans became a wake up call for the music community. Questions were bantered back and forth. How could we have allowed such a significant musician and teacher to leave the city? Why do we continue to take our most important artists for granted? Incidentally, despite Marsalis' opinion, the New Orleans Public Schools actually had a strong record of music education going back decades. He was protesting more recent decisions that reflected financial issues.

Ellis Marsalis returned to New Orleans in the fall of 1988. He was hired to start the Jazz Studies program at the University of New Orleans, thus beginning a new era in music education. A year later, Harold Battiste was recruited to join his old running partner from the late 1950s modern jazz scene after a highly successful stint in Los Angeles. Battiste worked on a number of high profile projects in California including serving as the musical director for the Sonny and Cher show, and he produced Mac Rebennack's first album as Dr. John. After more than twenty years on the west coast, he was the final ingredient in the new jazz program that grew under their leadership to become one of the best college jazz programs in the United States.

Within two years of the formation of the jazz program, the clubs of New Orleans were filled with students who studied under Marsalis and his ace staff during the day and experienced the real life of a jazz musician by night. It is impossible to overrate the significance of Marsalis' return and the influence the program has had on the development of the jazz scene in New Orleans to this day.

The University of New Orleans began showcasing student talent in a Wednesday series at the Sandbar on UNO's campus. The format in the early years had student combos playing first and then their teachers would join them. As the program got more successful, they began bringing in big name jazz stars to mentor the students. Ellis Marsalis and Harold Battiste occasionally performed together. One memorable evening at the Sandbar, they played an incredibly tasteful piano-sax duet that demonstrated their exceptional skill level and technique. The faculty improved immeasurably in November 1990 when the saxophonist Victor Goines signed on.

The national economy began a long period of resurgence at the end of the 1980s, and this upbeat mood was reflected in New Orleans as well. UNO and the other local colleges began attracting first-rate students from across the country, enhancing their status among the best places in the world to study jazz.

Wynton Marsalis was following in his father's footsteps and conducting student workshops while on the road. At a tour stop in St. Louis, he encountered a young trumpeter named Jeremy Davenport. They stayed in touch, and he encouraged Davenport to move to New Orleans and study with Ellis at UNO. Before Davenport even graduated, he was tapped by Harry Connick, Jr. to play in the piano player's hugely successful touring band. After completing four world tours with Connick, Davenport stepped out with a solo act. He released his first album on the well-respected Telarc label and played his first time as a leader at the Jazz Fest in 1997. He was 26 years old. He currently rules the roost at his namesake club in the Ritz-Carlton.

Loyola University was also ramping up its jazz studies program around this time. The faculty at Loyola was loaded with local talent including Astral Project's saxophonist Tony Dagradi, the guitarist Steve Masakowski and the drummer Johnny Vidacovich as well as other stalwarts from the modern jazz scene. The presence of these three players allowed the university to continue its development in jazz education. Dagradi is still at Loyola. Masakowski assumed the chair of the department at UNO after Ellis Marsalis retired.

In 1988, a drummer named Brian Blade moved to New Orleans to study at Loyola under the tutelage of Vidacovich. He became the first major jazz artist since the young lions of the early 1980s to emerge from the musical higher educational system in New Orleans. He is now among the most critically acclaimed and in-demand drummers in the world. Upon settling in New Orleans, Blade immediately dove into the scene. He has the deftest touch and an uncanny ability to feel the music and read other musicians. Those skills, though still developing, were evident the first time I saw him playing in the Earl Turbinton Trio in March 1990 at the Black Heritage Festival at the Audubon Zoo. James Singleton was the bass player.

For Harold Battiste, his homecoming was also a chance to revive his long-dormant record label, A.F.O. (All for One). The label is of extreme historical significance because it was one of the earliest attempts by African-American artists to control copyrights and means of production. A.F.O. had one giant hit, Barbara George's "I Know," and also released some of the only examples of late 1950s era modern jazz—New Orleans style. James Black, Ellis Marsalis and another great educator, the clarinetist Alvin Batiste, were part of the group of musicians recording under the A.F.O. umbrella.

Local tastemakers were also intrigued by the return of Battiste. In late August 1991, the wonderful New Orleans filmmaker, Jim Gabour, began his most ambitious project up until that point. He booked the brand new theater at the Contemporary Arts Center for an impressive video series he called "Music From New Orleans." He recorded Dr. John, Astral Project, Danny Barker and the Rebirth Brass Band.

But the show that stands out most in my memory was billed, "Harold Battiste with the A.F.O. Next Generation." The lineup of the band, in keeping with the pedagogical mission of A.F.O., was inter-generational. Faculty members, Victor Goines on saxophone and Ellis Marsalis on piano, joined Battiste. The rhythm section was two gifted students—Chris Thomas on bass and Brian Blade on drums. The show began with Marsalis and Battiste playing three duets. Then Tammy Lynn, the AFO vocalist and the only woman in the original organization, sang the blues. But it was Brian Blade who was the most impressive. His skills had grown considerably since I had seen him the previous summer, and it was even more obvious that he was going to be a major player in the jazz world.

Ironically, "The Music from New Orleans" series never aired. Hopefully, those tapes still exist because they would be a treasure trove for modern viewers.

The Jazz Studies programs continued to attract great talents drawn from the local pool as well as students from out of town. Another entire book could be written about all the players who matriculated through both programs throughout the1990s. I'll touch on a select group.

In mid-February 1995, the Donald Harrison Group performed at Snug Harbor. Harrison had three young musicians in his band—Victor Atkins on piano, Donald Edwards on drums and Roland Guerin on bass. They all went on to be major players on the scene. Harrison has continued the practice of hiring young musicians just like the legendary drummer Art Blakey, the first major performer who hired him.

The guitarist Todd Duke and the saxophonist John Ellis scored a major career coup when they were hired by the U.S. State Department for a tour of Africa following graduation. When they returned to New Orleans, Duke quickly became a significant part of the local scene. He is best known for his long tenure as John Boutte's bandleader. Ellis moved to New York where he has had a successful career as a solo artist as well as a sideman for the eight-string guitarist, Charlie Hunter. Educated by the trip to Africa, Duke and Ellis formed the New World Funk Ensemble around 1996 and set about creating a compelling original sound with other young players interested in exploring the deep connections between jazz and the various sounds of the African diaspora.

The first version of the band included Brian Seeger on guitar, Andrew Adair on piano, Karl Budo on drums, Michael Skinkus on percussion, Sam Price on bass and Loren Pickford on flute (he also plays saxophone, piano and sings). Pickford was the only veteran in the New World Funk Ensemble. He moved to the city in 1990 ending a peripatetic lifestyle that embodied the stereotypical notion of a beatnik musician.

Duke was also working in the jazz trio setting with two other young players, the drummer Geoff Clapp and the bassist Jason Stewart. Along with the pianists Andrew Adair, Charlie Dennard, who eventually replaced Adair in the New World Funk Ensemble, Glenn Patscha and Joshua Paxton, they represented the next wave of jazz players to invigorate the scene. Paxton did not play jazz exclusively. He also appeared regularly with Michael Ray, and the Wild Magnolias and is a disciple of James Booker.

Two short-lived funk bands were also active during this period, both of which would merely be footnotes in this tale except that their bassists eventually became key players on the scene. The Flavor Kings were the considerably more successful of the two outfits. Their bassist, Peter Harris, is now one of the A-list jazz players in town. Chunky the Most began gigging in 1996 at Café Brasil and the Maple Leaf. Their first bassist was Sam Price. Besides also working with the New World Funk Ensemble, he eventually went on to considerable local success with his Latin band, Otra!, as well as the roots rocking outfit, the Honey Island Swamp Band.

Charlie Dennard moved to New Orleans to study at UNO. He began gigging as a sideman almost immediately. By 1998, he was leading his own group, Five O'clock Charlie, which mined the jazz organ territory of the 1960s. Dennard has an uncanny ability to play the left hand side of the keyboard like a funk bassist. The way he used his pinky finger was mesmerizing. That single, least significant digit seemed to be working completely independently of the rest of his hand as if it had a mind of its own as he carved out bass lines that would have impressed George Porter, Jr.

Five O'clock Charlie shared membership with another new group which also became active around this time, Moore and More, a side project of Galactic's drummer, Stanton Moore. Though their memberships overlapped, both bands usually included Brian Seeger on guitar and Brent Rose on saxophone. It was a jazz-rooted band that gave Moore a chance to showcase his chops.

Dennard and Rose were also founding members of Quintology, a relatively short-lived band that formed when its members were students at UNO. The group also included the trumpeter Mark Rapp, the drummer Mark DiFlorio and the bassist Brady Kish. Quintology wrote original music and aspired to take a page from the career trajectory of Astral Project. Brian Seeger produced their first album and joined the band when Rapp left the city. The band produced their second album, *Blues for 5*, with Tim Green, but when Kish and DiFlorio moved on, the group gradually disbanded.

Dennard continued to play around town until he accepted a gig with Cirque du Soleil. He now travels the world as one of the musical directors of the acclaimed circus company. Rose and Seeger are still key elements of the thriving music scene in New Orleans. DiFlorio is an occasional visitor to the city.

In mid-October 1998, the Red Room, a swanky nightclub that opened on St. Charles Avenue a year earlier, hosted a tribute to Harold Battiste. It was one of those nights that featured young musicians and veterans. The clarinetist Alvin Batiste, one of Battiste's partners from the original A.F.O., led off the evening with a young band featuring the pianist Glenn Patcha, the bassist Roland Guerin, and the drummer Adonis Rose.

Dr. John followed with a rare solo performance. Between songs, he told a story about meeting Battiste in Los Angeles after being forced to relocate out of New Orleans because of running afoul of the local authorities too many times. Dr. John said, "At the time, all the cats were playing R&B and trying to learn jazz, Harold was playing jazz and trying to learn R&B."

Allen Toussaint followed with a short solo set before Nicholas Payton hit the stage with the same band as Alvin Batiste along with a brilliant young tenor saxophonist, Brice Winston, who was also studying in New Orleans. Winston has gone on to a successful career including a long tenure with Terence Blanchard. Payton was the most preternaturally gifted of the entire group of young players who studied at UNO. Reminiscing openly about Battiste, Payton said, "Harold is the only professor who gave me a 'D'. It was in music harmony—hopefully he'll see that I've improved."

I saw Guerin again when he performed at the Louisiana Music Factory to support his delightful debut album. He had perfected the slap bass style on his upright. Each performance was an opportunity to give the audience a lesson/demonstration on the history of that technique. I saw him again at Snug Harbor with a great band of young guns. Brice Winston was on saxophone, Geoff Clapp was on drums, and the rest of the front line was filled out with two other hot young horn players who were also emerging on the scene— Derek Douget on alto and Antonio Gambrell on trumpet.

While the jazz studies programs were churning out talent, they weren't the only proving grounds percolating with young gifted players. Ellis Marsalis famously said that in New Orleans the culture bubbles up from the street. Proving his point, new brass bands influenced by the success of the Rebirth Brass Band and the Soul Rebels began popping up in the Tremé and elsewhere across the city.

Two bands of high school students, the Looney Tunes and the Highsteppers, merged in 1995 and became the Hot 8 Brass Band. They burst on the scene with a tenacious energy that has allowed them to survive the deaths of four members and thrive in New Orleans. They first entered the consciousness of the second line community at a crowded event centered near Kemp's place at the corner of Lasalle and Washington Streets. The band had set up out of sight of the revelry on a side street near Shakespeare Park—the uptown epicenter of the brass band scene. At the perfect moment, they came charging across the grass with horns blaring and drums pounding.

It was a great entrance that had everyone immediately wondering about the band. They have been enthralling listeners ever since that day.

The Little Rascals Brass Band coalesced around two brilliant players, the trombonist Corey Henry and the alto saxophonist Charles Taylor. These two young talents were augmented by a rhythm section that practically grew up on the streets of the Sixth Ward, the sousaphonist Jeffery Hills and another pair of musicians from the gifted Andrews family, Eldridge on snare drum and Terrence on bass drum. The band also included Ezell "Money" Quinn and Dwon "Itchy" Scott on trumpets and Gregory Veals on trombone.

The Little Rascals suffered many of the same troubles inherent to inner city life that plagued the Hot 8 in their early years. By the time the Little Rascals released their first album in 2001, three of the founders of the band were dead.

Corey Henry comes from a traditional jazz family. His musical pedigree includes his uncle Benny Jones, the leader of the Tremé Brass Band, and his grandfather, the legendary Preservation Hall drummer, Chester Jones. Henry was preternaturally gifted on the horn at a very young age in the same mode as Derrick "Khabukey" Shezbie before him and Troy "Trombone Shorty" Andrews after him. Like so many in his large, extended family and other families from the musically rich Tremé community, he was soaking up the music at second line parades before he could walk. He gravitated to the trombone and was a quick study who mastered the "tailgating" style of the early jazz trombonists. Henry earned a spot in Kermit Ruffins' solo project while he continued to lead the Little Rascals. His potential as a soloist developed exponentially when he joined the Barbecue Swingers. When Henry closed his eyes, he seemed to be channeling the ancient musical spirits of New Orleans jazz. Ruffins soon took to calling his new musical foil "old man" despite the fact that Henry is ten years younger than Ruffins.

Charles Taylor was an equally gifted player who became known as "Alto" because he never went anywhere without his horn. His talent first became evident when he began showing up regularly at Ruffins' gigs where he would wait patiently to sit in with the band. Taylor was a humble, quiet person who rarely had much to say. But when he put the horn to his lips, his solos spoke volumes. He had a more modern sound than Henry and a rich, bright tone that belied his young age.

While Taylor and Henry played like older men, the rest of the Little Rascals were a bit raggedy in the early days. They began playing regularly at Kemp's and the Candlelight Lounge in the Tremé. An older relative actually suggested the name for the band because they sounded so rough. They garnered considerable attention literally because they were so loud.

The Little Rascals came out with a theme song, "Rascals Got Fire," that instantly captivated the Tremé community and the rest of the brass band musicians in the city. Though the members of the Little Rascals have moved on and rarely play under that moniker anymore, the song is now a brass band standard. Nearly every band playing the tune simply adjusts the refrain to feature their own name.

James Andrews and his younger brother, Troy "Trombone Shorty" Andrews, were also becoming more active with their own act, the Allstars Brass Band, which was also alternatively billed as the Trombone Shorty Brass Band. The group occasionally included another very young player, Travis Hill, who was one of Troy's childhood friends around the Tremé neighborhood. He was known as "Trumpet Black" and played quite well for a pre-teen. Sadly, he didn't escape the travails of the ghetto and spent years away from his horn before reemerging on the scene in 2012.

James Andrews is a gifted frontman who adopted the nickname "Satchmo of the Ghetto" in homage to the great Louis Armstrong and his Tremé neighborhood. His trumpet playing, like that of Ruffins and other players who sought to emulate the great Satchmo, has never reached the heights of talent of the legendary icon of the Crescent City, but Andrews is a strong soloist and is capable of delivering vocals in the same trademark rasp as Armstrong. His good-natured personality and strong musicianship made him a star on the scene at a very early age—but not as early as his younger brother.

Troy Andrews was toting a trombone to second line parades when he was four years old, and the trombone was longer than he was tall. He was also a regular at musical performances around the

Tremé. Never far from his trusty bicycle, he gravitated to parades and brass band performances as well as gigs of virtually every other musical style. His concentration as he listened to the music was eerie since he was such a young child. It is now clear that he was absorbing all the music around him and preparing himself to become an adult musician versed in every style from trad jazz to rock 'n' roll. Troy quickly became adept at all of the other instruments in a typical brass band except the saxophone. He still hasn't settled between trombone and trumpet. The Andrews brothers had a great gimmick that worked incredibly well at winning over fans when Troy was very young. Towards the end of a set, he made the rounds playing every instrument in the band. He played a bit on sousaphone, banged on the drums and played trombone and trumpet. It was an endearing piece of musical theater that grew tiring for the regulars but never failed to earn the band new listeners.

James Andrews was working nearly constantly during the mid-1990s. In addition to playing with his brother and occasionally with the Tremé Brass Band, he was also fronting the New Birth Brass Band.

By the late 1990s, yet another member of the Andrews' family musical dynasty began appearing on the scene playing second lines in the Tremé neighborhood and substituting in various brass bands. Glen David Andrews, a trombone player and vocalist, projected more of a carefree attitude about the music in the early days of his career. But he has developed into a charismatic frontman and talented trombonist with deep devotion to the traditions.

The New Birth included Tanio Hingle and Kerry "Fat Man" Hunter on bass drum and snare drum respectively, Stafford Agee and Reginald Steward on trombones, Derrick "Khabukey" Shezbie and Kenneth Terry on trumpets, and the irrepressible Kerwin "Fat" James, brother to Philip and Keith Frazier of the Rebirth, on sousaphone. The group of youngsters was hustling for gigs all the time while filling in for the Rebirth whenever they were touring.

It's actually funny looking back at the mid-1990s because the Rebirth was still on the road incessantly, especially during the summers, and the New Birth were ready substitutes. However, the switch was never advertised and many of their newer fans, and certainly all of the tourists who were flocking to the Maple Leaf and other clubs, never had a clue.

Though Rebirth was clearly the older, more talented ensemble, the New Birth could always hold their own primarily because of James' uncanny ability to sound like his older brother, Philip, and the thunderous combination of Hingle and Hunter on drums. Kenneth Terry, who eventually replaced Kermit Ruffins in the Rebirth, is a supremely talented trumpeter and vocalist in his own right. Hingle and Hunter also played in the New Orleans Nightcrawlers.

Over the years, the membership of the New Birth and the Rebirth overlapped considerably. In one curious case, during the summer of 1998, the conjoined world of the Rebirth and New Birth Brass Bands was turned upside down. Though there was always a lot of cross-membership in the two bands with musicians filling in or substituting for each other, a drastic change occurred overnight. The front lines of the two bands—saxophone, trombones and trumpets—switched places entirely.

Another new brass band also began playing around town during this period. The Coolbone Brass Band was led by trombonist Steven Johnson and featured three of his brothers. The group began playing traditional jazz and released their first recording, *Coolbone Swing Troupe,* independently. Like so many of their contemporaries, the group dabbled with hip-hop while playing traditional jazz. They dubbed their style "brass hop," quickly earned a deal with a major label, and released an adventurous recording centered on the infectious title cut and its telling chorus, "brass hop's for real."

The Paulin Brothers Brass Band was another group of young musicians who began playing more high profile gigs on the strength of their pedigree. Its leader, Ernest "Doc" Paulin, formed his first band in the 1920s and was well regarded for his ability to train youngsters in the tradition. His latest aggregation was loaded with his sons including Roderick Paulin of Rebirth fame. They performed a wonderful set in March 1998 at the Louisiana Music Factory. The leader, then a spry ninety years old, sang a dapper version of "When You're Smiling." Ernest "Doc" Paulin retired after the 2004 Jazz Fest and passed away in 2007, but his sons keep the torch burning.

The plethora of brass bands playing in New Orleans in the 1990s led to an enduring tradition. In 1992, The Krewe du Vieux, the irreverent Mardi Gras parading group, hired nearly every brass band in the city for their parade held two weeks before Mardi Gras. They had a huge blowout at the New Orleans Music Hall after the parade. Every brass band that marched was up on stage. It was a true testament to the growing size and musical prowess of the brass band community when nearly 100 musicians crowded the stage.

Talented musicians have also emerged from the gospel music scene in New Orleans. In 1994, Davell Crawford was beginning to come into his own as a charismatic performer and an idiosyncratic personality despite still being a teenager. He also had roots in the R&B world. His grandfather is the legendary singer "Sugarboy" Crawford. Davell was a child prodigy who amazed listeners with his stunning piano playing and compelling vocals. Like John Boutte, he was merging the secular and the sacred, often in the same performance. He could wail the blues or hit the heavens like a one-man gospel choir. At the Jazz Fest, he actually played with a huge choir, but he also often played solo piano or with small ensembles around town.

One story illustrates his volatile personality. At the Cutting Edge Music Conference's Pops Music Festival in Lafayette Square he began his performance by bemoaning the low fee he was earning. He then proceeded to introduce the missing members of his band who weren't there because he couldn't pay them. He called for a bassist from the audience and, amazingly, some guy got up to play. There was a small problem—he was a non-English speaking Russian! The show went on anyway with drummer Tony Dillon trying gamely to communicate with the bassist.

Crawford played a totally over the top set brimming with virtuosity on the keys and vocal pyrotechnics. When the stage announcer tried to cut him off since his time was up he shouted into the microphone, "I'm gonna sing for Jesus anyway," and he proceeded to launch into a spine-tingling version of "Amazing Grace." Davell Crawford has matured considerably since those days. He moved to New York after Katrina but still puts on incredible performances for the hometown crowd whenever he returns.

On September 1, 1997, Charles Dia Taylor, the brilliant young alto saxophonist known to all as "Alto," passed away in his sleep from complications related to asthma. At twenty-two, his talent was just beginning to bloom and his potential was unlimited. Had he lived, Taylor would surely have reached the pinnacle of a jazz musician. His talent was instantly evident to everyone who ever heard him whether as a sit-in with Kermit Ruffins, on gigs with the Little Rascals, or in Ruffins' big band where he was a featured soloist.

It was a very difficult loss for the Tremé community and his family. Most of the musicians in his orbit were profoundly affected by his death and went into a funk that lasted for months. On September 10, the Kermit Ruffins' Big Band played their first performance without Taylor.

The Little Rascals opened the show, and their entire set was a tribute to the fallen musician. Troy "Trombone Shorty" Andrews was playing tuba, and the trombonist, Gregory "Coon" Veals, led the band in an intense, cathartic jam that ended with everyone chanting "Alto, Alto" until they were hoarse. Less than a week later, during the Rebirth's regular Tuesday night gig at the Maple Leaf, the scene repeated itself at an even higher level of intensity. At the end of the first set, the Rebirth played a new tune inspired by Taylor. It was an extraordinary outpouring of emotions as the song ended with everyone chanting "We miss Alto" over and over. It was a heavy moment that deeply moved everyone in the club including numerous people who didn't even know Taylor.

I wrote these words as part of his obituary, which appeared on the front page of the Louisiana Weekly, "Charles Taylor still seemed a little unsure of his gifts. He was a humble musician who at times seemed just as amazed at the sounds coming out of his horn as those who were listening in awe." Though some might disagree, it would be fair to compare Taylor to Clifford Brown—another influential musician struck down at a young age.

His funeral was the saddest send-off that I have ever attended. The Little Rascals, young men supposedly hardened by life in the ghetto, were all in tears. Yet somehow they managed to play for their brother both in the Majestic Mortuary and for a short jazz funeral procession after the service. There was no police escort or parade permit, and the scene was positively heartbreaking with just a small group of mourners, his family and his band. Had he lived, even just to middle age, his funeral would have been a massive event with dignitaries paying their respects and the whole musical community in mourning.

Though the funeral itself was lightly attended, his extended musical family paid tribute later that night in a tradition that has existed since the dawn of the jazz age in the Tremé. A big parade started from "the lot" on the corner of St. Philip and N. Robertson Streets. Kermit Ruffins, with the barbecue pit still smoking in the bed of his pickup truck, provided light and security. The parade of a hundred or so Tremé residents and musicians wound around the neighborhood. It was a bittersweet scene that became even more moving when Ruffins joined in with the band and played a beautiful trumpet solo in tribute to Taylor.

Taylor was such a young man that he was basically unknown outside of the Tremé neighborhood when he died. He was never even recorded playing his horn, yet he left a legacy among those who knew him. The venerable arranger, Wardell Quezergue, was mightily impressed with his talents. He wrote specific parts for his alto horn when they worked together with Ruffins' big band. The Little Rascals recorded Taylor's composition, "Alto." They dedicated their first record to Taylor as well as to Ezell "Money" Quinn and Eldridge Andrews, his bandmates who followed him to the grave.

But perhaps the most significant dedication that best explains Taylor's talents to those who never heard him play came from Nicholas Payton, another young musician whose star was rising at the time. He wrote a moving tribute, "The Last Goodbye," that appeared on his album, *Payton's Place*. In the liner notes, the trumpeter wrote, "Charles Taylor was a talented alto saxophonist who died at the tender young age of twenty-two; God only knows what Charles might have done had he lived."

In New Orleans, music is life. Each generation feeds the next one. The children grow up and become the torchbearers. Though death is ever-present and the best musicians occasionally fall before their time, it cannot stop the endless stream of talent that bubbles up.

Some of the players chronicled in this chapter are world-class talents plying their art. Some are teachers instilling discipline and skills into the next generation to pass through the classrooms, clubs and cultural institutions of New Orleans. Others manage, like musicians from the beginning of time, to be both artists and mentors. They carry on a tradition that has helped New Orleans maintain its standing as the preeminent jazz city for over 100 years.

Chapter 13

JAZZ FUNERALS AND MARDI GRAS INDIANS

"We are the Indians of the nation, the whole wide creation, we won't bow down, on that dirty ground, because I love to call my Indian Red."— from the traditional Mardi Gras Indian song, "Indian Red"

Throughout this book, I have discussed musicians of many genres. Yet I have not touched enough on two of the most important components of the unique culture of New Orleans. Over the years, I have attended more than 200 jazz funerals and Mardi Gras Indian practices. I have also witnessed other occasions connected to the black Indians of New Orleans including weddings and funerals. This chapter tells some of those tales.

The first jazz funeral I attended was for the great pianist Henry Roeland Byrd, better known as Professor Longhair. For a peek back in time, scenes from his funeral are in the documentary, "Piano Players Rarely Play Together." I was a freshman in college, and though the experience was as unusual and overwhelming as anything I had ever witnessed before, I had no concept of the deep traditions connected with this ancient ritual. Like many Americans, I had seen the James Bond film, "Live and Let Die," so I had some vague notion that this unique manifestation of culture existed. But during that time period, even many lifelong New Orleanians were unaware of the pervasiveness and significance of the jazz funeral in the cultural and economic life of black New Orleans.

The tradition dates back to the antebellum period in New Orleans when release from the bonds of slavery was reason to celebrate even if that release came through death. However, its roots extend all the way back to Africa. There are analogous rituals all through the African diaspora. While working for the *Louisiana Weekly* on the Caribbean island of Antigua, I witnessed a similar procession that was so familiar it induced a feeling of déjà vu.

At the earliest jazz funerals in New Orleans, the brass band arrives at the house of the deceased (before the advent of funeral parlors, wakes were held in the home) and accompanies the family to the church while playing a mournful dirge. Following the service, the sad music continues as the band leads the procession of mourners to the graveyard. Before the automobile existed, most people lived, worked, worshipped, died and were buried in the same intimate neighborhood. After the final benediction at the gravesite, the body is metaphorically "cut loose" from the bonds of the "meat" world (Dr. John's expression for our earthly existence). The band commences an up tempo tune, and the dancing back to the family's home begins.

Since its beginnings, the jazz funeral has changed dramatically. Factors too numerous to detail here have influenced the way the ritual has morphed over the centuries. Suffice it to say that all jazz funerals are unique and the singular life of the deceased is reflected in specific aspects of the ceremony. Some jazz funerals are publicized events rife with media attention; others are private family affairs. Some are wild throwdowns; others are dignified send offs reflecting the early form. Some feature nearly every musician in town and hundreds of people in the second line; others include just a basic brass band followed by a small group of friends and family. Some wind all around town; others last just a city block. As Alfred "Bucket" Carter, the venerable leader of the Young Mens Olympian, Jr., the oldest active social aid and pleasure club, was overheard remarking at a recent jazz funeral, "You gotta bring him how he lived." That witty comment reflects another seldomly discussed aspect of the jazz funeral—a great majority are held for men.

As discussed earlier, these changes have not always sat well with tradition-minded members of the community. This conflict between custom and modernity came to a head on March 13, 1994 when Danny Barker, the patriarch of the modern brass band movement, passed away after a brief illness. The Tremé community was devastated.

Though he loved the younger generations and was always game for hijinks (he appeared on the cover of *Offbeat* magazine in a leather jacket more befitting a biker than a jazzman), he was sometimes critical of the latest generation of musicians and what he perceived as a lack of respect for the traditions. It was reported that he didn't even want a jazz funeral because of the lack of dignity at some of the more raucous ceremonies.

However, Gregg Stafford and some of the older players from Barker's early days back in New Orleans assured his widow, "Blue" Lu Barker, they would guarantee a dignified send-off. They promised all the musicians would be wearing the standard uniform of black shoes, black pants, white shirt and black tie. They would all wear the trademark cap of a brass band musician.

Two nights after he died, the mourning began in earnest. Kermit Ruffins and his fledgling solo act performed at Trombone Shorty's on the corner of N. Robertson and St. Philip Streets to a small crowd of Barker fans and neighborhood folks. The drummer Jerry Anderson was the most grief-stricken of the many musicians who gathered at the club. The expression on his face reflected what everyone was feeling—this is a loss of a man who can never be replaced.

Ruffins, along with Keith "Wolf" Anderson, Troy "Trombone Shorty" Andrews, James Andrews, Corey Henry and numerous others, paid tribute to Barker with a set list pulled from the great man's repertoire. Letting the music speak for their emotions, they played his now classic tune, "The Palm Court Strut," every other song for an entire set.

I had just begun my tenure with the *Louisiana Weekly* and was assigned the task of writing Barker's obituary. Overwhelmed with the obligation, I decided that, rather than try and write something profound, I would piece together quotes from local luminaries into a coherent story. Troy "Trombone Shorty" Andrews had one of the best lines even though he was just a four-year-old child. I used it to close the piece. He said, "If you knew Mr. Barker, you knew history."

Danny Barker's wake was held the following night at Gallier Hall—a place usually reserved for political figures of the Caucasian persuasion. The place was packed with musicians and mourners. The grief was palpable as if he had been stricken in his prime because, despite his advanced age, Barker still acted like a young man, carrying on and performing with people decades younger.

On March 17th, the funeral went off as planned. The procession, though crowded with thousands of onlookers, was dignified and aligned with the hundred-year-old tradition. The young players were conspicuously absent. But after Barker was interred in St. Louis Cemetery #2 and most of the older relatives and musicians had moved on to the repast, the next generation, led by Ruffins, took over. The streets of the Tremé erupted into a giant parade as the young musicians, including Kerwin James, Philip Frazier, John "Prince" Gilbert, and Corey Henry, paid their respects in their own fashion. Tributes to Barker including spontaneous street parades in the Tremé were ubiquitous over the months following the death of the great musician.

Just over a year later on May 26, 1995, 17-year-old Darnell "D-Boy" Andrews, an aspiring trombone player and the brother of both James and Troy "Trombone Shorty" Andrews, was shot and killed in the courtyard of the Lafitte housing project. His funeral was the most insane free-for-all I have ever witnessed in all my years in the Tremé. It was the exact sort of send-off Danny Barker was said to have feared.

After the service, a huge band made up of most of the sons of the neighborhood began playing the raucous hip-hop inflected style that was gaining in popularity among the younger brass band musicians. There was no dirge. The pallbearers, all teenage friends of the deceased, took his coffin out of the hearse and raised it high over their heads. Beer and liquor were poured copiously over the coffin in front of the family's home. Darnell's mother, Lois Nelson, led the young men carrying the coffin inside. When they emerged, she was in street clothes after shedding her funeral black.

All the while, thousands had gathered in the streets. Despite being friends with the family, I had no chance of getting close to the band. The throngs were out of control in their grief. The procession proceeded out of the Tremé proper along Orleans Avenue to the site of the murder. They pulled the coffin out of the hearse yet again and carried it into the courtyard of the housing project to the very spot where D-Boy was killed.

After they set the coffin down, D-Boy's mother climbed on top of her son's casket and slowly danced to the music of the brass band. It was a deeply moving moment exposing the intricate ties between the twin emotions of grief-stricken loss and joyous release that define a jazz funeral.

The folkie Michelle Shocked, who was living in the area at the time and became friends with the Andrews family, sang a song about the moment a year later at the Jazz Fest. The musicians in D-Boy's family were playing with her. Shocked introduced the song by describing the scene with Andrews' mother on the spot where he was killed. She told the crowd, "It was the most beautiful, saddest dance I have ever seen." Some of the lyrics of her song— "Lady Billie sure can dance the blues, she scraped his coffin with her shoes."

The status and age of a musician usually determines the reaction within the community. The funeral for Lady Linda Young, the long-time companion of Anthony "Tuba Fats" Lacen, illustrated the roles money and reputation play in insuring a proper jazz funeral. Two nights before she was laid to rest, a benefit was held at Donna's to raise money for the funeral. Despite being an icon of Jackson Square and mentor to dozens of younger musicians, Tuba Fats didn't have insurance or even enough money for a proper funeral. Young wasn't famous enough to warrant official intervention by the city or any benevolent organization.

When the day of the funeral arrived, there still wasn't enough money to pay for the police escort and parade permit necessary for the funeral procession to leave the Tremé and head to the couple's longtime stomping grounds in the French Quarter. Though illegal parades are common through the poorer parts of town, the rule of law is strictly enforced in the French Quarter.

The jazz funeral procession left the Charbonnet Funeral Home in the Tremé and headed to the French Quarter with many musicians and mourners fully intent on defying the law. But the parade broke up on Rampart Street—the boundary of the two neighborhoods. Family and friends were despondent; everyone really wanted to pass through the French Quarter. A plan was quickly hatched.

As the group of mourners disbanded, word went around that everyone was to gather in front of Preservation Hall in order to continue the ritual. Within a short time, all of the musicians and mourners regrouped and played the traditional songs in her memory. Wounded by the unfairness of the situation and still wound up, we then paraded back into the Tremé where the music could waft through the air unimpeded by the law.

Musicians and members of the city's social aid and pleasure clubs are the usual beneficiaries of a jazz funeral. But occasionally individuals who are not part of these two overlapping fraternities are recipients. Just before Danny Barker made his transition to the big band in the sky, Lawrence Fletcher, one of the most revered of the Mardi Gras Indian big chiefs, passed away. There was no brass band at his funeral on March 4, 1994, but the ritual had all the solemnity and mystique of a jazz funeral. Two esteemed big chiefs, Allison "Tootie" Montana of the Yellow Pocahontas and Donald Harrison of the Guardians of the Flame, led the procession as they brought the body out of the African Methodist Episcopal Church in Central City. Along with a number of other Indians, some in their colorful suits, they played tambourines and sang the prayer song, "Indian Red," in a dirge-like fashion before they lined up on either side of the hearse for the ritual of "cutting the body loose." The Indians gently sang "Shallow Water" and "Two Way Pocky Away" until one of the younger chiefs, Larry Bannock of the Golden Star Hunters, got into a brief shouting match with Harrison.

The gist of their debate was that Bannock felt that Harrison and the other elders needed to allow the next generation to honor the passing of the legendary chief in their own way. However, his meaning was deeper—your time has passed, and we are not going to wait in the wings. Yet time truly waits for no man. With all the Indians of the earlier generation now deceased, Bannock is the elder statesman of the uptown tribes and has had his own conflicts with the next generation of Mardi Gras Indians on the streets of New Orleans.

The response of the mourners often dictates the tenor of a jazz funeral. Another giant void was left when Charlie Bering, the impresario behind Lu and Charlie's, the most important contemporary jazz club during the 1970s, passed away. Though his second club, Charlie B's, was short-lived, he booked the jazz tent at the New Orleans Jazz and Heritage Festival for twenty years and was a very well respected figure in the community.

Bering's funeral on October 8, 1998 featured over twenty musicians including the trumpeter Gregory Davis who succeeded him at the Jazz Fest booking office. Only 62 when he passed, the band's repertoire after his funeral service reflected the profound loss. They played five dirges in a row as they made the slow walk along Rampart Street.

An incredible outpouring of grief accompanies any tragic death especially those like the saxophonist Charles Taylor who die so far before their time. In March 1998, the percussionist and bandleader Michael Ward passed away in his sleep after a long night of partying. He was 44.

His death left his large family and an even larger musical community in total shock. On March 26, two nights before his funeral, Henry Butler and a number of his musician friends gathered at the Maple Leaf to remember the fallen bandleader. The core group featured Russell Batiste on drums, Mark Brooks on bass, Renard Poché on percussion and June Yamagishi on guitar. Though numerous people were deeply affected by the untimely loss, Yamagishi was overwhelmed.

Yamagishi burst on the scene with a searing performance in the drummer Kerry Brown's band on the first day of the Jazz Fest in 1995. He had a successful career playing blues and R&B in Japan, but he longed to live in New Orleans. He moved to the city for good and quickly became an in-demand sideman. Ward had been his mentor in New Orleans, and he returned the favor when they toured in Japan. They were close friends who could often be found chowing down on a late lunch at the fabled Central City spot, Uglesich's.

There was a parade of special guests at the Maple Leaf that night including the violinist Michael Ward, Samirah Evans, George Porter, Jr., Bo Dollis and Marva Wright. Yamagishi fought back tears for hours, though he never left the stage. His face was completely contorted, torn between emotions, half-laughing and half-crying, the whole night.

The following evening, the Dragon's Den was the spot for another group of mourners. Alex McMurray spent considerable time in Ward's band, Reward, and his set with Royal Fingerbowl spoke volumes about Ward's life and the crazy times they spent together.

With Carlo Nuccio now playing drums in the band, McMurray wasn't the only one in the band who was close friends with the deceased percussionist. The vibe was over the top from the first note. They opened with "Junco Partner." It was a direct reference to the lifestyle that Mike Ward lived. As McMurray flailed away on his guitar, he added his friend's name to the lyrics.

Ward's funeral was the following morning, and nearly everyone there was bleary-eyed from late night partying, tears or both. The Tremé Brass Band led the jazz funeral procession along with Ward's close friend and percussion student, Chris Jones. After the send off, all of the drummers went wild playing hard for the memory of one of the most charismatic personalities on the scene.

The day after his funeral was the uptown Indian Sunday parade, which is part of the Mardi Gras Indians' St. Joseph's Day commemorations. The occasion was bittersweet since almost everyone in the tight-knit Indian and second line communities knew Ward. Later that night, a benefit was held at the Maple Leaf for Ward's extended family.

Though his funeral was just the day before, the vibe was one of celebration, not mourning. It was a wild and intensely crazy party that lasted until 6 AM. Smilin' Myron and Walter "Wolfman" Washington performed. But the highlight (it's hard to call it that given the circumstances) was an incendiary performance by a group billed as the Reward Allstars.

The core of the band included Alex McMurray, Glenn Hartman, and Keith Vinet—the keyboardist with George Porter, Jr.'s band. Numerous other musicians including Russell Batiste, Tony Hall, Willie Green, and George Porter, Jr. showed up to help the cause. At the end of the night, Mike Darby and Irene Sage, two musicians better known for screaming rock 'n' roll, got up on stage and played a pair of moving spirituals as the sun was rising outside.

Ward's influence extended to Galactic and other musicians as well. At a show in March at the House of Blues, the nouveau funk band put on one of its usual inventive sets. Davis Rogan got up on stage and performed a freestyle rap, and Mark Mullins and Craig Klein joined the band on trombones. Theryl DeClouet praised the late percussionist, his old friend and running partner, in a heart-felt dedication. Yet something was clearly missing from the performance; grief hung in the air like stale cigar smoke.

The first Rebirth show at the Maple Leaf after Ward's death was intense. The Maple Leaf was one of Ward's favorite hangouts. During a period when he was the percussionist in Harry Connick, Jr.'s band, he would always head to the bar after coming off tour dressed in fine threads, and he would buy everyone a round. Philip Frazier ran around the room while playing his tuba as the band vamped on a heavy blues-inflected jam. It was as if he were searching for any trace of Ward.

At the Uptown Free Street Festival, the dynamic soulful singer Sharon Martin dedicated "His Eye Is on the Sparrow" to Ward. Ward, who was everywhere all over town during life, was ubiquitous in death as well.

Though there are numerous overlaps and crossovers between the core cultural traditions of black New Orleans, use of the term "Mardi Gras Indian" developed separately from the culture. But since it is now common, I have chosen to use it throughout this work. The more proper terminology is "the black Indians of New Orleans." Musicians going back to the early part of the 20th century have sung songs about the black Indians. Over the years, many musicians have "masked Indian," and many Indians are also capable musicians. Additionally, many of the customs associated with second line parades, jazz funerals and social aid and pleasure clubs are similar to those in the Mardi Gras Indian community. The same people that are devoted to the Mardi Gras Indians are also followers of the second line clubs. The two parts of the culture are centered in the same parts of the city.

The roots of the Mardi Gras Indian culture are not as clear cut as those associated with second line community and brass band traditions. The origin of the first Mardi Gras Indian is shrouded in myth and lost to the annals of history. Three things are clear among various theories that are detailed elsewhere—Native Americans shared a kinship with enslaved Africans in Louisiana that was rooted in their animist belief systems, respect for nature, social customs and antipathy towards the European colonial mentality. Native American communities took in runaway slaves. The intermingling of the bloodlines is obvious among the faces of New Orleanians including many of the most revered Mardi Gras Indians.

The major difference between the two sides of these intertwined traditions concerns the visibility of the manifestations of the culture. While second line parades and jazz funerals are public events, the rituals of the Mardi Gras Indian community are more secretive. Their hidden nature reflects their roots as the product of outsiders and other marginalized members of society.

Though I was familiar with some of the traditions and culture of the Mardi Gras Indians through their music as well as public displays on Fat Tuesday and at the New Orleans Jazz and Heritage Festival, it took a connection with a man named Alton Green to allow me deep inside their world. He took me to my first Indian practices where I started learning about the ways of the Indians.

There exists a peripheral world among the Indians themselves—a world of assistants and gifted artists who have never worn an Indian suit themselves. Green was one of these Indians. His skills as a cobbler were put to great use sewing Indian suits, and he was highly respected in the community even though he never masked as an Indian. His place was as a designer and sewer of intricately beaded patches—the flat depictions of life in the Mardi Gras Indian world sewn onto various parts of the finished suit. He was also an excellent singer who could craft wicked lyrical improvisations about the other Indians.

Green had very specific knowledge about the individuals who make up the Mardi Gras Indian community. He could easily differentiate between the legitimate Indians who designed and sewed their own costumes and the many poseurs. He was aware of who knew the songs and, most importantly, he knew exactly how much respect each Indian had earned among his peers. He would point out the suits of Indians that included borrowed patches usually by saying something along the lines of, "See that patch on his apron? So-and-so had it on his crown last year." He could tell in an instant which Indians had done the hard work of sewing a suit with needle and thread versus those who chose the easier, cheaper route of using a hot glue gun.

He used the word "raggley" whenever he saw an Indian wearing a substandard suit or one wearing an old, beat-up suit. Best of all was when he referenced the iconic New Orleans drug store to denigrate a substandard suit. Displaying his usual understated disdain, he would say, "Now that there's a K&B Indian," suggesting he could have bought the suit in the Mardi Gras section of the local drug store chain.

The first time I went to Green's house in the 7th Ward, I watched intently as one of the Indians in his tribe got ready for practice, and I began to understand the dedication and commitment involved in being an Indian. From the moment I got there until the minute I left a couple of hours later, he was working diligently on his tambourine. The head had broken, most likely a victim of vigorous pounding the week before, and he was painstakingly cutting and placing strips of duct tape to replace the head. First the outer playing surface had to be reconstructed, and then the inside was carefully taped. All along the way, the tambourine was constantly tested to insure it had the sound he wanted.

Before leaving to head out to Indian practice, his small tribe had a short practice among themselves. I knew the prayer song, "Indian Red," since it appeared on the *Wild Tchoupitoulas* album and most of the tribes opened and/or closed their Jazz Fest performances with the tune. But I didn't understand the full significance of the tune until I heard this small group of young Mardi Gras Indians sing it in Green's living room.

It was more powerful than words can describe as they stood in a circle with their family members on the side. The emotions of this group of inner city men resonated deeply. They sang it as if it were a hymn. Each Indian sang his part in a raw voice as the others encouraged him with gentle taps on the tambourine and quiet shouts. We all sang the chorus until the three Indians were satisfied. Then we marched out of the house in a procession and headed uptown.

Our destination was an obscure corner at 2001 Dryades Street. The spot was a bar called Pop's Place, although everyone referred to it as "2001." It was the home of the Creole Wild West—the oldest Mardi Gras Indian tribe. The place was very dark, lit only by the Christmas tree lights that seem to be the lighting standard in many of these establishments, and some dim lights by the bar. I didn't see any other white faces, though nobody paid me much mind. I got a beer and inched my way closer to the circle of Indians.

The lyrics of Mardi Gras Indian music are based on boasting and improvised vocal rhymes. Each Indian took a turn until he ran out of words, began repeating himself or was pushed out of the spotlight by another Indian. This is the pattern they follow.

Within a half hour of our arrival, the front door burst open, but this was no quiet entrance to mirror ours when we slipped in. This was another gang arriving to play Indian. Their spy boy entered amid great commotion among the patrons and the practicing Indians. The circle instantly became a gauntlet, and the outsider had to dance his way through a number of other Indians before he got to meet the big chief of the Creole Wild West. Each Indian tried to push him down with words and dance. They tried to get him to back down, but he wouldn't, and after several minutes he had met the whole tribe. Now it was time to meet the big chief, but the big chief wouldn't have it. Chiefs only meet chiefs. He wanted to know—where's your chief? Within seconds, the door burst open again, and this time it was the whole tribe coming through.

All eyes in the bar were on the invading tribe. A wall of people had formed with everyone straining to get a glimpse of the makeshift alley the Creole Wild West had formed. One by one, they each danced their way down the gauntlet, and each was turned back like the first spy boy. Finally, the big chief appeared at the door. Amid the noise and confusion, he danced into the room, banging on his tambourine and shouting the ancient calls. He met each of the other members of the Creole Wild West in turn, and though they were not as menacing as they were with his underlings, it was obvious he had to prove he was indeed the big chief. The exchanges were perfunctory, but dead serious until he finally got to the big chief. Then the mood changed dramatically.

In an instant, it dawned on me—they know each other really well! It was all a game—they were playing Indian. The music stopped, and after all the posturing and veiled threats, everyone hugged each other like long lost friends. Then they were gone and the Creole Wild West returned to their practice.

This same scene has been repeated over and over with individual variations at neighborhood bars all over the city for decades. They are practicing for Mardi Gras. The songs, the dances and the percussion playing are all part of the practice, but meeting another tribe is the central preoccupation just as it is on Fat Tuesday.

On another night, we went down into the lower 9th Ward for the practice of the Ninth Ward Hunters at Silky's on St. Claude Avenue. As the practice at Silky's broke up, word went out that everyone was heading to another practice nearby on Forstall Street. We made our way to this remote location, but when we arrived there wasn't a soul in sight. The block was deserted, and the bar's front door was heavily chained and padlocked.

Green assured me, "If they said there's gonna be a practice, there's gonna be a practice." Sure enough, after a short wait someone showed up and unlocked the place. The lights came on, the jukebox was fired up, and a whole group of Indians showed up shortly thereafter.

The practice started, peaked, and within an hour it was over. Everyone left en masse, and as we drove away I could see the proprietor chaining the front door in my rear view mirror. We never even found out the name of the tribe that hosted the brief practice.

A week or so later, Green suggested we head to a practice in a different section of town at a neighborhood bar called Leroy's Lounge. The tribe in question was a gang I had never heard of—the Creole Osceolas. We took N. Broad Street into Gentilly, and when we arrived I immediately sensed something was different at Leroy's Lounge. To this day, I think I was the first Caucasian to ever walk into the bar. It wasn't that crowded, just a handful of patrons and maybe ten Indians. I headed straight to the bar and ordered a Heineken. "Sorry, no Heinekens." A quart of Bud or a Miller pony were my beer options.

I didn't want a quart of beer since I never knew how long we would be staying at any given practice. As I turned with my Miller pony to check out the Indians, I looked around the room at the other patrons—all the men had quarts, and all the women had ponies.

While this was one of the most low-key of all the practices I attended with Green, the evening was enlivened when Big Chief Rudy of the Ninth Ward Hunters walked through the front door. He was a legend before he passed away in 2003. The Creole Osceloas immediately stepped up the energy of the ritual, and Rudy joined the circle without any pretense of a ritual confrontation. He was a gifted singer I had heard perform at the Jazz Fest. He took a turn or two on lead vocals and left almost as quickly as he arrived.

When Mardi Gras arrived, I headed downtown at midday with a friend. We had a cooler full of beer as well as sandwiches and other supplies for a full day of chasing after Indians. As we approached Canal Street on Loyola Avenue, we spotted feather plumes on the neutral ground. It was an incongruous sight to say the least. Amid the skyscrapers of the Central Business District was a big gang of Indians. There were at least five men in full suits and a large complement of family and friends. They were downtown Indians, heading to the vast meeting place on N. Claiborne Avenue.

Without a second thought to where we were, I turned the car around, quickly parked in what I hoped was a legal spot, and bounded out intent on catching this tribe. In our haste, we left all of the beer in the car. After a few blocks we caught up to the Indians. The ones in suits didn't even acknowledge our presence, but as we tailed them across Canal Street, some of the support group gave us a cursory look and we engaged in enough small talk to find out their name. It was another tribe I had never heard of—the Morning Star Hunters.

They were moving with a purpose to the subtle beat of the tambourine. We were approaching the Iberville housing project, and my friend and I had some trepidation about following them into the notoriously dangerous development. But fear was trumped by discovery, and we followed them into the courtyard. Little kids were running everywhere as fathers tended barbeque grills. Everyone was outdoors enjoying the balmy weather, and the appearance of the Indians galvanized the tight-knit community in the project. Everyone wants to see an Indian on Mardi Gras.

From up on the balconies we heard laughing and revelry amid cries of, "Look at the white boys! Look at the white boys!" To our amazement, we were actually running with the Indians! When they reached N. Claiborne, the street was a crush of people. We went from being almost a part of the gang to just being two more bodies in the crowd.

By the late 1990s, a new generation of tribes was emerging on the scene, and none were more potent than the Young Cheyenne—a downtown tribe that practiced at a hole-in-the-wall called Club Yogi on Franklin Avenue.

On a Sunday in early January, I headed out to the various practices starting at Kemp's where the Golden Arrows held their practice. The place was packed, so we headed to a new place, the Star Line Lounge, also uptown, to check out another new tribe, the Wild Mohicans.

Young tribes sometimes have a hard time holding the momentum at their practices. The evening ended soon after the visiting Black Eagles tore through the place and virtually took over the practice on the strength of their big chief's vocals.

Following the advice of some of the Indians who were also moving on, we decided to head to Club Yogi. As spectators more comfortable in uptown practices, we were a little concerned the rivalry between uptown and downtown tribes might spill over onto us. When we got there, the streets were teeming with people. It was a downtown crowd, and the energy was crackling. A doorman actually checked my ID—a first in all my years of attending Mardi Gras Indian practices. The culture was changing with the passing of big chiefs like Lawrence Fletcher and Donald Harrison, Sr. Some of the other Indian bars eventually installed metal detectors to discourage individuals intent on wreaking real havoc.

As we entered Club Yogi, the intensity inside was so overwhelming it was palpable. People were spread out; not everyone was focusing on the circle of Indians who were chanting and playing percussion. The heat, even though it was January, was causing steam to rise off of people's heads. It was so packed that I couldn't even get close enough to the circle to see who was leading the practice.

After about 30 minutes amid a continually rising intensity level, the door suddenly burst open, and the Golden Star Hunters and the Black Eagles busted into the joint. There must have been twenty

Indians who stormed in, and upset the delicate balance of the huge crowd. I was pushed back against the far wall as the invading tribes tore into the circle whooping and hollering like they were trying to raise the dead.

When the ritual confrontation was complete and the uptown gangs made their exit, one of the younger members of the Yellow Pocahontas remarked to no one in particular, " Uptown just ripped through the practice." It was an absolutely crazy scene that foreshadowed the club being shut down because of drug violations and violence. Eventually, the big chief of the Young Cheyenne was banned from masking as an Indian because of a violent incident that ended with another chief on the way to the emergency room after a confrontation on St. Joseph's Night.

Ira "Dr. Ike" Padnos, now well-known as the visionary behind the Ponderosa Stomp celebration of the unsung heroes of American music, was also heavily involved in the Mardi Gras Indian community. In the late 1990s, he became friends with a number of the big chiefs and proposed a groundbreaking recording session. For the first time in history, downtown and uptown tribes would come together as the Indians of the Nation and record an album. It would be done on their terms with no outside producers.

The group held a benefit at Donna's to help pay for the recording. It included the chiefs of the Black Eagles and Golden Arrows representing uptown and the Black Feather and White Cloud Hunters from downtown. Big Chief Smiley Ricks of the Wild Renegade Hunters, Dr. John's longtime percussionist, represented the West Bank.

Besides the historic achievement represented by having the chiefs of five different tribes working together on a single recording, the Indians of the Nation also wrote several new songs which they performed on the album along with standards from the Mardi Gras Indian canon. Despite the success, in-fighting and ancient rivalries among participants cast a pall over any future joint endeavors. Old habits die hard.

When Carnival Day rolled around in 1995, word on the street was that a very special event was scheduled for Congo Square. Big Chief Walter Cook of the Creole Wild West was getting married on Mardi

Gras. But it rained all morning and it looked like the Indians were going to have to skip masking on Fat Tuesday. Rain and wind are the biggest fears for the Indians. Rain ruins the intricate beadwork and wind makes it hard to walk in the suits that can weigh hundreds of pounds. The event had to be moved into the Tremé Community Center, but miraculously the sun came out in the middle of the afternoon. By early evening, the streets of the Tremé were filled with Indians strutting their stuff.

It's hard to describe the level of intensity in the Tremé community on that Fat Tuesday. A dozen or so Indians, including members of the Creole Wild West, waited out front for the wedding party. The Zulu parade had broken up nearby, and the streets were filled with thousands of people celebrating the big day. Off in the distance, the faint rumble of an approaching brass band mingled with boisterous laughter.

The bride and groom arrived decked out in matching pink Indian suits befitting the nature of the day. Because of the chaos of Mardi Gras, there was some confusion getting the wedding started, but Cook waited patiently for his bride to walk down the aisle. She arrived to the accompaniment of drums, tambourines and chanting Indians. The ceremony was short, and then the entire congregation serenaded the couple with "Indian Red."

It wasn't even close to being a traditional wedding since everyone was in full Mardi Gras mode. After the brief ceremony, the Bayou Renegades began playing their searing Indian blues-funk, and the reception began. The sight of dozens of Indians with their bejeweled suits and massive feathered crowns was breath-taking. It was an absolutely amazing experience. When the service was over, the entire crowd, overwhelmed with the emotions associated with ritual, community and culture, returned to the streets, which were still packed with revelers.

Chapter 14

A NEW GENERATION GETS INTO THE MUSIC BUSINESS

"The music business is a cruel and shallow money trench, a long plastic hallway where thieves and pimps run free, and good men die like dogs. There's also a negative side."—Hunter S. Thompson

By the late 1980s, the national economy began rebounding. The reopening of Tipitina's marked the first wave in a new generational shift, reenergizing the careers of the legends while at the same time opening the door for new musicians, events and clubs to impact the culture of the city.

Earl King's career took off for yet another phase when he collaborated with the great Rhode Island band, Roomful of Blues. Their album, *Glazed,* exposed a whole new generation to the legendary R&B star's songwriting skills. He was on the cover of *Wavelength* magazine in November 1986 and appeared with Roomful of Blues at a record release party at Tipitina's. King was in fine form, and sounded great being backed by the horn-heavy, stop-on-a-dime outfit led by the guitarist Ronnie Earl, clearly an unabashed fan of King, and the keyboardist Ron Levy.

Because of the increased capacity of the renovated nightclub, the Neville Brothers began playing regularly at Tipitina's again. On the strength of their national and international success, the gigs became two-night stands that attracted thousands and added to the legend of the uptown club.

Within the first year of the new ownership, optimism reigned again for music lovers in New Orleans. Tipitina's was back! By the decade's end, a new crop of out-of-town musicians and celebrities would help to increase the club's profile on the national scene. New Orleans music was heading back into the spotlight.

As the recession eased, the music scene uptown was reaching a critical mass. Muddy Waters and the Maple Leaf were hopping nearly every night. Another new group that became a New Orleans icon, the Iguanas, debuted their Tex-Mex, retro R&B sound at the Maple Leaf on two Tuesdays in November 1989. The highly versatile band could play tejano-style music when Rod Hodges strapped on the accordion or rock out like the great R&B star, Lee Allen, when Derek Huston and Joe Cabral strapped on their saxophones.

By the end of 1990, the Iguanas were playing every Sunday night at the Maple Leaf. It quickly became a scene, and within a few months their shows on Sunday nights made the Leaf the place to be in uptown New Orleans. Every night, the bar was packed with dancers, and the group developed a dedicated fan base that still serves them to this day despite some personnel changes within the group's membership.

In 1992, Walter "Wolfman" Washington began a long-standing Saturday night gig at the Maple Leaf, and George Porter, Jr., after returning from a long tour with David Byrne, settled into a steady Saturday night gig at Muddy Waters with his new band, the Runnin' Pardners. His new label at the time, Rounder Records, insisted on the conventional spelling for his first solo album, *Runnin' Partner,* which was released in 1990, even though Porter said that he prefers the colloquial spelling,

Numerous people enjoyed an "only on Oak Street" ritual—spending a Saturday night bopping back and forth between the two clubs as both bands were on fire and attracted great crowds and numerous special guests. The clubs vied for which one would stay open the latest, and Washington's show routinely ended after 4:30 AM.

Benny's was also hitting on all cylinders and was packed every night. NOBD, the New Orleans Blues Department, had become something like the house band at the club. They were a competent outfit including Red Priest and Michael Sklar on guitars, Gary Rieger and/or J.J. Juliano on drums, and Spike Perkins on bass, and they were always wiling to play if another band cancelled or got a better gig. NOBD was also playing regularly at the Maple Leaf. They got a big shot of confidence right after the Jazz Fest in 1988 when Bruce Springsteen joined them on stage at the Maple Leaf.

Tipitina's was generating even more cachet among international music lovers who were descending on New Orleans in droves. The quirky British band, Hot House Flowers, had played at Tipitina's early in the year and returned in the fall for the specific purpose of filming a video at the club and capturing its magic. High profile shows at Tipitina's usually ended on the early side, and the night with Hot House Flowers was no exception. Since the music was far from over elsewhere in town—here's a look back at the rest of the night uptown after Tips closed around 1 AM.

Walter "Wolfman" Washington's gig at Muddy Waters was still in full swing. "Wolfman" had a hot new pianist, David Ellington, and the percussionist and vocalist, Andy Ambrose, playing with him. During the last set, the blues shouter, Mighty Sam McClain, sat in, and sang a killer version of "Stormy Monday."

Since Benny's was always the latest gig in town during this period, when the show at Muddy Waters ended, the corner of Camp and Valence was the next destination. The King Bees, a decent blues band that also featured the guitarist Michael Sklar from NOBD, were tearing the roof off the place with Ivan Neville and James Ledet sitting in on keys and drums respectively. Then, at 3:30 AM the entire band and entourage of Hot House Flowers arrived, set up their gear and played a bluesy three-tune set that included "Stormy Monday." It was just a typical night for the period.

Among the new faces hanging around the club at the corner of Tchoupitoulas and Napoleon was a wispy, dark-haired fellow in black jeans wearing an amulet around his neck. It was Daniel Lanois, the legendary producer, hot on the heels of producing smash hits for Peter Gabriel ("Sledgehammer" off the *So* album) and U2 ("I Still Haven't Found What I Was Looking For" off the *Joshua Tree* album). His vibe was genuine, and he looked like he was just another low-key individual soaking up the music of the Nevilles and other local acts.

At this point in time, Brian Stoltz had settled nicely into the guitar chair for the Neville Brothers. His solos were tasty—bluesy and blustery without the flash of Leo Nocentelli. He was capable of playing a searing lead but was also laid back enough to accompany Aaron Neville on a sweet ballad.

Unbeknownst to all but the most inside of insiders, Lanois was not hanging around town as a musical tourist; he was producing the latest Bob Dylan album, *Oh, Mercy*. The core of the Neville Brothers' rhythm section, "Mean" Willie Green, Daryl Johnson and Stoltz, along with Cyril Neville and other players on the fringe of Neville-land like the bassist Tony Hall, were secreted away in an uptown home that had been converted into a makeshift recording studio. Lanois went on to oversee the production of *Yellow Moon*, the album regarded by most critics as the Neville Brothers' most successful studio work, which came out in 1989. He also produced *Brother's Keeper*; the Nevilles' follow up recording.

In August 1989, it was reported that Lanois had purchased the former mansion home of Germaine Wells on the edge of the French Quarter at 544 Esplanade Avenue and was turning it into a recording studio that he called Kingsway. The conversion was complete a year later, and it became a sought after spot for recording that was hailed for its acoustics, location and intangibles such as its inviting vibe. Kingsway eventually became one of the leading studios in the world.

The list of performers who recorded at Kingsway (not all were produced by Lanois) include Emmylou Harris, R.E.M., Pearl Jam, Blind Melon, the Black Crowes, the Tragically Hip, Sheryl Crow, Ani DiFranco, Midnight Oil and many others. After Lanois sold the building following a ten-year run of successful recordings, the actor Nicholas Cage bought it.

Lanois wasn't just spending his time in New Orleans holed up in the studio; he was also playing a few low-key gigs around town. He performed at the Jazz Fest with Willie Green, Tony Hall and Mason Ruffner (who also played on *Oh Mercy*) on guitar. They did an eclectic set of folk ballads and Lanois originals including a great take on

"Little Sadie." Green toned down his attack, and he played the set with quiet taste using just his brushes. He even played off his own thighs on one tune. Hall and Ruffner were subdued and tasty as well.

A month later, Lanois played at a benefit for the New Orleans Free School. By this point, he had stripped the act down to nearly nothing. He played solo acoustic guitar with his "Willie in a Box." It was nothing more than a taped drum loop.

It wasn't just music fans roaming the streets of New Orleans with money in their pockets. The expanding economy also brought out businessmen eager to get in on the action. Five new clubs opened in 1988 alone, although only one is still in business. LeMoyne's Landing opened on Spanish Plaza and J.B. Rivers opened in the new mall, the Riverwalk. Both were short-lived experiments that presented local bands. J.B. Rivers was actually the home of trumpeter Al Hirt for a brief period. The Absolute Bar and Grill also opened uptown on Tchoupitoulas Street.

On a side street in the gradually gentrifying Warehouse District, a group of twenty-somethings decided the time was right for a new business that would cater to the latest generation of hipsters in New Orleans. The Economy Bar opened in a former industrial building on Girod Street. It had been five years since the World's Fair closed, and the neighborhood was beginning to change. Ironically, it stayed in business until residents at the new condominiums in the area complained because of the noise of the late night crowds. For a time though, the Economy, as everyone called it, was an important part of the music scene.

The setting was distinctly down home, and the place quickly developed a familiar vibe since it attracted like-minded music lovers and downtown slackers attracted by new music and cheap booze. In a sense, it was like Tipitina's without the residual memories of the '60s generation and the focus on older local musicians and touring acts. Tribe Nunzio became the default house band at the Economy, and a scene grew up around them. Times were clearly changing in New Orleans as a new generation was beginning to assert itself in the music community.

A night out at the Economy in those days was a treat because of how different it was from the uptown clubs and the burgeoning scene on Frenchmen Street. The Warehouse District was still a few years away from booming. The location, on a one-way street very close to the old World's Fair site, was desolate and difficult to find. But once on the block, it was hard to miss because the place was often packed. The Economy found a niche among hipsters disillusioned with other clubs and deftly exploited it.

The Economy Bar only lasted a short time; it was doomed by the forces of gentrification that reared up amid the development in the Warehouse District. But the same phenomenon repeated itself when a consortium, including two of the Economy's owners, opened the Mermaid Lounge a few blocks away and the scene gravitated there. The grand opening was on December 3, 1994, and featured Tribe Nunzio and the Iguanas. The Mermaid became the newest hip spot and was a successful business until those same neighborhood concerns about noise also forced them out of business. The space housing the Mermaid Lounge eventually reopened as the Rusty Nail. Somehow, they have managed to avoid the same fate as the previous tenant.

This pattern continues to this day. Each generation needs to find its own niche and make its own mark. It can be seen in 2012 in the success of clubs like One Eyed Jack's and the Hi-Ho Lounge. Undoubtedly, other new clubs will supplant them as the next generation moves into the music business.

John Blancher had never owned a nightclub when he purchased a dilapidated bowling alley in a rundown shopping center from the Knights of Columbus after returning from a pilgrimage to Medjugorje, Yugoslavia. He created one of the most enduring entertainment concepts in the city when he added live music and dubbed the place Mid-City Lanes Rock 'n' Bowl.

In 1996, he expanded Rock 'n' Bowl into the lower level of the building on the corner of Tulane and Carrollton. He dubbed the new space "Bowl Me Under" and began offering a Pay One Price (P.O.P.) policy that allowed patrons to see the bands at both venues without paying two cover charges.

Incidentally, Blancher is the rare club owner who has thrived without a guest list. A great story has circulated for years about an encounter between the longtime doorwoman and Mick Jagger a night or two before the Rolling Stones were to play at the Super-dome. When Jagger tried to get into the show for free, the woman reportedly asked him if he was going to let her into the Dome for free. Jagger promptly paid the cover.

New clubs continued to open in 1989 as well. Uptown, Mr. B's opened on Earhart Boulevard in the Hollygrove neighborhood. It was set up to reflect the style of the sorely missed Dorothy's Medallion. Walter "Wolfman" Washington held court in the early evening, although the band didn't start until after 1 AM. In keeping with the late night tradition, the band was still blazing at 4 AM on most nights.

The economy continued to percolate through the rest of the decade and into the 1990s, and new venues popped up in the Warehouse District, uptown and in the French Quarter. The Bourbon Street Gospel and Blues Club was an odd name for a place since, traditionally the two styles, though connected musically, rarely shared the same space. Marva Wright was the first regular performer at the club, which was fitting since she was a blues singer who got her start singing gospel in church.

While working as a secretary at McMain High School in uptown New Orleans, Wright began to test the waters of the club scene by night. Within a year or two, her career as a blues singer took off, and she was able devote herself to music full time. She was a well-regarded performer with a large following overseas who earned the sobriquet, "the Blues Queen of New Orleans," until her untimely passing in 2010.

Though the Bourbon Street Gospel and Blues Club didn't last, another club that has stood the test of time opened on Decatur Street in the revitalized lower French Quarter. George Buck, a traditional jazz aficionado and record label owner, opened the Palm Court Jazz Cafe with his wife Nina in January 1990. It has been the scene of hundreds of wonderful traditional jazz performances over the years and was home base for Danny Barker before he passed away.

A big space also opened on S. Peters Street called the New Orleans Music Hall. It has changed hands several times and is now the location of the Howlin' Wolf—a rock club that initially opened in a Metairie suburb before moving to its second location a mere block from the current one.

In 1991, the Warehouse Café, which was briefly located in the space that became Vic's, moved to Annunciation Street near the bridge overpass. The original owner took on a partner, Jack Leonardi, a veteran of the Coast Guard who had settled in the city. He has gone on to fame and fortune as the owner of Jacque-Imo's Café, the eclectic restaurant on Oak Street.

The Warehouse Cafe became another favorite among downtown hipsters, and its popularity expanded exponentially when the Rebirth Brass Band began playing there on Friday nights a couple of years after it opened. Part of the allure was Leonardi's *joie de vivre* and welcoming attitude. On the set break, he would put "El Rancho Rock" on the jukebox. The Champs' song was reminiscent of their biggest hit, "Tequila." Leonardi would climb up on the bar and run from end to end while pouring shots of tequila into the mouths of any willing customers. There were always plenty of them!

The two owners sold the Warehouse Café in 1996, and it became known as Monaco Bob's Touchdown Club. After that business closed, it became the well-regarded Italian restaurant, 1179.

In 1992, Charlie Bering, the proprietor of Lu and Charlie's, took another stab at club ownership when he opened Charlie B's in the Warehouse District. It was an upscale supper club with ambitious plans to feature local talent and touring acts too big for Snug Harbor. I first visited the new club on May 13 to see the trombonist Delfeayo Marsalis. He had a talented band of youngsters who were part of the growing contingent of college students gravitating to the new Jazz Studies program at UNO and the already existing program at Loyola University.

The young players were already beginning to make their marks. The Peter Martin Trio, with Chris Thomas on bass and Brian Blade on drums, made a serious impression when they played at Snug Harbor later in the year. Martin is a very percussive pianist, and his career has taken off, although he hasn't hit the stratosphere like Blade, his college drummer.

Dr. John appeared at Bering's club in June. Brian Stoltz from the Neville Brothers was on guitar. The crowd was positively enthralled when Dr. John brought up Danny Barker to sing "Bill Bailey" and then Big Chiefs Monk Boudreaux, Bo Dollis and Walter Cook. He was celebrating the release of his landmark album, *Goin' Back to New Orleans*.

Over the course of the next year and a half, a handful of other great shows took place at the downtown club including an appearance by the legendary organist Jimmy McGriff. Unfortunately, Charlie Bering made some of the same mistakes that doomed other clubs including an overly optimistic business plan featuring early morning jams reminiscent of the first incarnation of the Storyville club. Charlie B's closed unceremoniously in 1994.

The Crescent City Brewhouse on Decatur Street in the French Quarter began presenting bands around this time, and Delfeayo Marsalis was a regular performer. Another musical prodigy, the 16-year old Davell Crawford, made his professional debut at the Brewhouse in August 1992.

The RC Bridge Lounge, a dive bar that favored latter day punk and metal bands, also opened in 1992. The edgy bands playing there attracted huge crowds that spilled out onto the sidewalks of lower Magazine Street until they closed amid neighborhood concerns. A more upscale bar called the Bridge Lounge now occupies the spot.

One of the bands that played at the RC Bridge Lounge and also at Muddy Waters was a driving metal band called Oxen Thrust. The group would merely be a footnote in this tale if it weren't for the fact that their drummer was a young New Orleanian named Stanton Moore. Moore's musical direction would change considerably when he joined fellow students, Jeff Raines and Robert Mercurio to form Galactic Prophylactic—the precursor to the great funk outfit, Galactic.

In early 1993, a new club opened on the historic corner of St. Philip and N. Robertson Streets opposite Kermit Ruffins' lot. The building was the home of the Caldonia Inn, one of the legendary nightspots in the Tremé. Owned by the family of Troy "Trombone Shorty" Andrews, the latest prodigy to emerge on the New Orleans music scene, Trombone Shorty's quickly became another welcoming place in the Tremé. It was a hot spot where the younger generation of jazz musicians played and hung out.

The youngest of the brass bands, The Little Rascals and the Looney Tunes, soaked up the lessons of three generations of musicians. Danny Barker was a regular as was Big Chief Donald Harrison, Sr. and numerous other well-respected neighborhood luminaries. There was always someone with a story to tell holding court in the bar.

When Carnival time rolled around, it was natural for Harrison to start holding Indian practices at Trombone Shorty's with his tribe, the Guardians of the Flame. Held early in the evening, they were often raucous affairs.

Above all, Harrison was an educator. One of the few older Indians who did not regard outsiders with suspicion (as long as they respected the traditions and protocol of the Indians), he willingly discussed his life as an Indian, told stories about the old time Indians and fed the curiosity of anyone willing to ask. Harrison was also rare among the elders of the community because he embraced social and musical inclusiveness. He made a point of showcasing the connections between the black Indians of New Orleans and the original Native Americans. He even had a white woman masking in his tribe for a brief period.

Though Harrison was a revered chief who had led several tribes, he also was a contentious figure among some of the younger Indians who believed he needed to step aside. One time, an Indian who was clearly not welcome at Harrison's practice strode through the door. Though Harrison was getting up in years, he quickly grabbed a baseball bat he had stashed behind the bar and chased the man out into the street. It was hard to believe that a man his age could move so fast and was willing to challenge someone who was considerably younger. But Harrison was an old time Indian who believed that the ancient protocols were to be completely respected.

The Tremé Music Hall opened later in the year, a block away at Ursulines and N. Robertson, and the neighborhood became a treasure trove of Mardi Gras Indians. Big Chief Franklin "Wingy" Davis, Jr. and the Wild Apaches practiced at the Tremé Music Hall; Big Chief "Little" Charles Taylor and the White Cloud Hunters were at the Candlelight Lounge; and the Guardians of the Flame were at Trombone Shorty's. Lorraine's Dugout, the home of the Yellow Pocahontas for a period and then the Monogram Hunters, was nearby on St. Claude Avenue. After a renovation it opened as the jazz club, Sweet Lorraine's, and is still in business today.

The practices were staggered so it was easy to walk back and forth from the three bars and check out all of the Indians. If you tired of the ancient rhythms and chants, the blues singer Big Al Carson held forth at Joe's Cozy Corner on the same block.

However, none of these new business ventures created as much of a stir among New Orleans music lovers and musicians as did the opening of the House of Blues on upper Decatur Street in January 1994. The club scene in New Orleans began expecting major fallout in mid-1993 when it was announced that the management of the House of Blues had decided that their first satellite club, to complement the original location in Cambridge, Massachusetts, was to be located on a rundown section of upper Decatur Street in the French Quarter. No club was affected more by this watershed moment than the venerable uptown institution of Tipitina's. The House of Blues hired away Sonny Schneideau, the long time talent buyer for Tipitina's. Schneideau maintained in the press that the decision was amicable and was based on his desire for a change in his career. But the choice hit hard among the devotees of Tipitina's, and almost immediately the House of Blues was cast as a villain aiming to destroy one of the city's most beloved institutions.

While fans of Tipitina's were fretting over the impact of this major competitor, the management behind the scenes at the House of Blues was working diligently to woo virtually every other segment of the New Orleans community. The marketing department courted the local media, and virtually every outlet produced fawning stories about the new venue. They marveled about the folk art on the walls, the state of the art sound system, and the menu at the adjoining restaurant. Special note was made of the refrigerated garbage holding area.

A slew of special pre-opening events in early 1994 targeted various sections of the local community. Like an astute politician, the club presented shows, free of charge with complementary beverages and hors d'oeuvres, for its various constituents for a full week before the official grand opening. On Wednesday, January 19, Herman Ernest, the slamming drummer from Dr. John's band, played for Musician's Night. The next night, the traditional jazz clarinetist, Dr. Michael White, performed with his band featuring Lucien Barbarin and Maynard Chatters on trombones, Don Vappie on banjo and Steve Pistorius on piano. It was filmed for a program called Mo' Jazz.

Friday night, the guitarist Norman Brown and Foley, Miles Davis' former bassist, performed for another episode of Mo' Jazz. Saturday night was Film and Video Industry Night with Walter "Wolfman" Washington and the Roadmasters. Monday was Hospitality Industry Night, and Kermit Ruffins put on a jumping set with special guest, Carl LeBlanc. The following Thursday, George Porter, Jr. and the Runnin' Pardners played at the club for another private gig. Reportedly, the management also hosted other private non-publicized nights for the police department, taxi cab drivers and other crucial constituents necessary for building a successful business.

Taking a page from the reopening of Tipitina's back in 1983, the official grand opening of the House of Blues was scheduled for Super Bowl weekend. On Saturday, January 29, 1994, the doors opened to the general public for the first time with a stellar lineup. John Mooney opened the show with David Torkanowsky on keys, Carlo Nuccio on drums, David Lee Watson on bass and Cranston Clements on guitar. Marva Wright joined the band for two songs and tore the roof off the sucker with her soulful vocals. Up next, Dr. John put on a compelling performance complete with his ace horn section of Alvin "Red" Tyler and Eric Traub on saxophones and Charlie Miller on trumpet. The headliner was the Blues Brothers Band led by Paul Schaffer of David Letterman fame. Dan Aykroyd, an investor in the new club, revived the shtick complete with dark suit and sunglasses, and the late John Belushi's brother, Jim, capably filled his role. The band featured two stalwarts of the Memphis soul scene, Donald "Duck" Dunn on bass and Steve Cropper on guitar.

Despite the hype, it was actually a great set and a wonderful opportunity for music freaks to hear the players behind so many great hits by the likes of Otis Redding and Booker T and the MGs. Gospel crossover stars Mavis and Pops Staples were also on the bill as special guests along with Delbert McClinton on harmonica. Despite the grumblings about corporate outsiders, more expensive drinks, higher cover charges and the perceived menace to Tipitina's, the opening was an unqualified success.

The threat to Tipitina's never materialized in any significant way, although initially, the uptown club appeared to be reeling from the juggernaut of the House of Blues. Management placed an ad in the summer of 1994 stating unequivocally that the club was not closing or being sold. They slogged through some tough times and were forced to adjust their booking policy as bands that were previously regulars began playing at the House of Blues.

One of their first business strategies was to capitalize on the cachet of the club's patron saint, Professor Longhair. They came up with a new concept to draw weekday crowds to the club. It was called "Fess-tival," and a newcomer to town, the pianist Tom Worrell, organized the Wednesday concert series.

Worrell has an uncanny ability to play like "Fess," and he was able to put together an all-star band that included a number of play-ers who performed with the great pianist. Among them were the rhythm section of Johnny Vidacovich and James Singleton, the sax-ophonists Alvin "Red" Tyler and Tony Dagradi and Professor Long-hair's longtime percussionist, Alfred "Uganda" Roberts.

The concerts were hit or miss affairs, but they ignited a resur-gence of interest in Longhair's career. Another generation of musi-cians and music lovers was now ready to embrace the great man's legacy. Worrell was in the right place at the right time, and he played in Longhair's style at many gigs until he tired of the act and began focusing on his own sound.

In 1996, despite the owner Jim Green's protestations over the previous two years, Tipitina's was sold to a group of investors led by a real estate developer and property owner named Roland von Kur-natowski. Still the owner today, he has greatly enhanced the profile of the club with a foundation to support the music of New Orleans.

The new company, Eighth Floor, LLC, immediately began address-ing some of the problems plaguing the club since its inception in the 1970s. A state of the art sound system replaced the old system that was over ten years old. The dressing room was upgraded and was air-conditioned for the first time. The dance floor was redone, and as an added touch, the Tips logo was inlaid in tile near the stage. The bathrooms, always notorious, were completely renovated. They also began developing the Tipitina's Walk of Fame and set about putting the names of the legendary musicians of New Orleans on lighted insets on the sidewalk in front of the club.

In the long run, both Tipitina's and the House of Blues found their own niche, especially in more recent years when the House of Blues grew into a national chain catering to a much wider music demographic.

The other clubs in town were not really impacted by the House of Blues. New venues continued to open including the Dragon's Den over the Siam Café on Esplanade Avenue. Though initially featuring generic blues bands and other pedestrian musical fare, the Dragon's Den gradually developed into a venue that featured cutting edge hip-hop and avant-garde jazz.

In 1995, following his recovery from alcohol and drug-related problems and his marriage to Antoinette, the legendary R&B star Ernie K-Doe opened a club named after his biggest hit, "Mother-In-Law." He had a new lease on life after years of hard living. Before his career revival, he played sporadically around town, mostly at Jazz Fest and at various 1950s R&B reviews, but his performances were usually rough, and his voice was mostly shot.

But in the friendly confines of his own club, surrounded by his various acolytes and running partners, he could usually be counted on to put on a good show. One particular evening bears revisiting. He had a great backing band, led by the guitarist Ernie Vincent, and they were on fire. Musically flashing back to his heyday, K-Doe was clearly in his element. At one point, he took the microphone, on a super long cord, right out into N. Claiborne Avenue—one of the busiest streets in the city. Half the crowd followed him out the door, and he sang in the middle of the street as cars swerved to avoid him.

Uptown, the venerable neighborhood bar, Le Bon Temps Roule, started presenting bands for the first time in their recently renovated back room. Pasquallie's opened in the bar formerly known as Benny's, and they began presenting the same or similar acts creating an intimate walking scene between the two bars that were located two blocks from each other.

By 1996, the club scene was shifting yet again in New Orleans. A

walking tour operator in the French Quarter named Richard Rochester told everyone in town that Danny Barker had suggested he open
a jazz club, so he did just that. The Funky Butt took over a space on
N. Rampart Street that had been the home of the much-lauded Restaurant Jonathan in the 1970s.

The club was beautifully decorated in a style reflecting its geo-
graphical and musical connection to the old Storyville Red Light
District. There was a small downstairs room for intimate performances and a larger space upstairs. On April 25, 1996, they had their
grand opening at the beginning of the Jazz Fest season.

The Little Rascals Brass Band put on a decent, though strangely
lackluster opening set before Henry Butler took the stage. He was
playing a grand piano specifically ordered by Rochester for the
great musician who intended to make the Funky Butt his main base
of operations.

Butler's first set was solo in keeping with Rochester's high-
minded concept for his club. He played the part of a Storyville piano
professor with a stunning display of musical virtuosity. For the second set, which began at 2:30 AM, Butler had his regular rhythm section during this period, Chris Severin and Herman Jackson, along
with a new saxophonist on the scene who had been studying at
Loyola University with Tony Dagradi. Clarence Johnson III played
with finesse and balance and, despite his youth and relative inexpe-
rience, was also capable of almost frightening displays of power. He
was an equal player among the other musicians and proceeded to
blow away the crowd.

Perhaps attempting to take a page from John Blancher at the
Rock 'n' Bowl, Rochester banned the guest list. His efforts to enforce
the policy included a smugly worded sign to that effect posted at
the entrance to his upstairs room. It was just one example of his
unwillingness or inability to simply get along in the tight knit music
scene in New Orleans that eventually doomed his business.

Rochester alienated many musicians and most of the music
community with his poor interpersonal skills and weak understanding of the local mores. However, for a time he did decent business
within the tourist market that was his bread and butter as a tour
operator before getting into the club business. He sold the club to

the trombonist "Big" Sam Williams and his wife before permanently leaving town.

As the 1990s came to a close, new clubs opened. Some like the Caldonia 2000, located in the Tremé, and Levon Helm's Great American Café barely made it a year. Others like the Red Room and Quint Davis and Ralph Brennan's Storyville District, a grand attempt to bring jazz back to Bourbon Street, did decent business before floundering.

The Old Point Bar, a neighborhood joint in Algiers on the riverfront, and the Banks Street Bar and Grill, a neighborhood barroom in Mid City, quietly began presenting bands. The Old Point became a focal point for several musicians who were branching out into gigs as bandleaders. When the keyboardist John Gros decided to start his own band, he left George Porter, Jr.'s band and formed Papa Grows Funk with June Yamagishi and Russell Batiste. Yamagishi is also in the Trio with George Porter, Jr. and Johnny Vidacovich. Both of those bands called the Old Point home before they outgrew the out-of-the-way bar and relocated their regular gigs to the Maple Leaf.

The Shim Sham Club opened in the French Quarter in the old Toulouse Street Theater. They featured a new generation of burlesque dancers and live music of the indie variety while catering to a new, younger demographic. The club eventually morphed into One Eyed Jack's, which still actively presents live shows appealing to downtown hipsters.

Clubs weren't the only businesses to take advantage of the booming economy and the rising profile of New Orleans music. One of the most important businesses related to music in New Orleans, the Louisiana Music Factory, opened in early 1992 on N. Peters Street in the French Quarter. The record store, started by the entrepreneur Barry Smith and Jerry Brock, one of the founders of WWOZ and a local music expert, quickly became an alternative to the chain mentality of Tower Records located three blocks away.

The Factory, as everyone calls it, caters to the New Orleans musician, and it became the go-to spot for young bands with music to sell as well as veterans with deep catalogs. By the end of the year, Abita beer was sponsoring in-store performances at the store. In the early years, these performances pulled from the Tremé community and traditional jazz, but by the time the program reached maturity, the store was hosting touring acts during Jazz Fest, and a veritable who's who of New Orleans musicians have now graced the tiny stage.

One of the first in-store performances at the Factory was by Troy "Trombone Shorty" Andrews. He was a seasoned veteran at fourteen who had been leading bands since he was six. The band included his older brother, James Andrews, on trumpet; another relative, Clarence Andrews, on bass drum; Davis Rogan on piano and Arthur Kastler on bass.

John Sinclair, the grizzled Sixties veteran, poet, author and revolutionary who had visited the city for years, left his native Michigan and settled in New Orleans for a long run. He quickly established himself as a fixture at the Factory in addition to becoming a radio personality on WWOZ. His late night blues and roots show quickly became a favorite of the denizens of the nightlife. An idiosyncratic entertainer, Sinclair is also an erudite writer whose work began appearing in *Offbeat* magazine. He began performing his poems with Walter "Wolfman" Washington and members of his band in early 1993 at Buffa's, a neighborhood joint on Esplanade Avenue.

Tower Records had been presenting a strong schedule of in-store performances during what came to be called the "daze-in-between" Jazz Fest weekends since they first opened. In 1993, the Louisiana Music Factory joined in and started a long tradition that has outlived the national chain. They had music all day Monday through Wednesday and showcased artists like Anders Osborne, John Mooney, Earl Turbinton, Donald Harrison, Jr., and Anthony "Tuba Fats" Lacen and his trad jazz band, the Chosen Few.

The highlight of the in-stores was the Trombone Shorty's Brass Band Blowout on Wednesday. All of the Tremé musicians performed in various combinations, and Big Fritz of Trombone Shorty's bar provided food. It was the beginning of another tradition that lasted for a number of years. Of course, Rebirth closed the day out in fine style.

By 1996, the Louisiana Music Factory was developing into a force on the local scene. They had no trouble competing with Tower Records based on their superior customer service and deep knowledge of local musicians and the music community. In August, the owners of the record store announced they were moving the business from N. Peters Street to Decatur Street across a narrow alley in the French Quarter. The new location was situated directly across the street from the House of Blues and offered more space for the growing company. It also opened the door towards considerably more regular in-store performances because the new spot had a permanent stage.

On September 14, the grand reopening of the Louisiana Music Factory featured a great lineup that defined the open, eclectic nature of the store. Anders Osborne and Theresa Andersson performed first as an acoustic duo. Then Kermit Ruffins and the Barbecue Swingers performed with Marie Wantanabe on piano and Richard Payne on upright bass. They opened with "Struttin' With Some Barbecue," the classic from Louis Armstrong's canon that has become one of Ruffins' signature tunes.

The legendary bandleader and composer, Dave Bartholomew of Fats Domino fame, was in the house since he was up next on the schedule. He was in a feisty mood, and he jumped up on the stage with Ruffins' band to add a verse during "I Still Get Jealous." Then Bartholomew played his own set featuring stalwarts of Domino's band, Fred Kemp, Ed Frank, Erving Charles, and Charles Moore, doing piano-less versions of many of the songs he co-wrote with Domino.

The Louisiana Music Factory had entered a new era, and over the course of the next decade they began presenting in-store performances almost every Saturday afternoon. Saturdays at the Factory are now an integral part of the fabric of the New Orleans musical community where you can always count on seeing incredible sets by veterans and newcomers alike.

The French Quarter Festival began to really heat up around the mid-'90s as the organizers tried to pitch the annual event as a more local, laid back alternative to the growing behemoth of the Jazz Fest. The vocalist Samirah Evans played a really sweet set with a band of veteran players that included Ed Frank on piano, Walter Payton on bass and Fred Kemp on saxophone.

But the highlight that day was an appearance by a son of the Tremé who had the musical bug that was epidemic in his family. John Boutte, whose sister Lillian was already a significant presence both in New Orleans and in Europe, possesses a voice that is instantaneously recognizable. He is slight and slender, but his vocals sometimes seem like they are coming from a much larger frame. His musical roots are in the church, but he is equally comfortable with secular songs. He sings with an inherent passion and truly inhabits each song. He can wail or growl depending on the song and the moment. He is equally adept fronting a band or performing, as he has done in recent years, with a single accompanist.

On this particular day, Boutte had Loren Pickford on sax, Ed Frank on piano and "Luscious" Lloyd Lambert, another venerable local musician, on bass. The set was spiritual, but not overtly religious. Since then, many have marveled at the understated way he has created a career for himself. His work in 2000 with the band Cubanismo was a groundbreaking amalgamation of New Orleans and Cuban music.

In the months leading up to the summer of 1995, the music community was buzzing about a new festival scheduled for the 4th of July holiday at the Superdome. There was good reason to be excited; the event was being produced by Festival Productions, the same company that produced the Jazz Fest. The Essence Festival was supposed to be a one-off event tied to the 25th anniversary of *Essence* magazine, but the three-night concert series was an instant hit. After some touch-and-go negotiating with the city in the early years, it has become an eagerly anticipated annual affair.

Though I prefer to spend my time listening to the local bands in the more intimate Superlounges during the Essence Fest, one main stage performance needs to be recounted. In 1996, Stevie Wonder set the tone for this new love affair between the city and the Essence Festival with his closing set on the first night in the Superdome. He played all of his hits from *Songs in the Key of Life* plus great versions of "Signed, Sealed and Delivered" and "Superstition." The highlight of his incredible set was when he split the Dome up into sections and then taught us all to sing with each section doing a different part. At the end of the lesson, the entire crowd was doing the beginning of "My Cheri Amour" in three-part harmony!

* * *

By 1997, Kermit Ruffins' relationship with Justice Records, the label that released his first two solo records, had run its course. But conveniently, a new face, part of the next generation of entrepreneurs with new ideas, was on the scene.

Mark Samuels formed Basin Street Records, and Ruffins was the first act he signed. Having decided that Ruffins needed to record a live album, a date was set for November 14 at Tipitina's. The place was packed, but unfortunately the band played the same set twice, and the crowd's energy dissipated the second time around.

Known in the early days of his business for his creative marketing techniques, Samuels has since gone on to become a significant player on the scene. Though the Ruffins disc sold well, Basin Street's biggest success came a year later.

During the summer of 1997, Bill Summers, an energetic percussionist who was a member of Herbie Hancock's legendary fusion group, the Headhunters, returned to New Orleans. Besides gigging with some of the greatest musicians in the world, he also worked behind the scenes in television and film. He collaborated with Quincy Jones on the music for the groundbreaking television mini-series, *Roots,* and he was an arranger and percussionist on *The Color Purple* soundtrack.

His first performance at Jazz Fest was in a trio with the muscular Chicago-based saxophonist Ed Petersen (now a professor of music at UNO) and David Torkanowsky. The music was fascinating. Towards the end of the set, Summers' wife at the time, Yvette, appeared in a gossamer dress and added haunting Afro-Cuban chanting to the eclectic set.

Summers' arrival in the city after a 30-year absence began to pay dividends within a year when he hooked up with Irvin Mayfield and Jason Marsalis to form Los Hombres Calientes. Here's the story of the band's beginnings.

On February 7, 1998, they played their first gig at Snug Harbor. David Pulphus was the bassist, Victor Atkins was the pianist and Yvette Summers played percussion and sang. The show was reportedly one of wildest in the history of the Faubourg Marigny nightclub. By the end of the second set, tables and chairs were pushed out of the way and people were dancing with wild abandon to the group's compelling Afro-Cuban grooves.

By the time they played at the House of Blues on March 12, they had already developed some incredible word-of-mouth attention among the local music freaks. Everyone on the scene, especially those who had been observing the development of Mayfield and Marsalis in various settings, was excited about the gig. People wanted to understand how they had become the talk of the town so quickly, so the club was packed.

Summers was the wild card since he had only recently returned to New Orleans. His extensive résumé spoke volumes about his career but left some doubt about how he would fit in with such young talent. The doubt was erased immediately upon seeing how they interacted at the House of Blues.

The band had yet to write any significant amount of original material, so the songs were long, percussion-heavy jams and reworked versions of jazz standards. Atkins and Mayfield took the bulk of the solos, and they pushed each rising crescendo into the stratosphere. Marsalis and Summers were locked in tight as Summers displayed his on-stage effervescence by bouncing around his huge percussion rig and playing every instrument with child-like aplomb.

Clearly, Mayfield's youth was not going to be an impediment to the group's success. He was poised on stage and his solos indicated he had been practicing this material that differed so greatly from the feel-good cutting contests with Kermit Ruffins at Donna's and Vaughan's. This was another style of music with depth and history, and Mayfield was intent on mastering its intricacies.

Summers was clearly the elder statesman in the group as his musical experiences surpassed those of everyone else in the band combined. However, he allowed the younger musicians plenty of space to experiment and grow musically, and they rewarded him with loyalty and dedication. The band became another supergroup of sorts coalescing around Bill Summers' encyclopedic knowledge of the rhythms of the African diaspora and the insatiable hunger for musical knowledge of the co-founders of the band, Irvin Mayfield and Jason Marsalis.

Los Hombres Calientes was a great concept from the beginning, and Mark Samuels immediately signed the band to Basin Street Records. In what may have been the shortest time from the formation of a group until their first recording, *Los Hombres Calientes, Vol. 1* was released in time for the Jazz Fest. The album was a best seller and immediately launched the group and the label onto the A-list.

Mayfield became another of Basin Street Records' acts when he recorded his first album in 1998. He released five more recordings, four of them on Basin Street, before he was 25 years old.

His relationship with Ruffins, which stretched back to when he was a high school student at NOCCA, was an important one. When the two trumpeters hosted the second Battle of the Bands, Mayfield upped the ante by arriving with a ringer of a band featuring David Pulphus, Victor Atkins, Aaron Fletcher and another new face around town, the drummer Jaz Sawyer.

Hot on the heels of the runaway success of Los Hombres Calientes, Mark Samuels and his Basin Street Records booked the ornate Orpheum Theater for a night show during Jazz Fest. The featured acts were Los Hombres Calientes and Kermit Ruffins and the Barbecue Swingers with special guests.

The night started with a straight-ahead jazz set from the members of Los Hombres minus Bill and Yvette Summers. Delfeayo Marsalis and Wes Anderson, the alto saxophonist from Wynton Marsalis' group, joined in. Then Summers joined the proceedings and put on a high energy Afro-Cuban set with the full band.

The finale was left to Ruffins, the more established artist. He had Shannon Powell on drums and was joined by Delfeayo Marsalis and a young saxophonist, Aaron Fletcher. Despite this powerhouse lineup and the strength of the musical performances, the decision to rent the Orpheum was a rare business miscue for Samuels. The elegant theater was practically empty.

Los Hombres Calientes continued to grow musically, and the personnel in the band changed over the course of their five albums on Basin Street Records. The trumpeter Leon Brown and the trombonist Steve Walker began playing more regularly when the group expanded to include a full horn section. The two friends were natural additions to the unit. A couple of years later, they also formed their own band, Funkin' Horns, which approached the music from the perspective of the instrumental funk master Maceo Parker. Leon Brown also began a long association with the traditional jazz drummer Bob French. He took over Kermit Ruffins' Monday date at Donna's, and Brown began honing his trad chops as well as taking a vocal turn now and then.

The bassist Edwin Livingston became the newest face around town when he replaced David Pulphus in Los Hombres Calientes. They played a super hot show at Tipitina's with Ricky Sebastian filling in on drums for Jason Marsalis who was on the road with the pianist Marcus Roberts. Marsalis eventually quit the group and was replaced by Horatio "el Negro" Hernandez before he was ultimately replaced by Sebastian. Los Hombres Calientes continued to perform regularly until Hurricane Katrina and Mayfield began focusing his attention on his New Orleans Jazz Orchestra.

Elsewhere on the business front, a group of young music aficionados, Kerry Black, Rick Farman, Richard Goodstone, and Jonathan Mayers, formed a company called Superfly Productions. Within a short period of time, they became major players on the local scene by presenting acts rarely heard in New Orleans and by hosting their own shows at a new venue, a warehouse space attached to the Contemporary Arts Center. They also began promoting shows at local clubs.

Superfly's first advertised concert series was dubbed "Take Funk to Heaven—Mardi Gras 1997." The first of the two shows was the initial example of what has become their forte—pairing lesser-known acts with successful bands and using the synergy between the groups to develop a fan base. Superfly booked the Funky Meters with Galactic, a group that was already beginning to break out of New Orleans due to an ambitious tour schedule and a burgeoning fan base.

Galactic is a band that rose up quickly because of three factors. They are arguably the most important band in the second wave of funk acts that developed after the demise of the original Meters. Secondly, their emergence coincided with the expansion of the national jam band movement following the death of Jerry Garcia of the Grateful Dead in 1995. Thirdly, they were essentially tri-coastal with a small, but dedicated fan base on the east and west coasts and in New Orleans.

Here's a look back at their first several months. After shortening their moniker from the sophomoric Galactic Prophylactic to simply

Galactic, the young group of collegiate funksters met a producer from San Francisco who was looking for the next big thing out of New Orleans and began a ride that continues to this day.

Dan Prothero recorded Galactic's debut for his Fog City Records. It was released at the end of July 1996. *Coolin' Off* represents an early stage of the band's music, but because of Prothero's connections on the West Coast and the incipient jam band scene, the record helped propel the group to national success.

However, the membership of the band was still in flux. Two early members, the singer Chris Lane and the guitarist Rob Gowen, had left before the band met Prothero. They had no permanent horn players, and the role of Theryl DeClouet, who was as much a mentor as a member of the band, had not yet solidified. They played regularly during this period, but the personnel were rarely the same. However, the shows were consistently stellar and the musicians improved incrementally between each and every performance during their early career.

Despite having an album that opened doors nationally, they were still mostly an unknown quantity around New Orleans. After all, the musical cognoscenti had barely quit laughing at their original name.

One of their first relatively high profile gigs was opening for the great Johnny "Guitar" Watson at the House of Blues on February 2, 1996. Tom Fitzpatrick and Mark Mullins played saxophone and trombone respectively. On March 8, they opened for the more established Smilin' Myron at Tipitina's. This time around, they had Joe Cabral on sax and Mark Mullins on trombone. DeClouet only sang a few songs, but the core band was really tight and the jams were huge.

On March 16, Galactic appeared at the WTUL Rock On Survival Marathon on a day that also featured the aforementioned incredible set by All That as well as great sets by Lump, a short-lived edgy rock band that usually included the future Galactic saxophonist, Ben Ellman, and the Rebirth Brass Band. It was a beautiful, sunny, early spring day, and the atmosphere on the quad added mightily to the proceedings. After their set, I wrote in my journal that Galactic represented a new kind of groovy. Interestingly, Stanton Moore was unavailable, so Johnny Vidacovich played the gig.

On May 5, Galactic played for the first time at the New Orleans Jazz and Heritage Festival. The fest's organizers had them booked as the second act on the smaller Stage 4—known as the House of Blues/Dr. Martens stage at the time. The spot was jammed shoulder to shoulder with people who had heard about this hot young funk band.

A little over two weeks later, Galactic appeared as the middle act on a three-band bill at the House of Blues. All That opened and the Soul Rebels were the headliners. This time it was Galactic's Jeff Raines who was missing. Alex McMurray, who had roared during All That's opening set, donned a black wig and ably played guitar with the nouveau funk outfit.

A week after the show at the House of Blues, Galactic did a show at the Mermaid Lounge with the veteran saxophonist Eric Traub playing vintage New Orleans style soul. Traub was a major force in the early days of the band. He co-wrote three tracks on the first record and appeared, along with the trumpeter Eric Jekabson and Mark Mullins, as a guest artist on the album.

By the end of the year, Galactic was the hottest band in town. In an interview in *Offbeat* magazine, Jim Green, the owner of Tipitina's, raved about the young band's drawing power and presciently opined that, "If some national or major label could get a hold of Galactic, I think they could do tremendous business, not just in New Orleans."

By the next summer, Ben Ellman was playing saxophone regularly with the band. He also played the harmonica, broadening the group's already expansive sound. He is now a key member of the band and has helped expand their sonic palette through his stellar production work. DeClouet left the band in the early part of the 21st century.

When Superfly Productions made the brilliant decision to pair the young band with the Funky Meters, it increased the size of their fan base by exposing the young band to an older generation of music lovers and Meters' devotees. That double bill proved to be a major factor in Galactic's meteoric rise.

The following night, the Saturday before Mardi Gras, Superfly brought the great saxophonist Maceo Parker to town on a bill with George Porter, Jr.'s Runnin' Pardners and the Rebirth Brass Band. The company has grown famous for their ability to match musicians and create compelling double and triple bills.

Following the success of the Mardi Gras shows, the company's plans grew more ambitious, and though they only presented three shows during Jazz Fest that first year, it was clear from their beginnings that this was a business destined to make an impact on the music scene in New Orleans.

During Jazz Fest, they booked two bands with large underground followings among the younger generation of music lovers—Bela Fleck and the Flecktones, and Medeski, Martin and Wood. Neither of the bands played New Orleans music per se, but they attracted a similar demographic of music fans. Fleck is a banjo virtuoso whose music crosses genres, and MMW is an organ trio that was one of the first of a younger generation of musicians to be signed to the venerable Blue Note label.

Superfly also got tongues wagging among the growing legion of critics of the booking policy of the Jazz Fest itself. They contended that both Bela Fleck and MMW deserved to be playing at the Fairgrounds. It was not the last time the company stimulated discussions about the booking policies of the Jazz Fest.

On November 28, 1998, Superfly Productions presented their first SuperJam at Tipitina's. The concept behind the super jam was to team up like-minded (read jam-happy) musicians and just let them play. Of course, the young company didn't invent the concept; they just created a way to capitalize on it. The inspiration may lie with another supergroup that performed a couple of years earlier.

Anders Osborne and Theresa Andersson had been sitting in with the Radiators quite a bit during 1996. Osborne's guitar work neatly complemented the band, and everyone seemed eager to have the comely Andersson on stage, She added great backing vocals and sparred with the guitarists on her violin. It was inevitable that the two Swedes would eventually join forces with members of the Radiators in a side project.

After briefly functioning as the Blue Jackal in 1995 and against incredible odds, Benny's reopened for the umpteenth time in October 1996. It was the final incarnation for the club, and given all the intense music created between those dingy walls, the place was destined to go out with a bang.

Monkey Ranch played their first show at Benny's on December 20, 1996. The band consisted of Osborne, Andersson, Dave Malone and Reggie Scanlan of the Radiators, "Mean" Willie Green on drums, Mark McGrain on trombone and Glenn Hartman on keys. The show was a total free-for-all that lasted until 5 AM. The modern day bluesman, Keb Mo, played the whole second set instead of Malone. There were other sit-ins as well including Tommy Malone on guitar and Tony Hall who played both bass and drums. The set list was very loose with long wide-open jams and collaborative efforts on cover songs. There were a few other performances by Monkey Ranch, but that first show was the kind of concert musicians and fans alike dream of experiencing. There was no ego in the room, and the musicians were as enthralled by each other's music as was the rabid audience. They stood by the side of the stage, itching for a chance to play as if they were school children waiting in line for the restroom.

It was a wonderful last hurrah for the neighborhood bar that had nurtured members of the Neville family and countless other musicians, but the battle against gentrification was finally lost. The building that housed Benny's is now an upscale middle class home without so much as a sign indicating the significance of the corner.

Superfly's first SuperJam featured John Mooney, Henry Butler, George Porter, Jr. and Stanton Moore. For Moore, playing in a rhythm section with one of his musical heroes was a dream come true. Porter and Moore locked into an impenetrable groove almost immediately, but both Mooney and Butler had a hard time shaking their individual styles. In the end, it was an up-and-down set that had a lot of energy but never reached the same heights as the musicians playing with their individual bands.

A month later, Superfly presented their second SuperJam on New Year's Eve at the Howlin' Wolf. The band included Zigaboo Modeliste, Walter "Wolfman" Washington, Jon Cleary and Tony Hall, and it set the template for future collaborations. Though Washington was the default frontman, he left plenty of space for the other musicians. Modeliste sang some of his songs from the Meters while locking in tight with Hall. Cleary delivered rippling New Orleans keyboard lines while also taking a few turns on lead vocals. The music was classic Meters-inspired New Orleans funk played with deep soul by four masters of the genre. An added bonus for those who stayed late was a guest turn by Art Neville. He led the band through a spirited jam on "Hey Pocky Way" that segued into the finale—"Iko Iko."

Barely a year in business, Superfly Productions had hit its stride. The business grew exponentially expanding into theater space on Canal Street as well as wonderfully intimate concerts on riverboats that recalled the heyday of the Riverboat President during Jazz Fest. Within three years, the company changed the face of the music business in New Orleans with creative bookings, a forward-looking business plan that took advantage of the new media infrastructure, and bigger and better SuperJams including a celebrated concert at the Saenger Theater in 2001 featuring Stewart Copeland of the Police, Les Claypool of Primus and Trey Anastasio of Phish. By the summer of 2002, Superfly Productions began to outgrow their beginnings in New Orleans. In partnership with a more established production company, they hosted the first annual Bonnaroo Music Festival on a giant farm outside of Manchester, Tennessee selling 75,000 tickets on word of mouth alone. Superfly Productions has not looked back ever since their local launch. Regarded as one of the country's premier grass roots music companies, they currently sell a successful business model to bands, festivals and other music-related businesses.

Superfly Productions was not without competition with respect to the newest generation of music lovers. The new owner of Tipitina's announced a grand expansion. Two new clubs were to open— a larger space in the Warehouse District, previously a dance club called City Lights, which would allow the club to book bands too big for the uptown venue, and a French Quarter location on N. Peters Street.

Tip's Big Room debuted with an impressive lineup during the second weekend of Jazz Fest in 1997. They had four nights of music including a performance by another band, Leftover Salmon, which was mining the same territory of Bela Fleck; a blues night with Jimmy Rogers and Mason Ruffner; a Historic Jazz Summit with Kermit Ruffins' Big Band, Henry Butler plus Shannon Powell and the

Tremé Jazz Ensemble as well as the Tremé Brass Band. The grand finale on the closing Sunday of the festival was a performance by the Funky Meters. The Rebirth Brass Band and Jo "Cool" Davis, the gospel singer and longtime doorman at Tipitina's uptown location, were the supporting acts.

The company had a short tenure in the warehouse space. However, they did have one huge show. James Brown played and the place was packed wall to wall. Brown was late getting on stage; a sore reminder of the debacle of his Jazz Fest appearance years earlier. But his performance was mesmerizing. Though long past his prime as a dancer, his voice was in top shape, and he worked the crowd as if he still had something to prove.

Tipitina's French Quarter opened on New Year's Eve with a performance by Galactic. Henry Butler opened the show with a great set featuring his new band, Orleans Inspiration. But it paled in comparison to the energy emanating from the stage while Galactic was performing.

The show lasted until 4:30 AM, a late night tradition that the band continues for special shows. Scott Messersmith, Keng and Chaddy, the vocalists from Iris May Tango, and the trumpeter Eric Jacobsen, who played with the band at Jazz Fest, all sat in for a fine evening of jamming. They had reached the pinnacle of their first phase and began experimenting with new directions in the coming years.

Following the grand opening of Tipitina's French Quarter location, they began an impressive series of concerts in March that were booked by two New Orleans musical icons. Allen Toussaint presented Thursday night's bookings, and Cyril Neville was responsible for Friday night's musical offerings. Toussaint used the opportunity to book bands he had recorded for his label, NYNO Records, which was formed in 1996 and put out a small number of well-received albums before being placed on the back burner by the celebrated producer. Some of the acts included the vocalist Larry Hamilton, the gospel prodigy Raymond Myles, and the irrepressible "Satchmo of the Ghetto," James Andrews. Toussaint's relationship with the French Quarter location lasted until June 1999.

Neville booked his own band, the Uptown Allstars, Los Hombres Calientes, the Iguanas, and Iris May Tango among others. He often appeared with his featured acts playing kit drums or percussion.

The trombonist Mark Mullins, a member of Harry Connick, Jr.'s band, had formed a rock band called MuleBone with the keyboardist John Gros, and he began booking gigs on Wednesdays at the Tipitina's French Quarter location. He used his new musical outlet to perfect an innovative technique that involved playing the trombone through various effects usually associated with electric guitar. MuleBone gradually disappeared from the scene after Gros formed his own group, Papa Grows Funk.

But on June 10, 1998, Mullins debuted the first version of another band at Tipitina's French Quarter that eventually became a successful touring act and provided pundits with an unanswerable question—are they a rock band or a brass band? The first incarnation of Bonarama included the trombonists Corey Henry, Craig Klein, Rick Trolsen, Freddie Lonzo and Steve Suter. The rhythm section featured Glenn Patscha on keys, Russell Batiste on drums and Matt Perrine on tuba. Curiously, there was no guitar player even though Bert Cotton became an integral part of the band in later years.

The show was excellent. The tunes, originals and covers, had crafty arrangements. They were funky, high-energy workouts for the band. The trombone players, much maligned in the music world (there's a joke—what do you call a trombonist with a cell phone? — an optimist), seemed to be totally enjoying the very idea of a group of trombonists. At the end of the show, four other trombonists including Steve Johnson from Coolbone, Gregory "Coon" Veals from the Little Rascals and Andy Galbiati from the Algiers Brass Band all joined in for a wild finale.

Though Henry and Lonzo didn't last in the group for long, the other players have built the band into an institution. Batiste played in the early years along with Stanton Moore before the lineup solidified with Eric Bolivar on drums.

Klein, Suter, Trolsen and Perrine were also key members of the New Orleans Nightcrawlers, a brass supergroup of sorts. Interestingly, the pianist Tom McDermott organized them and wrote arrangements despite the fact he did not actually play in the group.

Fredy Omar, a sophisticated vocalist from Honduras who had been fronting Ritmo Caribeno, one of the longest-standing Latin groups in New Orleans, started his own band in 1997. He became a regular at Café Brasil in October. His stage presence, ace band including veteran Latin percussionists Humberto "Pupi" Menes and Cristobal Cruzado, and killer vocals were a sign the young man had a bright future in New Orleans. Fredy Omar con su Banda is now one of the most popular Latin bands in the city.

New bands continued to emerge as the 1990s came to a close. Some, like Los Vecinos, a Cuban music-inspired band with membership that overlapped with Mas Mamones, are fondly remembered footnotes in the bigger picture. Others, like the Morning 40 Federation, boozy rockers who took their name from the habit of drinking 40 ounces of beer each morning, presided over a whole new scene before combusting into the ether. They occasionally play reunion shows. Still others, like Papa Grows Funk and The Trio, featuring Johnny Vidacovich, George Porter, Jr. and June Yamagishi (or special guests), have become institutions.

Scott Billington, the acclaimed producer for Rounder Records, spent much of 1997 assembling a great compilation, *Ain't No Funk Like N.O. Funk*, which was released in the summer of 1998. It featured the cream of the crop of the second generation of funk bands including Galactic, All That, the New Orleans Nightcrawlers, Davell Crawford, the New World Funk Ensemble, Smilin' Myron, the Flavor Kings, Iris May Tango, and Billy Iuso's first band, the Brides of Jesus. For added pleasure, they also included two cuts by Walter "Wolfman" Washington.

At this point in time, Rounder had already significantly reduced their New Orleans output. Earlier in the year, the company ended its decades-plus deal as distributor for the local Blacktop Records. But Billington still had his finger on the pulse of the scene in New Orleans. In an interview in the August 1997 issue of *Offbeat* magazine he said, "I think people are going to look at New Orleans and Louisiana right now in 1997 as being a whole new golden era for New Orleans music."

Chapter 15

JAZZ FEST IN THE 1990s

"There are a lot of places I like, but I like New Orleans better."—Bob Dylan

The Jazz Fest went through one of its most significant periods of development during the late 1980s and the early 1990s. Despite booking more and more national acts, the organizers continued to pay homage to the local R&B greats of the 1950s. Artists like Ernie K Doe, Jessie Hill, Bobby Marchan, and Frankie Ford participated in reviews saluting the music's heyday. However, one extremely important player from that era was missing from the stages at the Fairgrounds.

The funk pioneer Eddie Bo was mostly just a legend to the new contingent of fans crowding the infield at the Jazz Fest though numerous bands played his well-known songs. But Bo himself was in semi-retirement because of problems he had with the business of music. He didn't play at all through most of the 1980s, although he was listed in *Wavelength* magazine's band guide in 1985.

He emerged from his self-imposed retirement in 1989 and appeared at the Jazz Fest on the first Saturday. It was an early time slot on Stage 1, and the billing read, "Ernie K-Doe with Blue-Eyed Soul Revue & Eddie Bo." He also appeared at Tyler's with the great saxophonist Fred Kemp during the Jazz Fest. But it wasn't until October 5, 1989 when Bo played a much-anticipated show at Tipitina's that his comeback really began. He had an all-star band backing him with George Porter, Jr. on bass, Hurley Blanchard on drums and Alonzo Bowens on sax. Jon "King" Cleary played guitar—his original instrument—since Bo is a pianist.

He played all of his classics including "Every Dog Got His Day" and "Check Mr. Popeye." Clearly in an ebullient mood, he covered Jessie Hill's "Ooh Poo Pah Doo." Though the show was sparsely attended, the jams were precious. The highlight of the night was a fifteen-minute version of Chris Kenner's "Land of a 1000 Dances" to open the third set. That song became a staple of his live set. However, Bo wasn't completely back in the public eye after this show.

A month before Mardi Gras in 1990, he debuted a new band at Tipitina's. Since Bo was back in the business, it was clear that using pick-up bands, even if George Porter, Jr. led them, was no longer acceptable. This group included the venerable Walter Payton on bass, David Lee on drums, Eugene Ross, a guitarist who played regularly at Benny's with the band Blue Lunch, and Red Morgan on saxophone and flute.

Though they didn't have the pedigree of Porter, they were Bo's band, and it was obvious they had been rehearsing. Since it was early in the Carnival season, Bo jammed one of his biggest hits, "Check Mr. Popeye," into the Professor Longhair classic, "Mardi Gras in New Orleans." He dedicated the whole show to the great patron saint of Tipitina's.

Of all the players in his band, Morgan's performance was memorable for his unique ability to scat sing while still playing the flute. Morgan played regularly with Bo until the great pianist's death in 2009. Bo and his new band made a statement—he was back on the scene, and he was taking no prisoners.

At the Jazz Fest in 1990, Bo was still being billed with Ernie K-Doe, this time as "special guest." But it is significant to note that he also gave an interview at the Music Heritage stage expounding on his long absence from the scene.

At the Jazz Fest, the great R&B veteran Ernie K-Doe's sets were notoriously uneven. He could be idiosyncratically brilliant or he could be a washout. Eddie Bo virtually took over K-Doe's B-list backing band, and the set went straight over-the-top. K-Doe appeared resplendent in a colorful suit that reflected the nickname he gave himself—the Emperor of the Universe. He sang his hits, "Mother-In-Law," "'Tain't It the Truth" and "A Certain Girl," with verve and gusto that recalled his 1950s heyday.

By 1994, Eddie Bo was becoming an active participant on the music scene once again. He began playing a regular gig at Margaritaville in the small saloon-like space fronting Decatur Street. He worked the crowd like a pro and usually ended his sets with a guest from the audience sharing the piano bench on a crowd favorite like "Mustang Sally" or "Proud Mary." But he didn't pander to the baser sensibilities of the tourist crowd; he was always aware of the musically informed in his audience.

On February 26, he played a rare date at Café Istanbul. Despite a weak crowd mostly sitting in the back, Bo was up dancing on stage during "Mustang Sally." He then rhetorically asked the crowd, "Who's from New Orleans, who's from out of town?" He then answered himself, "Well, you people in the back (sitting down) are going to have to do something to prove it (that you're local)". He then launched into "The Land of 1000 Dances" and confirmed to himself and the small group on the dance floor that there were no other locals in the house.

Bo remained a vital part of the New Orleans music scene for the next fifteen years. He mentored young artists including the guitarist Marc Stone and numerous others. His already stunning career comeback was burnished by his performances at the Jazz Fest. They became renowned since he would always leave the stage with a second line umbrella in his hand and dive deep into the crowd; his trademark turban bobbing on his head and an impish grin covering his face.

The first day of the Jazz Fest in 1990 was deluged with thunderstorms. Rain was coming down in droves during Tribe Nunzio's set, but the hardcore festers, who actually prefer the threat of rain because it keeps the rookies and tourists at home, were dancing with wild abandon as the rain poured, the wind howled and umbrellas turned inside out. Holden Miller, the group's irrepressible lead singer, was awed by the dedication of the crowd. She yelled in admiration, "Y'all look groovy, all wet and all!"

Charles Neville debuted his new jazz group, Diversity, on the second Friday of the 1990 Jazz Fest. He had Patrice Fisher on harp, a cello player, three backing singers, a guitarist and a saxophonist. The music varied widely and their press materials described the sound as "from Charlie Parker to Fess." They did a wicked version of "God Bless the Child" and closed with a barely recognizable, jazzy version of "Hey Pocky Way."

For the night shows, the Jazz Fest brought back the River Tent for the second year. It was a different style of tent that was supposed to be more comfortable and safer than the one that blew down in 1989. One of the best bills scheduled at the new River Tent featured Ladysmith Black Mambazo, Arrow and the Neville Brothers.

Ladysmith Black Mambazo is the South African vocal group that played a prominent role on Paul Simon's landmark album, *Graceland*. He was backstage for their set, and when he responded to the call of the group's leader, Joseph Shabalala, he joined the group sans guitar. They performed "Homeless," one of the songs off of *Graceland,* as well as "Amazing Grace" and the African anthem, "God Bless Africa," which they sang in Zulu. Simon was very animated and seemed to be truly enjoying himself. Of course, the crowd went crazy. It would be two decades before he appeared again on a stage at the Jazz Fest.

As the Jazz Fest grew, it became more and more of an economic engine fueling other businesses. Tower Records had recently opened a franchise on Decatur Street in the French Quarter. In 1990, they had a full schedule of in-store performances during the "daze-in-between" to capitalize on the increasing number of out of town visitors who elected to make their pilgrimage to the Crescent City a ten-day affair.

On Wednesday afternoon, I witnessed one of the most intimate performances I have ever seen. Snooks Eaglin and Earl King appeared together at the downtown store. Because of some technical problem, there were no microphones. The two carried on, trading licks on their guitars as if they were back at some dive thirty years earlier, while performing a stunning duet on King's Carnival anthem, "Big Chief".

On Thursday night, Rounder Records celebrated their 20th anniversary with a party at a new venue that had opened the previous fall. The Riverboat Hallelujah, formerly a cinema, was actually a land-locked hall on Tulane Avenue. The Rebirth Brass Band opened the show to an empty room. But the place quickly filled up for Snooks Eaglin (with George Porter, Jr. and Russell Batiste) followed by Bo Dollis and the Wild Magnolias with Big Chief Monk Boudreaux. George Porter, Jr. and the Runnin' Pardners closed the show.

Porter's new group was beginning to gel although the personnel had yet to stabilize. Russell Batiste was already the regular drummer, and Alonzo Bowens was playing saxophone. Brint Anderson, a smoldering guitarist from Natchez, Mississippi, eventually took over the guitar chair in the Runnin' Pardners.

Art Neville sat in on "People Say" at the end of Porter's set at the Riverboat Hallelujah. The crowd was buzzing as the tantalizing thought of half of the Meters on stage coursed through the cavernous room. These near reunions, the growing importance of their music to younger musicians, and the continuing personnel drama of the Meters still dominated many people's minds even though Zigaboo Modeliste moved to the Bay Area during the summer of 1986 and Leo Nocentelli was based out of Los Angeles. They both returned home regularly, and the rumors of reunions were staples of every visit. Here are some anecdotes from the period.

In the fall of 1986, Nocentelli announced he was returning to town to debut his new band in late October. They were scheduled to open for the Neville Brothers at Tipitina's along with George Porter, Jr.'s latest aggregation. Would there be a reunion of the three members of the Meters?

Nocentelli's band, called Nocentelli, included other New Orleans transplants to Los Angeles. Ivan Neville was on keyboards and vocals, Nick Daniels was on bass and Earl Smith was on percussion and vocals. The drummer was a session player named Tony Braunagel who was unfamiliar to the Meters' fans in attendance.

In a word, Nocentelli was horrible. The leader had completely abandoned his groundbreaking rhythm guitar style and transformed into a flashy over-the-top lead player. He was loud and obnoxious, and his repetitive, lightning fast licks dominated the mix. The qualities in his playing that so appealed to fans of the Meters just a few short years earlier were nowhere to be heard. To add insult to injury, the new songs were equally as horrid. Nocentelli released one 45-RPM single, the title of which sums up all that was wrong with his new band, "We Put the Rock in Your Roll." Needless to say, there was no reunion that night.

The band Nocentelli returned to New Orleans for the Jazz Fest in 1988 and appeared on a double bill with George Porter, Jr.'s Funksters at Jimmy's on April 30. This time around, the guitarist and the bassist played together during a late night jam at the end of the show. They played the Meters' classics, "Hey Pocky Way," "Ain't No Use," and "People Say." The legendary singer/songwriter, Alex Chilton, joined them on stage. The energy was electric, and the two musicians were as energized by their reunion as the crowd was overjoyed to witness it. The stage was set for future collaboration.

On the night before Mardi Gras in 1989, their new act, Geo-Leo, debuted at a short-lived venue called the Absolute Bar and Grill on Tchoupitoulas Street. It was billed as "The Night Two Meters Meet." Jon Cleary opened the show on solo piano. Carnival time always brings out the best in local performers, and the show at the Absolute was no exception despite the non-traditional setting of playing in a restaurant. The band ripped it up, and expectations were high after Mardi Gras passed.

Leo Nocentelli was back in New Orleans, at least temporarily, and he sat in everywhere during the months between Carnival and Jazz Fest. He jammed regularly with a variety of players including Henry Butler and the bassist Daryl Johnson and his new band, Trouble. By the time Jazz Fest rolled around, Geo-Leo had a full slate of performances, and Nocentelli continued to sit in whenever and wherever he could. He joined Porter on a rousing version of "Africa" at the record release party for the bassist's first solo album at Tyler's Beer Garden and sat in with Trouble at the Fairgrounds on the first Friday.

Geo-Leo played at Jimmy's the night before their performance at the Jazz Fest on the first Sunday. The show was heavily hyped and was overflowing with a new generation of fans eager to hear the music of the Meters even if there were only two original members on stage. The crowd was positively delirious when Art Neville showed up for a late night jam.

Leo Nocentelli was very late the next day for their set at the Fairgrounds, and everyone had to chill while waiting for him. He arrived sporting dark shades and looking as if he hadn't had much sleep. The group instantly hit its stride, picking up right where the show left off the night before. The only downside of the set was when Nocentelli broke one string and then another and was forced to change them himself.

Though Art Neville did not join Geo-Leo at the Fairgrounds, the late night appearance set the stage for another big reunion of members of the Meters. On December 2, 1989, three-quarters of the Meters reunited with Russell Batiste taking the place of Zigaboo Modeliste at the Riverboat Hallelujah. Cyril Neville and the Uptown Allstars and Tribe Nunzio were the opening acts.

The show was over the top, and though Batiste didn't have the finesse of Zigaboo Modeliste on the drums, he certainly knew the music and powered the band in his own youthful fashion. Art Neville's voice was in fine form, and it was clear to longtime followers of the band that his vocals were the missing ingredient in all the other incarnations of the Meters. During the second set, Ivan and Cyril Neville both sat in with the band.

The highlights of the evening included great versions of all the classics including "Love Slip Up On Ya," "Lovey Dovey," "Chug-A-Lug" and "Be My Lady." Though it wasn't the original foursome, the music was awesome and plans were laid to reprise the concert during Carnival of 1990. The Meters, albeit three of the original quartet, were back complete with new merchandise—a t-shirt picturing an eerie-looking, afro-wearing skull emblazoned with the words, "The Meters Will Funk You to Death."

This new version lasted barely four years, although they didn't play together very often. Art Neville was much too busy touring with the Neville Brothers who were achieving unprecedented success following the release of *Yellow Moon* in 1989 and its follow-up, *Brother's Keeper*, a year later.

In late 1993, Leo Nocentelli quit the Meters leaving George Porter, Jr. and Art Neville as the remaining original members. They recruited the guitarist Brian Stoltz, who had played with the Neville Brothers, to fill Nocentelli's big shoes. The new group was christened the Funky Meters, and their tenure eventually completely eclipsed that of the original band.

Zigaboo Modeliste returned to play at the Jazz Fest in 1999 with a band he was calling Zigaboo's Revue. The group featured the guitarists Camile Baudoin (of the Radiators) and Renard Poché along with Nick Daniels on bass. They blazed through an amazing set as Baudoin and Poché traded lead lines.

At the end of the set, George Porter, Jr. joined his estranged bandmate on a couple of songs from the Meters' catalog. The reunion of the classic rhythm section helped pave the way for the first full-fledged Meters performance in fifteen years.

Throughout the 1990s, there was occasionally talk of more full reunions. But with the Funky Meters on the scene, the collective urge disappeared for the most part from the communal consciousness of the funk diaspora. Eventually a small group of diehards persuaded the foursome to get on stage together in 2000 in San Francisco leading to a 2001 performance on the Fairgrounds, a performance at the Voodoo Music Experience in 2006 and more reunion shows in 2011.

* * *

The Jazz Fest continued to grow almost exponentially. A day was added in 1991 and the Thursday before the second weekend came to be known as "Slacker's Day" because very few out-of-towners, excepting those with the wherewithal to come early for the second weekend or take a full week off of work, were in attendance. There weren't even that many locals at the Fairgrounds, and hardcore festers relished an atmosphere that brought them back ten years.

National touring acts were beginning to hire New Orleans talent. George Porter, Jr. recorded with David Byrne and went on a long tour with the former Talking Heads' frontman in 1992, the great jazz vocalist, Dianne Reeves, hired David Torkanowsky to be her musical director. She put on a great set on the first Sunday, and the band also included locals Chris Severin and Russell Batiste.

The last Sunday in 1991 set a record of 75,000 people on the Fairgrounds. It wasn't just crowded at the Fairgrounds. Saturday night, the hordes of visitors fully overwhelmed the clubs on Oak Street.

Carrollton Avenue was so packed with cars that the entire neighborhood was gridlocked. Marcia Ball was playing at Muddy Waters, Beausoleil was at the Maple Leaf and NRBQ was at Jimmy's.

The New Orleans Jazz and Heritage Foundation started a series of free neighborhood festivals in 1992; a move seen by some as an attempt to assuage some of the ill will generated among locals as the Jazz Fest grew. As a non-profit, they also were required to give back to the community a percentage of the monies that were now filling up the foundation's coffers.

The Uptown Street Festival was held on the corner of Napoleon Avenue and Magazine Street and featured George Porter, Jr. and the Runnin' Pardners and Cyril Neville and the Uptown Allstars among others. The saxophonist Tim Green and the keyboardist Terry Manuel, who was in and out of Neville's side project, threw down a massive improvisational jam to end the day.

A new band that put a unique spin on the uptown funk also played that day. They were called DEFF Generation and featured members of the next generation of Nevilles including Aaron's youngest son, Jason. They were one of the first New Orleans bands to mix hip-hop and funk. They put on a high energy set with Jimmy Ives, who also played with Michael Ward and Reward, on bass and George Sartin, who also played with Cyril Neville and the Uptown Allstars, on guitar.

Their only album, which came out in 1994, is a tour-de-force of this early blending. It includes a great rap tune about the urban culture of New Orleans called "Runnin' with the Second Line."

The following year, the Uptown Street Festival featured the jazz vocalist Phillip Manuel. He put on a deeply soulful set with Donald Ramsey and Tony Dillon backing him up along with an elegant pianist named Daryl Lavigne. Manuel is one of the true vocal geniuses of the Crescent City and never ceases to amaze the audience with his improvisational abilities and his intuitive sense of the feeling behind a song. The idea behind the free festivals was to showcase local talent hailing from each area of the city. Three other neighborhood festivals were scheduled throughout the year in the Tremé, Carrollton and the 9th Ward. Discontinued after several years, these festivals were sorely missed until the foundation revived the idea by sponsoring smaller, local festivals in the early 21st century.

The Jazz Fest kept growing and hiring more and more national and internationally known talent. The rosters in the mid-1990s were the first to feature such a wide range of high-dollar talent. The 1992 fest featured Al Green, Boz Scaggs, Blues Traveler, Rickie Lee Jones, Hugh Masekela and Carole King with her special guests, Aaron Neville and Slash. Bob Dylan appeared for the first time in 1993. Dickie Betts of the Allman Brothers joined the '60s icon on two songs. The saxophone colossus, Sonny Rollins, also played that year. Of course, it was impossible to see them all. I coined a phrase to help face this conundrum that has become popular among festers—"You can't judge a day at the Jazz Fest by who you saw, you have to judge it by who you missed."

There were downsides to this exponential growth. The long run of top tier African and Caribbean bands appearing at the Jazz Fest began to end in 1993. Though the festival continues to present bands from the diaspora, the focus was clearly shifting to more mainstream acts appealing to the baby boomer demographic.

Appearances in 1994 by both Tabu Ley Rochereau, the legendary bandleader from Zaire, and Ali Farka Touré, a Malian griot touring with Ry Cooder in support of their great record, helped redeem the reduction of African bands at the festival. In 1996, they continued to woo back world music lovers by developing a new concept— each year's festival was dedicated to a separate country from the diaspora. They brought in bands of various styles to highlight each nation's musical diversity. Haiti was the first country to be honored, and the concept continued for several more years.

As the booking policy of the Jazz Fest skewed further towards national touring acts, an underground faction arose to promote the preservation of the "jazz and heritage" concept behind the origins of the festival. Some longtime fans of the event, curmudgeons in the music community as well as outspoken musicians began to complain about slots going to bands that have nothing to do with the jazz or the heritage of New Orleans and south Louisiana. Festival organizers pointed out, as they do to this day, that the great majority of performers are still local.

Despite this persistent undercurrent of grumbling, new performers fitting within the rigid framework of the cranky locals began earning gigs at the Jazz Fest. Sonny Landreth and the Goners played for the first time at the Jazz Fest in 1992. Landreth has a technique that is instantly fascinating to any fan of the slide guitar. Kenny Blevins accompanied him on drums with David Ransom on bass. The trio absolutely killed, and his unique style of playing behind the slide dazzled the crowd. The fact that he performed "Congo Square," a song long associated with the Neville Brothers that he actually wrote, only added to his appeal.

John Campbell, a self-styled hoodoo bluesman who died young after years of hard living, played in 1993. He has become an underground legend in blues circles because he was just beginning to earn a modicum of recognition for his genius before his untimely death. His set was like a blues clinic. Before playing each song, he described its style, history and origins in his gravelly understated voice. He then proceeded to completely shred his six-string on each sub-genre from Texas boogie-woogie to the Delta blues.

On December 17, 1993, the grandstand and the clubhouse at the New Orleans Fairgrounds burned to the ground leaving behind a twisted metal skeleton and an anxious public. Though the grandstand was not used in the early days of the New Orleans Jazz and Heritage Festival's tenure at the Fairgrounds, as the festival expanded the inside space and the sprawling outdoor seating area became crucial to the event's continued growth.

Over the course of the next four years, the hulking remnants, which conjured images of the wreck of the Hindenburg, remained a visible, if somewhat surreal, reminder of the fire. During this time, the Fairgrounds' owners slogged through legal, insurance and rebuilding issues. However, the fire turned out to be a blessing in disguise because it allowed the Jazz Fest to expand into the parking lots around the grandstand.

In the long run, the movement of the jazz, gospel and blues tents to the parking lot allowed the festival space to grow even further resulting in the epic day in 2001 when over 100,000 people crammed the Fairgrounds in order to see the Dave Matthews Band and the New Orleans rapper, Mystikal, who were booked at nearly the same time. Looking at a photo taken from the air, there does not appear to be an inch of open space.

By the mid-1990s, the daytime activities during the "daze-in-between" and the night shows at various clubs proved to be some of the best music being played in the city. The Louisiana Music Factory moved beyond their usual staple of brass and blues musicians to present some truly scintillating sets.

On Monday, April 25, 1994, John Sinclair appeared on the tiny stage performing his poetry with the drummer Johnny Vidacovich backing him. Sinclair put on a totally insane, over the top show early in the afternoon. It looked like his whole head was on fire and smoke was about to come out of his ears as he screamed over and over at the climax of one of his poems, "Bud Powell, Bud Powell!" Vidacovich provided powerful punctuation on his drums.

Henry Butler followed and stuck to a program of jazz tunes. When someone in the crowd yelled for him to sing, he replied back in a voice that was clearly worn out from other gigs, "If anyone's gonna sing, it's gonna be you." Jazz Fest doesn't just exhaust the audience.

Theresa Andersson and Anders Osborne were still trying to find their way amid the tight knit New Orleans musical community at this point in their career development. They had some success performing as a duo, but Andersson was moving away from their common musical ground and venturing into jazz. She put on a delightful set at the Factory with Brian Seeger backing her on guitar. Osborne followed with an acoustic set.

One-off venues began emerging to capitalize on the increasing number of out of town music lovers flocking to New Orleans. Once such venue was a wonderful, underused theater space on the thirteenth floor of a building at 333 St. Charles Avenue in the Central Business District.

The highlight of the ambitious schedule at the theater was a performance that has since been dubbed, "Astral Funk." The contemporary jazz band, Astral Project, joined Big Chiefs Monk Boudreaux and Bo Dollis along with Norbert "Geechie" Johnson, the Wild Magnolias' longtime percussionist, in a landmark concert that merged Astral Project's scintillating modern jazz with the ancient rhythms and chants of the Indians. They tore through two sets of improvised

286

Indian grooves and loose versions of Astral Project's songs as the music shifted back and forth between the two distinct styles. They repeated the experiment a couple more times, but sadly, the only record is a bootleg recording of that first fateful night.

In retrospect, the show was as groundbreaking as the synthesis between the Indian music of the Wild Magnolias and Willie Tee's New Orleans Project 25 years earlier. Tee was the mastermind behind the now legendary recordings that featured his brother, Earl, as well as the guitarist, Snooks Eaglin, backing the same two big chiefs. He mixed the Indian rhythms with 1970s-era New Orleans funk.

While the idea of mixing the ancient Indian rhythms with electric guitars and a funky bass was revolutionary, the Wild Magnolias continued to be a percussion ensemble for a number of years until they hooked up with a group called the Bayou Renegades.

June Victory, a guitarist so raw that he once played at Tipitina's without an amp—he just plugged straight into the PA system—led the group. They first played together at the Jazz Fest in 1993. The set was laced with dripping-acid blues, bare bones funk rhythms and sizzling Indian chanting.

Victory was a scorching player, but his work ethic and lifestyle made him unreliable. He even ran afoul of the powers-that-be at the Jazz Fest, a serious faux pas, when he refused to stop playing despite the fact that time was up and the Indians had long left the stage.

When June Yamagishi eventually took over the lead guitar role from June Victory, the Wild Magnolias improved immeasurably, and they quickly became an in-demand stage act. Yamagishi has established himself as one of the most versatile guitarists in town.

By 1998, other Mardi Gras Indian tribes began augmenting their sound with other non-percussion instruments and musicians. The Creole Wild West, with bluesman J. Monque 'D as their frontman, welcomed back Second Chief Howard Miller, one of the stalwarts of the tribe who had missed the last few Jazz Fests. Monque 'D bellowed in his introduction, "He's back from his incarceration in the war with the blue coat soldiers!"

However, many of the traditionalists stuck with the core sounds of various percussion instruments. When Big Chief Larry Bannock of the Golden Star Hunters assumed the mantle of a Mardi Gras Indian elder following the death of his mentor, Lawrence Fletcher, he began a long string of many memorable sets at the Fairgrounds. He dissed all of the so-called Indians who talk all year long about their new suit and then fail to come through. He dedicated "You Talk That Shit or You Better Get Your Mind Right" to the posers.

In 1994, Allison Miner, one of the driving forces behind the Jazz and Heritage Festival and a tireless advocate for the musicians of the city, was struck with bone cancer, and several benefits were organized to aid in paying her medical expenses. The most impressive, with respect to musical talent, was held on January 10, 1995 at the House of Blues. The Rebirth Brass Band, a group Miner was representing, opened the show with a short, energetic set. Then Willie Tee hit the stage with Alfred "Uganda" Roberts and Steve Masakowski from Astral Project on guitar. They played a few of Tee's songs including the classic, "Teasin' You," and then Big Chiefs Monk Boudreaux and Bo Dollis emerged onto the stage. They proceeded to recreate history with Masakowski tearing out lines that would have made Snooks Eaglin proud. Yet there was no saxophonist—Tee's brother, Earl Turbinton, was a crucial part of the old recordings—and he was missing in action.

Following the Mardi Gras Indian funk, the Radiators hit the stage raring to go. They performed a mini five-song set before George Porter, Jr. and Monk Boudreaux joined them for a smoking version of "They All Axed For You." Then Eddie Bo, a musical hero of the members of the Radiators, joined in the fun before John Sinclair hit the stage with poetry in hand. He did his poem, "Tommy Johnson," while the supergroup wailed on the blues classic, "Spoonful". The performance was intense, only to be outdone by the finale, which featured Kermit Ruffins, Corey Henry and Monk Boudreaux joining the Radiators for "Jump Back".

Nearly everyone who donated his or her time to Miner's cause had a personal relationship with her. She was a central figure on the scene for decades. Sadly, she passed away at the end of the year. The Jazz Fest honored her legacy by rechristening the Heritage Stage, where interviews and intimate performances take place, the Allison Miner Music Heritage Stage.

Every so often, a band appearance impacts the Jazz Fest and affects the bookings that follow. Though they had played at Tipitina's in the '80s, the back story of the jam band Phish's show at the festival in 1996 begins in 1992.

The trumpeter Michael Ray, a veteran of both Sun Ra's avant-garde jazz band and Kool and the Gang, had recently relocated to New Orleans. He didn't really have a regular band until he debuted his long-running group, the Cosmic Krewe, at the 1992 Jazz Fest. Ray liked to challenge his listeners by playing in the mode of Sun Ra. He also liked to funk it up in the fashion of his other longtime employers, so the band opened with a New Orleans second line tune before heading into musical cosmos.

The following year, Ray appeared at the fest on a set billed as Michael Ray's Tribute to Sun Ra with Kidd Jordan and Carl LeBlanc. They stayed in outer space mode the entire set as Jordan and LeBlanc wailed away.

By 1995, Ray had fully established himself on the local scene with "anything goes" style performances that often included numerous guest appearances. At the Jazz Fest that year, Ray took a foray into the burgeoning jam band movement when he invited the guitarist Trey Anastasio and the drummer Jon Fishman of Phish to join him on stage at the Fairgrounds.

The members of the band had been quietly digging into the New Orleans scene for a few years. So when the invitation to perform at the New Orleans Jazz and Heritage Festival came in late 1995, they knew the significance and came off of hiatus for the single show.

Their legion of Deadhead-inspired fans converged on New Orleans the following spring and completely upended the status quo. Their late night bongo jams in Jackson Square were the catalyst for a new phase in the decades-long struggle of wills between street musicians and residents seeking peace and quiet in the French Quarter. Thousands of these latter day hippies were everywhere—camping in people's backyards and even sleeping in the streets.

Even the old hippies who organized and controlled the basic ambiance at the Jazz Fest were appalled at this new generation of freaks. In their memories of their younger selves, the Phish heads just seemed a little dirtier, much more asocial and a lot more closed-minded. Plus, many of them stunk of days-old funk. It was as if the entire 1960s contingent of New Orleanians was thinking, "they're nothing like we were." But from a financial viewpoint, the appearance of Phish was an unqualified success as Stage 3 was packed back to the track. However, it's telling that Phish has never been asked to return.

Though never confirmed, there were reports of rampant stealing from craft vendors, and piles of human fecal waste littering the Fairgrounds after the group's appearance. The band laughed it off at their next New Orleans appearance when they opened the performance at the UNO Lakefront Arena with the Rolling Stones' song, "Sweet Virginia," and its telling lyric, "got to scrape that shit right off your shoes."

There are so many memorable shows at each and every Jazz Fest that everyone has their favorites. Here are a few performances, and one notorious absence, that stand out in my mind from the 1990s.

Musicians are willing to brave all sorts of obstacles in order to earn a coveted gig at the Fairgrounds. Therefore, cancellations are virtually unheard of. But in 1994, Bob Weir of the Grateful Dead and the great jazz bassist, Rob Wasserman, cancelled their appearance on short notice reportedly because Weir was suffering from insomnia. The Meters performed in their place, and Deadheads all over the world laughed at the incredulousness of the excuse. After all, any in-demand musician barely sleeps over the ten days of the festival.

It rained on and off over the course of the first weekend in 1996. One of the highlights demonstrating the festival's hallmark blend of audience support and artist commitment was a performance by Zap Mama. The group is a female vocal ensemble that plays a danceable blend of African and European pop. The day got a late start because of the rain, which kept up throughout the afternoon in varying intensity, and some acts had their performances postponed or cancelled. As the rain picked up during the middle of Zap Mama's set, members of the production crew scrambled to keep the stage dry. The crowd didn't mind one bit. The singers, obviously impressed with the crew's dedication and the crowd's energy, used scat vocals and sweeping sounds to good-naturedly imitate the sound of the stagehand who was busy sweeping water from the stage. It was an incredible display of vocal improvisation that had everyone in the crowd astonished.

Chaka Khan played a brilliant set at the Fairgrounds; it was one of the best shows of the entire festival. Her band was super tight, and her voice was big, bossy and soulful. The producer/director Quint Davis' quote at the end of the set said it all, "This one's for the judge—next time it'll be the Soul and Heritage Festival."

King Floyd was one of those underrated New Orleans vocalists though he had a couple of monster hits with "Groove Me" and "Feel Like Dynamite." He put on a killer set, and when the crowd went nuts the stage manager rewarded him with the rare Fairgrounds encore—he sang "Iko Iko" a cappella.

Fats Domino's reclusive nature had caused him to miss performances in the past including one infamous appearance in the '80s. His bandleader, Dave Bartholomew, repeatedly called him out as the band vamped, and the crowd waited eagerly. But sadly, his efforts were for naught. However, there was no waiting in vain for him to appear in 1997. He closed out Stage 4 with a performance that was simply astounding. His band, stocked with horn greats like Herbert Hardesty and Roger Lewis, was on fire, and he tore through dozens of his hits the crowd knew by heart. The songs came so fast and furious that Domino barely stopped to breathe. At the end of his set, he moved the grand piano across the stage by bouncing it along with his belly. It took five guys to move it back!

Bartholomew was rumored to be reluctant to play the Fairgrounds as a headliner because of various issues including payment for rehearsals. But he was on the bill in 1998 and brought his big band that closely resembled Domino's band in personnel. He had at least seven saxophonists including Kidd Jordan, and the group was smoking with incredibly tight arrangements and strong solos. They clearly had rehearsed.

When the gates to the Jazz Fest opened in 1998, festers were met with a welcome sight. After a four-year delay because of litigation and construction, the gleaming new grandstand was open, and it immediately became part of the fabric of the festival. The building is air-conditioned, has great big windows providing panoramic views of the outside portion of the festival, and most importantly for one coveted demographic, it has restrooms with running water. The paddock area became the home of the Lagniappe Stage. The many floors of the building were used for food heritage, music heritage, folk heritage and the international pavilion. Additional areas featured displays of other aspects of the unique culture of New Orleans.

However, another development accompanying the opening of the grandstand tempered the enthusiasm of a lot of long time festers. The jazz and gospel tents were moved from the infield into the parking lot. Patient fans of the New Orleans Jazz and Heritage Festival had gotten used to changes each and every year, yet there were still a fair percentage of grumblers hung up on the earliest incarnation of the event. The curmudgeons were up in arms yet again when the gates to the Fairgrounds opened a year later.

The move that put the jazz and gospel tents in the parking lot was considered a travesty, but when the blues stage followed them into a tent on the pavement, another blow was dealt to the original concepts behind the festival. While sound bleeding from stage to stage was a chronic issue from the festival's beginnings, many thought that moving the blues into a tent was actually more of a problem than a solution. The music under the tent just didn't sound right. Also, now fans of the blues had to sit in chairs rather than dance under the vibrant sun. For many it was the final blow to the dancing ethic that defined the early years of the festival.

The sheer number of chair people at the other stages also began to upend the perceptions of longtime festers and musicians as well. It didn't help when the grumblers realized that the Jazz Fest itself was selling chairs emblazoned with the iconic logo. The legendary South African trumpeter and vocalist, Hugh Masekela, was a regular at the festival performing on and off over the years. He appeared visibly upset about all of the inattentive chair people lining the rail during his set on the second Saturday. They were waiting for Will Downing, the closing act on the Congo Square stage.

Angelique Kidjo, the great diva from Benin, was also affected by the lack of dancing and crowd participation. She delivered a spot-on performance with a killer band. Yet, she seemed confused by the crowd, as if the reports of the wildly participatory audiences in New Orleans were only a rumor. Again, the problem lay with the programming at the Congo Square stage. They had another staid act, Jeffery Osborne, booked to attract another coveted demographic following Kidjo.

While the movement of the blues stage and the increased problem with uninvolved audiences adversely affected the vibe at a couple of the stages, the addition of a giant television monitor at Stage 3 actually made some fans quite happy. It has now become another welcome amenity at the fest. When a notoriously photoshy Bob Dylan performed in 2006, *Offbeat* magazine ran an image of the singer performing on the big screen in the issue recapping the Jazz Fest. Now fans can watch scintillating close ups at Stage 1 as well.

Of course, while these changes were noted by longtime festers with a mix of grumbling and acceptance, they didn't really affect the average fan or the huge majority of the musicians. Incredible performances, rooted in the wonderful ambiance and vibe that have been thirty years in the making, continue to be the norm.

In 1998, Bonnie Raitt demonstrated her deep New Orleans roots by simply letting her musical friends sit in. At the end of her set, John Mooney, Art Neville, Zigaboo Modeliste and Earl Palmer had all joined her for some spirited jamming. The Panamanian jazz pianist, Danilo Perez, was dazzling. The James Andrews Allstar Band dedicated "Who Dat Call the Police" to New Orleans' finest. Phil DeGruy cracked up the guitarists in his audience with a comment about being in Tuners Anonymous—" You know, AA 440." Little Queenie was introduced as the "embodiment of God as white woman."

The Jazz Fest set a new attendance record when 98,000 people crowded the Fairgrounds on the second Saturday of 1998, although the new set up made it seem like there was a bit more room especially around the smaller stages. The growth of the festival did not go unnoticed by other promoters and clubs in town.

The "daze-in-between" the two weekends of Jazz Fest continued to feature incredible music during the day at various in-store performances while night shows were beginning to be dominated by outside promoters.

In 1998, the Maple Leaf Bar and an independent producer named Henry Petras set the bar higher than any other club in town and established a new paradigm during Jazz Fest. Petras scheduled a performance by Zigaboo Modeliste to begin at 4:20 AM. It sold out.

The Maple Leaf began scheduling music until 7 AM on the weekend nights during the Jazz Fest. Many of those dates were successful as well. A new era had dawned, and over the ensuing years, late night sets have become standard at most of the clubs in town during Jazz Fest and Mardi Gras.

Superfly Productions placed Galactic with the Lil Rascals Brass Band on the Cajun Queen Riverboat during the 1999 festival. Ben Ellman and Skerik, a crazed saxophonist from Seattle with serious avant-garde, eclectic musical leanings, traded riffs at an amazing, high-energy show loaded with deep funk grooves. The Lil Rascals opened the show and played the break. Ellman, who played with them during his early days in New Orleans, joined them for a number. It felt like a show on the sorely missed Riverboat President; performed in front of a crowd that had no problem dancing up a storm on a boat rocking on the river.

Skerik also sat in with Galactic at the Fairgrounds. They had graduated to the biggest stage at the Fairgrounds. He took one of the most astonishing solos I have ever witnessed at the Jazz Fest. Standing on the edge of the stage, he leaned down and fed his saxophone back through the massive PA system. The sound was monstrous in volume and depth. It shook the scaffolding and blew back the hair of the ecstatic fans in the front rows.

Fats Domino reunited with Dave Bartholomew, his longtime writing partner and bandleader, for the first time in twelve years to close out the first Sunday in 1999. His big band, stocked with the cream-of-the-crop of local players, was rehearsed to a sharp edge like a chef's best knife, and its members were positively ebullient basking in the rapport of the two old friends. After a stop-on-a-dime set of hit-after-sing-along-hit under the strict musical attention of Bartholomew, Domino poured all of his emotions into his show-stopping closer—a rollicking, piano-driven, barn-burning version of "When the Saints Go Marching In." Suddenly, towards the conclusion of Domino's last performance in the 20th century, while the horns were blasting and the rhythm section was pounding, the music sounded like it was veering off the band's written charts into the musical unknown. Domino is a genuine musical legend, however group improvisation is not part of his repertoire. But without a moment's hesitation or a missed note, the big band just kept on grooving; just like the Jazz Fest and just like the city of New Orleans.

Epilogue

Over the course of the thirty years covered in these pages, I have seen literally thousands of performances by acts large and small, well known and unknown, fondly remembered or barely recalled. I like to think I have heard it all, but given the breadth and depth of talent in this most musical of North American cities, that would be an unconscionable boast.

What remains true are these facts. I have watched and listened as hundreds of musicians found the muse, matured, and developed their gifts into individual voices. I have also observed the breakdowns; talented musicians in free fall because of their personal demons, and gifted players who quit when confronted with the bleak realities of an artist struggling to survive. I have marveled at numerous musicians who achieved a modicum of success through sheer tenacity despite possessing lesser abilities.

I have stood humbly among so many wonderfully exceptional players. I watched dozens of the early greats peak musically and then pass on; some whose skills atrophied slowly and others who retired or died suddenly. I witnessed men and women, youngsters when I arrived in New Orleans, mature into masters. And I have seen hundreds of young players, some really just children, blossom into the standard bearers of the culture and the music.

Since individual musicians rarely operate in a void, I have seen the humble beginnings of many bands and watched as they developed the communication, both on stage and off, that is a necessary component for developing an audience and achieving success. I have also witnessed the sad demise of groups unable to navigate the rough road of interpersonal relations in a business that spits out the seeds in favor of the fully formed fruit.

I have witnessed myriad changes, large and small, in infrastructure, demographics, personnel, and organization within dozens of institutions from festivals and music clubs to universities and the media; from Mardi Gras Indian tribes and brass bands to second line organizations and non-profit foundations.

Over the years, I changed as well. I moved to New Orleans as a seventeen-year-old with scarcely a sense of the vibrant culture existing here for over two hundred years. I feel privileged to have arrived in the city when remnants of an age-old way of life, before air conditioners, televisions and the other elements of the creeping homogenization of America, still existed.

I embraced the culture of New Orleans in all its complexity and contradictions, and it has hugged me back. I always carry with me this quote from Robbie Robertson, "There are these veils in front of this place, and it keeps revealing itself more and more. The more you look, the more you know—and the more you don't understand." I continue to be amazed at the depth of expression of her artists.

I moved here with near total naiveté about the music and became a rabid fan. Yet for over ten years, I was just another face in the crowd (usually dancing up front and center). Then I became a cog in this wondrous world. I learned the nuts and bolts of the music business working for a small publication in a small market. I found a niche, and I am grateful for the opportunities the business has provided me.

But most of all, I am grateful for the musicians. Not only for those who have successfully integrated life as art; not only for those who have reached a level which allows them to pursue their work without regard to finance, public fancy or fear of folly; but especially for those who still struggle…with the rent, with the muse, with the very concept of being a musician in the modern world. As another wise man once said, "Without music, life would be a mistake."

Acknowledgements

Numerous people were of great assistance over the long history of this book. I would like to specifically thank Derek Houston, Danny "the Poet" Kerwick, and Steve Wolfram for their thoughts on the earliest draft of this project. The Hogan Jazz Archive at Tulane University provided indispensable support. I am also deeply grateful for the editing efforts of Ann Marie Brennan, Alice Horowitz, Rob Rudner and Reggie Scanlan. I would like to thank the anonymous reader who was hired to review the manuscript by the University Press of Mississippi. Your margin notes were very helpful in cleaning up the final version. I would also like to acknowledge Kimberly Krohn for first pointing out that I am always "up front and center" at shows. Special thanks go out to Kermit Ruffins, Sue Marchman at Nutshell Indexing, Isabelle Jacopin, Zach Smith, Nijme Rinaldi Nun, Jonny O and Brian Boyles as well. Finally, I would like to say thank you to the fine folks at the Threadhead Foundation. Your efforts on behalf of the musicians of New Orleans deserve a standing ovation.

Index

.

Made in the USA
Charleston, SC
29 March 2012